EXPOSURE AND LIGHTING FOR DIGITAL PHOTOGRAPHERS ONLY

By: Michael Meadhra
and Charlotte K. Lowrie

1807
WILEY
2007

Wiley Publishing, Inc.

Exposure and Lighting For Digital Photographers Only

Published by
Wiley Publishing, Inc.
111 River Street
Hoboken, N.J. 07030
www.wiley.com

Copyright © 2007 by Wiley Publishing, Inc., Indianapolis, Indiana

Published by Wiley Publishing, Inc., Indianapolis, Indiana

Published simultaneously in Canada

ISBN-13: 978-0-470-03869-7

ISBN-10: 0-470-03869-1

Manufactured in the United States of America

10 9 8 7 6 5 4 3 2

1K/QY/RR/QW/IN

For general information on our other products and services or to obtain technical support, please contact our Customer Care Department within the U.S. at (800) 762-2974, outside the U.S. at (317) 572-3993 or fax (317) 572-4002.

Wiley also publishes its books in a variety of electronic formats. Some content that appears in print may not be available in electronic books.

Library of Congress Control Number: 2006934802

about the authors

Michael Meadhra earned a bachelor's degree with area of concentration in art, with media specialty in photography. After an apprenticeship with a leading commercial photographer in Louisville, KY, Michael went on to open and run a studio in Nashville, TN where he developed a reputation for his lighting on advertising illustration assignments, some of which won ADDY awards from the American Advertising Federation. He also worked as a graphic designer and media producer and gained experience creating still images, animation sequences, and title effects using both traditional artwork/photography methods and digital technologies. After moving into management, Michael spent much of his time teaching and training others, and began writing to create the training materials he needed. That lead to a writing career in which he has authored, coauthored, or contributed to more than 40 computer book titles and hundreds of articles, including articles, chapters, and books on leading digital imaging software such as Adobe Photoshop, Corel Painter, Ulead PhotoImpact, and many others.

Charlotte Lowrie is an award-winning freelance journalist and professional photographer based in the Seattle area. She shoots portraits and editorial assignments as well as stock photography. Her writing and photography have appeared in newstand magazines, newspapers, and on industry Web sites including the Canon Digital Learning Center on Photoworkshop.com and TakeGreatPictures.com. She also teaches photography classes at BetterPhoto.com. Charlotte is the author of four books including the *Canon EOS Digital Rebel Field Guide, Adobe Camera Raw Studio Skills, The Canon EOS 30D Field Guide,* and *Teach Yourself Visually Digital Photography, 2nd Edition,* all published by John Wiley & Sons.

To Don Young
Thanks for giving me such a great start.

preface

When I talked to some of my photographer friends about this book, they were surprised by the "For Digital Photographers Only" part of the title. They usually made some comment to the effect that, although digital imaging has revolutionized many things about photography, exposure and lighting are still pretty much the same whether you shoot digital or film.

That's an understandable response from a bunch of former film photographers who gradually migrated to digital photography. They learned to do everything manually with film, and they've adapted that knowledge and experience to the new digital photography tools.

However, the title makes more sense for the new generation of photographers who may have never used a camera without auto-focus and auto-exposure capabilities. All those automatic features are great, but sometimes even the best automation fails, and the photographer must override the camera's automatic settings to get the shot. And sometimes you just want to exercise more creative control. The problem is that the automation that makes normal shooting so much easier can actually make manual overrides harder. Today's highly automated digital cameras tend to hide and disguise fundamentals that were obvious on old manual cameras.

For example, unless you're old enough to have gray hair and bifocal glasses (like me), you've probably never used a camera just a few mechanically timed shutter speeds, each of which doubled the previous speed. Modern cameras with electronically controlled shutters have many more shutter speeds that provide more precise exposure control. However, all those extra shutter speeds also make it harder to visualize which ones are a full stop (one EV) apart and which ones are intermediate steps.

In the past, photographers had to learn certain fundamentals in order to use a camera effectively to take pictures. But that's no longer the case. Today's cameras are capable of handling many details automatically, leaving the photographer free to concentrate on the subject and the composition. As a result, photographers can get to a moderately advanced level without mastering some of the basics — either because they never had to learn the basics to take a picture, or more likely, because the knowledge of the basics got rusty from lack of use.

This book is for digital photographers who have been relying heavily on the automatic features of their digital cameras, but are now ready to begin exercising more creative control over their images by selecting or overriding the camera's automatic exposure controls. But it's not just about exposure controls. It's also about the lighting on the subject you're photographing — whether it's finding good natural lighting or creating photographic lighting from scratch in the studio. And it's all from the perspective of a photographer who now shoots digital images instead of film.

I've tried to make this book as camera-brand agnostic as possible. The information on these pages is applicable to any digital camera with manual controls. That includes all the digital SLRs from Nikon, Canon, Olympus, Fuji, and other manufacturers, as well as many of the higher-end consumer zoom cameras. Many of the lighting tips will work with any camera — even point-and-shoot digital cameras and those antique film cameras.

acknowledgments

Writing a book is a team effort. Although it's the principal author's name that appears on the cover, the book would not exist without the contributions of many different people. I'm glad that tradition allows me this opportunity to acknowledge some of those people for their efforts.

A special thanks to all the photographers who so generously contributed images to serve as examples. They include Dan Dry, Tony Guffy, Dean Lavenson, Charlotte Lowrie, Randy McCaffery, Alicia McGinnis, Bryan Moberly, Fred Reaves, Ramon Rodriguez, and Rob Sheppard. Their talents, and their images, made this book possible. On the other hand, I bear sole responsibility for the real and simulated bad examples.

I'm very grateful for the assistance of fellow author, Charlotte Lowrie, who stepped in to help ensure that the book met its publishing deadlines by contributing text in Chapters 9 and 11.Thanks to Mike Roney, acquisitions editor, for giving this book its start. Beth Taylor, served as both project editor, managing the editing process, and as copy editor, making sure my prose was readable and grammatically correct. Mike Sullivan, technical editor, helped ensure the accuracy of the text. I didn't have much direct contact with the rest of the Wiley staff working on this book, but their contributions are appreciated nonetheless. My thanks to all of you!

And finally, I wish to thank my agent, Carole McClendon of Waterside Productions, for getting me this gig.

contents at a glance

contents

chapter **2 The Color of Light   23**

Part II What's Your Exposure   39

chapter **3 Balancing the Elements of Exposure   41**

chapter **4 Measuring Your Exposure   57**

chapter **5 Making Creative Exposure Choices 83**

chapter **6 Controlling Motion with Shutter Speed 99**

chapter **7** **Taking Control of Aperture Selection** **113**

chapter **8** **Dealing with Digital Film** **125**

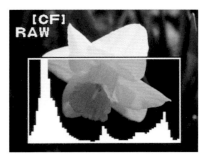

Part III Put a Little Light on the Subject   141

chapter 9 Lighting Tools and Approaches   143

chapter 10 Making Light Available on Location   173

Part IV Lighting and Exposure for Specific Subjects   215

chapter **11 Making Pictures of People**   217

chapter **12 Getting into the Action 243**

chapter **13 Photographing Nature 257**

chapter **14 Taking Pictures of Objects   277**

chapter **15 Approaching Architectural Subjects   299**

Appendix A Contributing Photographers   317

Pro Glossary   325

Index   331

Chapter 1

THE NATURE OF LIGHT

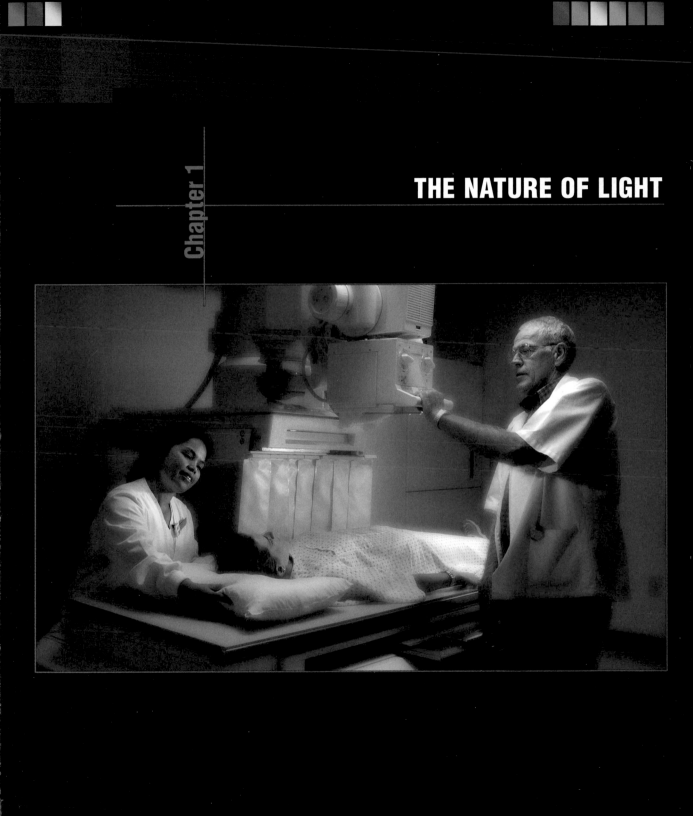

The art of photography is often referred to as painting with light. Although the subject of a photograph such as figure 1-1 may appear to be a landscape, it's the light reflected from that landscape that makes the photograph, not the subject itself. Without light, you simply can't make a photograph.

RECORDING REFLECTED LIGHT

Simply stated, capturing a photograph is recording the light reflected from a scene by means of a camera, which uses a lens to focus an image onto a photosensitive recording medium. For generations, that medium was photographic film, which created an image through chemical reactions. Now, digital image sensors are rapidly replacing chemical-based film as the preferred photographic medium, and photographers typically record images as computer files instead of film negatives. Although the photographic recording medium is new, the essence of photography is the same — it's still about recording reflected light.

Cameras have come a long way over the years. Early cameras, such as the one in figure 1-2 were little more than a lens holder in the front, a film holder in the back, and a flexible bellows in between that created a light-tight enclosure. The technical process of making a photograph with such a camera was arduous. The introduction of the box camera in figure 1-3 reduced the size of the contraption so that it was easier to transport and popularized multiframe rolls of film instead of single sheets.

1-1
© Charlotte K. Lowrie | wordsandphotos.org

small package. The evolution continued with the addition of convenience features such as automatic film advance, automatic focusing, and automatic exposure in cameras like the one shown in figure 1-5. The sophisticated features and slick design of these electronically controlled cameras makes them fast and easy to use. Much of the technical process of taking a picture is automated, leaving the photographer free to concentrate on aesthetic decisions such as framing the image, and of course, the lighting.

1-2
Photo from Wikipedia, GFDL

1-4
Photo courtesy Photopath

1-3
Photo from Wikipedia, GFDL

The 35mm SLR (single lens reflex) further reduced the size of the camera while adding a much more sophisticated focusing system, interchangeable lenses, and a built-in exposure meter. As a result, cameras such as the venerable Nikon F2 (see figure 1-4) gave photographers lots of creative control in a

1-5
Image provided by Dreamstime

In some respects, today's digital cameras have revolutionized photography. Digital sensors have replaced film as the image recording device, and images are stored on a memory card instead of in a film cassette. Digital images can be viewed instantly on a display screen on the back of the camera instead of waiting hours or days for film processing. Editing and printing images can be done on a personal computer instead of in a specially equipped lab.

However, in spite of all the changes brought about by digital photography, a digital camera such as the Canon Digital Rebel in figure 1-6 looks and operates a lot like its film-based predecessor. At its core, the camera is still a light-tight box with a lens that focuses reflected light from the scene onto a photosensitive recording medium. You still need to frame and focus the image the same way, and control the exposure with aperture and shutter speed in the same way, so it's not surprising that those parts of the camera design remain unchanged. The only feature that has really changed is the technical details of the recording medium. Granted, that's a significant change, but it doesn't alter the fundamental truth that photography is the art of recording light and that the camera is basically just a simple recording tool.

1-6
Photo from Wikipedia, GFDL

To be sure, there are some differences between recording a photographic image digitally and recording it onto film, and I explore some of them in other chapters. However, those differences, while they do exist, don't make a profound difference in photographic lighting and exposure for most photographic subjects. Photography by natural light is pretty much the same whether you record the image on film or digital. In the studio, you can use most of the same lighting technologies and techniques for both film and digital (with some exceptions), and a given exposure will produce equivalent results on both film and digital of the same ISO (with some exceptions and limitations). Of course, there are numerous small details that are different in digital photography, but they usually require minor tweaks in a lighting technique or exposure, not a major change in approach.

X-REF

See Chapter 8 for more information on the differences between film and digital photography.

The area where digital photography has the greatest impact is on the photographer's workflow. And I'm not referring only to the processing and printing workflow after a photograph is taken. I'm talking about changes in the shooting workflow as well.

By necessity, the workflow for film-based photography had to allow for the fact that film processing takes hours. If the film had to be sent to an outside lab for processing, it could be days before the photographer could see the results. Consequently, testing new equipment and lighting techniques was a painfully slow process, which required tedious testing procedures and meticulous record keeping to match test conditions with the results that weren't available until hours or days later. The process usually goes something like this:

1. Set up a test situation to test a new camera, lens, or lights. You may need to repeat or refine the tests, so you must either leave the test setup untouched while you wait for results, or you must make careful notes that will enable you to replicate the test conditions exactly at a later time.

2. Shoot a series of test exposures. Because of the time lag before you can see results, you must try to anticipate and test as many variations as possible, which means keeping meticulous notes of the exposure settings and other variables for each exposure.

3. Send the film to the lab for processing. Wait hours or days to see the results.

4. Evaluate the results, taking time to carefully match each exposure to your notes.

5. Repeat the whole process as needed. Each test cycle takes a few hours if you shoot color transparency film and have access to an in-house processing lab, much longer if you use outside processing.

In contrast, digital photography produces instant results. You can view your image immediately on the camera's display screen and get important exposure information from the histogram display. It takes just minutes to transfer an image to a computer for detailed examination. This makes for a fast and efficient feedback loop that is changing how photographers work. Digital photographers can confirm each shot and reshoot immediately if necessary. For complex studio shots that require testing, refinement, and retesting, the test cycle time has been reduced from hours to seconds. When working with studio flash, some digital photographers find that it's faster to fire off a test shot and adjust from there than to meter the scene with an external flash meter. The working pace is quicker and experimentation is faster and easier. The test process is reduced to something like this:

1. Set up a test situation to test a new camera, lens, or lights. Your test will be complete in minutes, so there's no need to take precautions that will enable you to replicate the test conditions later.

2. Shoot a quick test exposure. You can see each result immediately, so you don't need to structure elaborate procedures to test several variables. And you can probably dispense with the note taking because you're dealing with only one thing at a time, and the camera automatically records most exposure variables if you need to refer to them.

3. View and evaluate the results on the camera's display screen. Or, for a more detailed examination, download the images to your computer.

4. Repeat the process as needed. Each test cycle takes less than a minute if you evaluate the results on the camera's display. If you transfer images to a computer, it might take five minutes.

X-REF

See Chapter 4 for more information on using light meters to measure light and calculate exposures.

EXERCISING CREATIVE LICENSE

Photographers are observers and recorders of light. The camera is the tool that records the light reflected from the subject, but it's the photographer that observes that light and decides what to photograph and when; what to include and what to exclude. The photographer can choose to simply capture an image of pleasant scene, such as the wildflowers in figure 1-7, or look for an interesting interplay of light and shadow, such as figure 1-8.

Artists have been observing light and making it a major component of their art for hundreds of years. Painters have long used dramatic contrast of light and shadow to highlight a portion of the subject and create a distinctive mood, and the trend continues today. For example, consider the low-key portrait of a welder in figure 1-9. The side-lit face standing out from the overall dark tones of the rest of the image is reminiscent of the lighting in paintings by the old masters, such as the Rembrandt self-portrait in figure 1-10 (*Self Portrait as the Apostle Paul,* by Rembrandt van Rijn, 1661, oil on canvas, Rijksmuseum, Amsterdam).

1-10
Photo courtesy DirectMedia and Yorck Project, GFDL

Even mundane subjects can become striking images when the lighting is right. Consider too, the photograph of the Irish coastline in figure 1-11 and compare it to the painting of the Normandy coast by French realist painter, Gustave Corbet, in figure 1-12 (*Seacoast in the Normandie*, Gustave Courbet, 1867, Oil on canvas, Puschkin Museum). Both are pictures of rather nondescript sections of beach. What makes these images appealing is the quality of the light and how it plays across the clouds in the sky, the water, and the rocks on the shore.

1-9
Photo by Den Lavenson

1-11
Photo courtesy PDPhoto.org

1-12
Photo courtesy DirectMedia and Yorck Project, GFDL

The French impressionist painters were known for their obsession with light and their attempts to capture distinctive lighting in their paintings. They created beautiful artwork by painting ordinary scenes in extraordinary light. The anonymous photographer who shot the fields and trees in figure 1-13 captured a lighting effect that is very similar to the lighting in the Alfred Sisley painting in figure 1-14 (*Small Meadows in Spring*, by Alfred Sisley, 1881, Oil on canvas, National Gallery, London, UK). In both images, the light coming from the left side of the frame at a low angle causes each tree limb and tuft of grass to stand out with a distinct highlight on one side and shadow on the other.

1-13
Photo from Wikipedia, GFDL

1-14
Photo courtesy DirectMedia and Yorck Project, GFDL

BEING SELECTIVE

What makes a great photograph is not a great subject; it's great lighting. No matter how interesting or spectacular the subject may be, you won't get a good picture without decent lighting. For most photographic subjects, that means choosing the season, time of day, and other conditions for best results.

For example, figures 1-15 and 1-16 show nearly identical scenes of Monument Valley. The dramatic difference is the lighting from the last rays of the setting sun in figure 1-16. What a difference a few hours make!

1-15
Photo courtesy PDPhoto.org

1-16
Photo courtesy PDPhoto.org

MANIPULATING LIGHT

When shooting landscapes and other outdoor subjects, photographers have little choice other than waiting for nature to change the lighting conditions. However, when shooting indoors, you have the option of taking an active role in manipulating the light to create the desired effect.

If the goal was to simply record the medical scene in figure 1-17, the photographer could have taken the picture with the light from the overhead fluorescent room lights or an on-camera flash. Instead, he chose to create a much more dramatic effect with some carefully placed photographic lights. By selectively lighting certain areas and keeping other areas relatively dark, he drew attention to the people and subdued the distracting background and overpowering bulk of the machinery.

NOTE

Lighting is the biggest difference between a typical tourist picture of a spectacular scene and the postcard or magazine images of the same scene taken by a professional photographer. The tourist typically shoots the scene in whatever light is available at the time. The pro has the patience and perseverance to wait for the light to be right, sometimes returning to the scene repeatedly in search of the best light.

X-REF

See Chapter 11 for more information on location lighting.

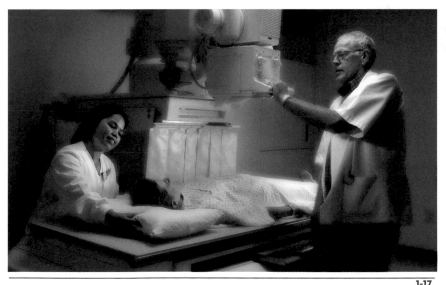

1-17
Photo by Dean Lavenson

In the photographic studio, you have total control over lighting. You can create and control the entire environment, adding and taking away lights at will.

The advertising illustration shown in figure 1-18 was shot on a studio tabletop set that was designed around the planned lighting effect. The highlights on the black rocks were created by the main light, a large soft-box positioned above the subject. Other soft lights and reflectors filled from the sides and front. The background effect was created by a spotlight positioned behind a sheet of rear projection material. All this to provide a mood setting for the museum-quality freshwater pearls that are the subject of the photograph.

X-REF

See Chapters 10 and 12 for more information on studio lighting.

EXAMINING THE CHARACTER OF LIGHT AND SHADOW

There's more to photography than just getting enough light focused onto your camera's digital sensor to form a recordable image. The amount and character of the light establish the creative mood of the photograph and define the subject.

PRO TIP

The image sensor in a typical digital camera isn't as sensitive as the human eye, so your camera needs more light for a successful photograph than the minimum light level you need to see objects in your environment. As a general rule, if the ambient light is too dim for you to read the labels on your camera's buttons comfortably, you need to resort to flash or other supplemental lighting.

The overall lightness or darkness of an image goes a long way toward creating its general mood. You can see that clearly in the fashion shots shown in figures 1-19 and 1-20. The dark tones of the low key lighting in figure 1-19 create a very different first impression from the predominantly light tones of the high key image in figure 1-20.

1-18
Photo courtesy of American Pearl Company and Latendresse Family, TN

1-19
Photo by Alicia McGinnis

1-20
Photo by Alicia McGinnis

Note that the flesh tones in both images are similar in value. The difference is the way the flesh tones contrast with their surroundings in each image. They are the lightest areas of the low key image in figure 1-19, but the flesh tones are darker than the white background and shirt in figure 1-20.

HARD LIGHT AND SHADOWS

One of the essential characteristics of light that can have a profound effect on the images you create is the relative hardness or softness of the light.

Hard light is kind of light you get from a point source, shining directly on the subject. It's a highly directional light that produces crisp, bright highlights and dark, sharp-edged shadows. Figure 1-21 shows a studio test setup lit by a single light placed about 30 degrees to the left of the camera and pointed directly at the subject. Notice the distinct shadows cast by the toy, the nose on the head, and the stem of the glass.

1-21

1-22

Direct sunlight is the best example of hard light. The sun is a huge light source, but it's so far away that it's essentially a point source. The high contrast light created by direct sunlight is good for some subjects, such as the landscapes earlier in this chapter, but the harsh shadows aren't usually very flattering for people, as you can see in figure 1-22.

SOFT LIGHT AND SHADOWS

Soft light is the kind of light you get from a large, diffuse light source or an indirect light that is bounced and scattered before reaching the subject. It's characterized by relatively broad highlights and open, soft-edged shadows. Figure 1-23 shows the same studio test setup from figure 1-21, but with a large translucent white diffuser placed between the light and the subject. Notice that the nose shadow is much softer, and the shadows of the toy and glass stem are almost gone.

1-23

1-24

The classic real-world example of a soft light is called *open shade*. That's when the subject is placed in the shade, out of the direct sunlight, but lit indirectly by a large expanse of sky. Compare figure 1-24, which I shot in open shade, to figure 1-22. Notice that the harsh shadows are gone. The left side of the face is lighter because it's exposed to more light from the sky while the foliage blocks some of the light from the right side. The transition from highlight to shadow is smooth, and the contrast between lightest and darkest areas are much less severe.

DEFINING SHAPE WITH LIGHT

A photograph is usually a two-dimensional rendering of a three-dimensional subject. The three-dimensional forms are defined by the way the light reflects off different angles and curves of the surfaces, creating highlights, shadows, and gradations in between.

Without the subtle shading created by good lighting, you wouldn't be able to see the model's muscle definition in figure 1-25. (And the model would be disappointed if all those hours in the gym were wasted by a misplaced light.)

To create the kind of shading required to define three-dimensional forms, you need a directional light — one that shines across the subject from a definite direction, creating lighter areas on the side closest to the light and darker areas on the side away from the light. It's the differences that define the form.

If a subject is evenly illuminated, with almost no shadows, you don't get the shading that defines the form. To illustrate the point, I lit figure 1-26 with two lights placed equal distances on either side of the camera and surrounded the test head with diffusion material. The result is a kind of flat, nondirectional light that makes it difficult to see the shape of the features.

1-25
Photo by Alicia McGinnis

1-26

Compare that to figure 1-27. The overall illumination level is the same, but now the light is coming from one light, positioned high and to the left so it has a distinct direction going across the subject instead of straight on from the front. This creates shadows on the right side to contrast with the highlighted left side. The light source is still diffused as before, but I placed a black card on the right side of the head to block some of the reflection into the shadows, which increases the contrast. Forms that were lost before are clearly visible now.

The position of the light source relative to the subject is also a critical factor in defining three-dimensional form. You get very different results when the light comes from different directions, even when the subject is exactly the same. To illustrate this point, I shot another series of the test head in figures 1-28 through 1-30, this time without the light background diffusers surrounding it.

1-27

1-28

In figure 1-28, the light source is positioned level with the camera and almost 90 degrees to the right. Placing a reflector on the left side of the subject bounces some light back into the shadows, so they don't go completely black.

In figure 1-29, the light is at the same level, but I moved it around to the left of the camera, just far enough to create some shadow on the right side of the nose. Doing this creates a markedly different look from the side-lit head in figure 1-28. Notice that the right side of the face beyond the jaw line disappears into deep shadow because there's no reflector or supplementary light to fill in areas that aren't illuminated by the main light.

In figure 1-30, I kept the light at approximately the same angle to the left of the camera, but moved it in and up so that it pointed down at about a 60-degree angle. Notice how that change creates shadows under the eyelids, nose, and lips that weren't there before. A reflector placed under the camera lens bounces some light back into the shadows so the right side of the face no longer disappears into blackness. The last version looks more natural because it comes closest to the normal overhead lighting that we see every day.

Q&A

What are the differences between point-source and hard light, and between diffuse and soft light?

The terms *point-source* and *diffuse* describe light sources, whereas the terms *hard light* and *soft light* describe the character of the light striking the subject. Because point-source lights produce hard light with stark highlights and crisp, dark shadows, the two terms are often used interchangeably. Likewise, because diffuse light sources produce soft light with lower contrast and open, soft-edged shadows, those terms are also used interchangeably by some people.

You say that great lighting makes great photographs, but what about framing and composition? Aren't they important too?

There are many factors that go into making a photograph, and the quality of the framing (selecting what to include and exclude from the image) and composition (using good design principles to achieve a pleasing arrangement of the objects in the image) are both major contributors to the overall quality of the image. However, photography is the art of recording light, so the quality of the lighting is what defines the image. You need good framing and composition too, but it doesn't matter how magificent the framing and composition are; if the lighting isn't good, you don't have a decent photograph, much less a great one.

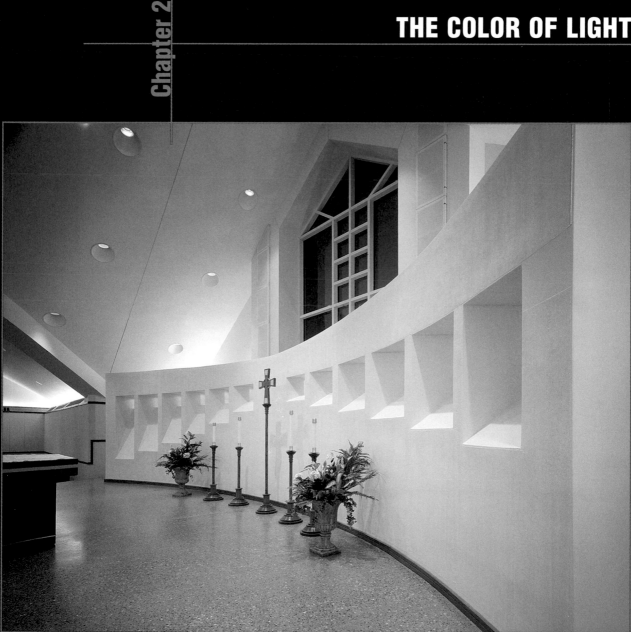

Photography started out as a black-and-white medium. Photographs simply recorded the brightness level of the light reflected from various portions of the scene and represented it as shades of gray. As a result, a black-and-white photograph is an abstraction of the original scene on two levels. First, it's a two-dimensional representation of a three-dimensional scene. Secondly, it's a representation of a full-color scene as a study in light values — shades of gray with no color. This dual level of abstraction gives black and white photography an enduring visual quality that causes it to persist as a medium of artistic expression long after photographers gained the technical capability to record full-color images.

Adding color to a photographic image gives the photographer the ability to make a more complete and accurate representation of the original scene. Color simultaneously enhances realism and removes one level of abstraction that is present in a black-and-white photograph. Additionally, a photographer can use color expressively, deliberately manipulating the colors in the photograph for artistic effect instead of accurately representing the original scene.

Fortunately, in today's world of digital photography, photographers can create images in black and white, as shown in figure 2-1 and in full color, as shown in figure 2-2. Colors can be controlled and manipulated at will, provided you understand some of the mechanics of the color of light.

2-1
Photo by Fred D. Reaves

2-2
Photo by Fred D. Reaves

UNDERSTANDING COLOR PERCEPTION

Let's start by looking at some of the basics of light and how humans perceive color. You may have encountered some of this information before, but a quick refresher of the key points will make it easier to understand how your eye and your camera deal with color, and that can help you make better color pictures.

The spectrum of visible light is the portion of the electromagnetic spectrum that humans can see and perceive as a range of brightness and color. The electromagnetic spectrum includes nonvisible light, radio waves, and other energy frequencies, but in this book, I'm concerned only with the range of light wavelengths that fall within the visible spectrum. Figure 2-3 shows the wavelengths of light in that spectrum as different colors, ranging from magenta through red, orange, yellow, green, cyan, and blue, to violet.

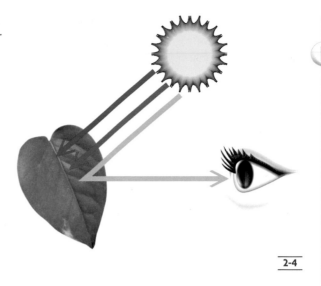

2-4

If the light falling on the leaf is red instead of white, the leaf doesn't look green anymore. In the absence of any green light to reflect, the leaf would be gray or black. So, changes in the color of the light source (actually, changes in the mix of colors in the light) can significantly change the colors reflected from objects.

2-3

The sun, and most other light sources, emits light across the entire spectrum. When all the colors of light mix together, white is produced, and an absence of color makes black. So sunlight is white light, which is a mixture of all the colors of light.

When you look at an object, what you see is the light that is reflected off that object and into our eye (see figure 2-4). If the object reflects all portions of the visible spectrum equally, the object appears white or gray. If, on the other hand, the object absorbs some wavelengths of light and reflects others, then the object takes on the color of the light it reflects. So, a green leaf looks green because it reflects mostly green light and absorbs most of the other colors.

COLOR TEMPERATURE

If all light sources emitted light in equal amounts across the entire visible light spectrum, then colors would always be consistent and my discussion would end here. However, light sources are not consistent. Light sources, such as incandescent lamps, emit disproportionately larger amounts of light in one portion of the visible light spectrum (yellows and reds) and less light in others (blues). The sun as a light source is consistent, but different angles and atmospheric conditions change how sunlight is filtered and reflected before it reaches us, which changes the effective composition of the light.

To help describe and manage the differences in the color makeup of different light sources, we use the term *color temperature.* Light is said to have a given color temperature when it matches the spectral characteristics of the light that would be radiated by a *theoretical black body* heated to that surface temperature. The theoretical black body is a hypothetical construct, but it closely approximates the light emitting characteristics of both the sun and the filament in an incandescent light bulb.

NOTE

Color temperature is measured on the Kelvin temperature scale, which is named after William Thompson, 1st Baron Kelvin, a 19th-century scientist and engineer.

The useful portion of the color temperature scale, shown in figure 2-5, ranges from 1500 kelvin to around 20,000 kelvin. Color temperatures at the lower end of the scale represent reddish light such as the last glow of the setting sun or the light of a candle flame. Figure 2-5 shows the color temperature scale progressing through brighter orange and yellow to the white of the mid-day sun. The higher color temperatures represent the increasingly blue cast of the light from the north sky.

2-5

The color temperature scale works very well for describing the various stages of daylight and for light sources such as incandescent lamps, arc lights, and photographic flashes. However, not all light sources have light emitting characteristics that closely approximate that of the theoretical black body, which is to say a continuous wide spectrum of light, with color distribution that transitions smoothly from more to

less abundant colors. (The chart on the left in Figure 2-6 diagrams the light output of an incandescent lamp.) In contrast, some lights are monochromatic (emit only one color of light) or exhibit a discontinuous spectrum, which means that they emit only a few colors of light with multiple sharp transitions between colors that are abundant and others that are almost nonexistent. Fluorescent lights have a mildly discontinuous spectrum. Notice the sharp spikes in the chart of a fluorescent lamp's light output, shown on the right side of figure 2-6. The Mercury vapor lights in figure 2-7 and the sodium vapor (lights in figure 2-8) are more severely discontinuous in their light output, which results in strange color shifts. Notice that the colors of the yellow machinery and copper coils in figure 2-7 are washed out due to the lack of yellow and red light from the mercury vapor lights.

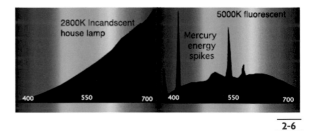

2-6

Because lights with a discontinuous spectrum don't behave like the theoretical black body, they can't be described as having a color temperature. However, because color temperature is so widely used to describe light sources, it can be useful to know where these lights fall on the scale. The *Correlated Color Temperature* (CCT) maps the average color of a discontinuous spectrum light source to its approximate location on the color temperature scale. Table 2-1 lists the color temperatures or correlated color temperature of some common light sources.

2-7

© Bryan Moberly | moberlyphotography.com

Table 2-1: Color Temperature

Light Source	Approximate Color Temperature in Kelvin
Candlelight	1500
High pressure sodium vapor	2100*
100w incandescent lamp	2800
Warm white fluorescent	3050*
Sunrise/sunset	3200
Tungsten photoflood	3200
White fluorescent	4000*
Neutral white fluorescent	4500*
Arc lamp	5000
Noon sun	5500
Photo flash	5600
Mercury vapor	3500-5900*
Bright sky	6000
Daylight fluorescent	6600*
Overcast sky	7000
Blue north sky	10,000 - 20,000

* Correlated Color Temperature

2-8

(Photo by Randy J. McCaffery

HOW WE PERCEIVE LIGHT

If an object can reflect only the light that falls on it, and there's a big difference in the color of light from an incandescent lamp, a sunny day, and an overcast sky, then it makes sense that an object, such as a red apple, would look different in different light. However, that's not what happens in real life. If you look at an apple inside the house, outside in direct sunlight, and again on a cloudy day, you probably won't notice any change in the color of the apple at all.

Actually, the color of the apple changes significantly. You don't notice it because of a phenomenon called *chromatic adaptation*. The human eye and brain automatically adapt to changing lighting conditions, adjusting color perception so that all but the most extreme color changes go unnoticed. As a result, you see the colors that you expect to see, regardless of changes in the light.

About the only time you notice differences in the color of light from different light sources is when more than one light source is visible at the same time. When you look at a scene, such as the one in figure 2-9, you can see the green cast of the light coming from inside the arched windows of the building because it contrasts with the streetlights in the foreground and the sky in the background. But when you enter the building,

chromatic adaptation makes that greenish light look normal and you won't notice any green cast to your surroundings.

2-9
© Bryan Moberly | moberlyphotography.com

HOW THE CAMERA SEES LIGHT

Unlike humans, cameras record light objectively. There's no chromatic adaptation process automatically making subjective adjustments so that colors match expectations. The camera has no expectation of what the colors of an object *should* look like, so it simply records the colors actually reflected by the object.

This is both a blessing and a curse. Objective color rendering makes the colors recorded by the camera much more accurate, but it means that those colors may not match human perceptions and expectations. In other words, the photograph may not contain the colors you thought you saw.

For example, figure 2-10 shows a building lit by artificial light, color corrected to look the way it appeared to the human eye. Figure 2-11 shows the same scene as recorded by the camera. The camera's image sensor is calibrated to normal daylight (color temperature of about 5500 kelvin) and the different color temperature of the artificial lights (probably around 3400 kelvin) creates a pronounced yellow-orange cast.

2-10
Photo by Rob Sheppard

2-11
Photo by Rob Sheppard

COLOR TEMPERATURE AND WHITE BALANCE

The digital image sensor in your camera produces optimum color results under lighting conditions that match mid-day sunlight, which is a color temperature of about 5500 kelvin. Under those lighting conditions, a digital camera produces an image with colors that match the colors you see with the human eye. However, if the distribution of colors in the light source changes, so will the colors of the image recorded by the camera. Therefore, if you take a picture in the shade or on an overcast day, the image recorded by the camera has a distinctly blue cast, which creates the pale flesh tones in figure 2-12. Similarly, a picture taken indoors by incandescent light has a strong yellow cast, as shown in figure 2-13.

2-12

2-13

When you take a picture under any lighting conditions other than mid-day sunlight, those images need color adjustments to remove the color cast caused by the different color composition of the light source. Fortunately, digital cameras have the ability to apply those color adjustments right in the camera, using a feature called *white balance*.

PRO TIP

Perhaps the simplest way to deal with white balance selection is to shoot in Camera Raw format and just ignore the camera's white balance setting. You can adjust the color balance of the image easily when you process the Raw file to convert it to another format. The camera's white balance settings are necessary only when you record your images directly to a finished image format, such as JPEG.

SELECTING A PRESET WHITE BALANCE

The camera's white balance setting allows you to select one of several lighting profiles, which tells the camera the color temperature of the light source for the scene you're about to photograph. Once the camera knows the color temperature of the light source in the scene, its built-in image processing software can automatically apply the appropriate color corrections to restore normal color rendering before saving the image file.

Getting the white balance selection right is very important. A good match between the camera's white balance setting and the actual color temperature of the light source for the scene produces clean neutral colors, such as those in figure 2-14, even though the lighting was obviously not the standard sunny day. On the other hand, a mismatched white balance setting

31

can cause blatantly off-color results such as figure 2-15, which shows what happens when you use tungsten white balance in daylight. The effect is exaggerated by the fact that the scene is in the shade, which is bluer (higher color temperature) than mid-day sunlight. For comparison, figure 2-16 shows the same scene with the correct color balance.

PRO TIP

Remember, you must set the white balance *before* you take a picture. The camera applies the color adjustments immediately after you click the shutter, and the image file is recorded with the color balance you specified. If you shoot Camera Raw, you can make further color balance adjustments when you process the Raw file. However, if you shoot JPEGs, changing the color balance after-the-fact is much harder. You can edit the colors in Photoshop, but it's hard to get good results with large-scale color changes.

The available white balance profiles vary with the different makes and models of cameras. Some typical preset white balance profiles include:

> **Daylight:** 5300 Kelvin

> **Cloudy day:** 6000 Kelvin

> **Open shade:** 7500 Kelvin

> **Tungsten:** 3000 Kelvin

> **Fluorescent options:** 4000, 4500, 6600 Kelvin

Your camera may offer different selections or use slightly different color temperatures for some profiles. You pick the one that most closely matches the light source for the scene and the camera applies the corresponding color balance adjustments.

2-14
© Bryan Moberly | moberlyphotography.com

2-15
Photo by Rob Sheppard

2-16
Photo by Rob Sheppard

The technique for selecting white balance also varies with the different makes and models of cameras. Some cameras give you quick access to the white balance setting with a button or dial, and it's usually available somewhere in the camera's menu system as well. For example, here's the way you set the white balance on an Olympus E-500:

1. Press the WB button on the back of the camera. (The WB button is also the Up navigation button.) The white balance selection screen appears on the display screen on the back of the camera.

2. Use the selection dial on the top of the camera to scroll through the icons representing the white balance settings. Highlight the desired selection.

3. Press the OK button on the back of the camera to set the camera for the highlighted white balance.

AUTOMATIC WHITE BALANCE

In addition to the white balance presets, almost all current digital cameras offer an automatic white balance mode. It's sort of a digital camera version of a human's chromatic adaptation and it's the default operating mode for most digital cameras.

The automatic white balance feature typically works by detecting white or near white areas in the image and automatically applying color adjustments to remove any color cast from those areas. It usually works pretty well as long as you're photographing an average scene that includes some clean white or very light neutral gray. However, if there's no white in the scene, the automatic white balance has nothing to work with and the camera's attempt to color balance the image may produce surprising results.

MANUAL WHITE BALANCE

If you don't trust the automatic white balance to give you good results in a difficult situation, and none of the white balance profiles match the light source in the scene (or the color temperature of the light source is unknown), then you can use manual white balance. Most digital cameras offer at least one manual white balance option in addition to the assorted profiles and automatic white balance.

Some cameras allow you to create a white balance point with a user-definable color temperature. The option may be labeled something like Kelvin or Custom, and allows you to create a white balance profile for a color temperature that isn't covered by one of the standard profiles. After defining the color temperature, you select and use this white balance just like any other white balance profile. The procedure for setting the color temperature for the user-defined white balance varies from camera to camera, so refer to your camera manual for instructions.

The user-defined white balance option works best for situations in which you know the color temperature of the light source, or you need to use the same non-standard setting repeatedly. When you don't know the color temperature of the light source, you want to use another manual white balance option provided by many digital cameras — one that allows you to set the white balance by sampling the light reflected off a gray card. (See figure 2-17.) This feature may be called white balance preset, custom white balance, or one touch white balance, or something similar. Refer to your camera manual for the name of the feature and specific procedure for how to select it. The following steps outline the general process:

2-17

1. Place a standard gray card in the scene you want to photograph, illuminated by the light source you plan to use for the finished image.

2. Aim the camera at the gray card and zoom in so that the card fills the frame completely. Make sure that no glare or shadows show on the gray card.

3. Follow the procedure for white balance sampling as specified in your camera manual. For an Olympus E500, you press and hold the One-Touch button while you press the shutter release, then press the OK button on the back of the camera when the One-Touch screen appears on the display.

Setting white balance by sampling the light at the scene automatically compensates for unpredictable variables such as atmospheric conditions, mixed light sources, and reflected light from the surroundings. It takes just a minute or so to do and it guarantees the best possible color reproduction. Just be sure you reset the white balance for each new lighting situation.

▶ **How can I use the white balance selection to give my pictures a slightly warmer tone?**

Many people prefer a slightly warmer color rendition to the neutral colors of a "correct" white balance. Traditionally, photographers achieved that warmer look by shooting in the "golden hour" before sunset or by using a warming filter on the lens. However, you can also achieve a similar effect with the white balance selection. To get warmer (more reddish) colors, select a white balance with a color temperature just a bit higher than the actual color temperature of the light source. For example, when shooting in mid-day sun (5500 kelvin), selecting the cloudy day (6000 kelvin) white balance gives your images a slightly warmer color cast. Telling the camera that the light is bluer than it really is causes the camera to compensate by making the image a little redder.

How do I know when to select a different white balance if all the colors look normal because the human eye adapts automatically to the color of different light sources?

You're correct in concluding that chromatic adaptation normally makes subjective color perceptions undependable when it comes to detecting white balance changes that the camera will see. However, you can teach yourself to see color changes in the light sources around you by simply being conscious of colors from different light sources and observing the change as you transition from areas lit by one light source or another. With practice, you can become remarkably proficient at detecting a change in the color of the light, although you probably won't be able to identify its specific color temperature by eye alone. Often, you can guess what white balance setting to use by observing the light source. Outdoors, it's easy to differentiate direct sunlight from shade or a cloudy day. Indoors, you can readily tell the difference between the tungsten-balance incandescent light of the table lamps in most homes and the fluorescent tubes lighting most offices. However, it's not so easy to distinguish a warm white fluorescent from a cool white fluorescent. The only sure solution is to shoot a test and evaluate the results each time you enter a new lighting situation. Fortunately, the camera's preview image is usually accurate enough to confirm an approximate white balance match. It'll alert you to major mismatches such as selecting tungsten white balance in daylight. If the white balance is close enough that you can't see any problem in the preview, then it's probably close enough to be corrected easily in an image editor. Still, if critical color rendition is important, you should download your test image to a computer for careful evaluation.

How do I know what color temperature to use for a user-defined white balance?

In order to use the user-defined white balance effectively, you must know (or be able to guess) the color temperature of the light source. If you have access to a color temperature meter, you're all set, but that's not a likely scenario. If you're shooting under artificial light, try to find out the brand and type of lamps used to light the scene. If there are spare bulbs sitting around, the lamp's specifications (including its color temperature) may be printed on the packaging. Otherwise, you may be able to find the information on the manufacturer's Web site. As a last resort, there's always trial and error experimentation. Try all the white balance profiles and find the two that come closest to producing the desired color. Then set the color temperature of the user-defined white balance in between the color temperatures of those profiles. Shoot a test, evaluate the results, refine your settings, and test again as needed. Better yet, record your shots in Camera Raw format and do the color correction when you process your Raw files into another format.

How do external filters affect my camera's white balance?

If you're using preset white balance settings, then any external filters you add to your lens will have exactly the effect you would expect. A warming filter (such as a Wratten 85) gives the image a warmer cast, a cooling filter (such as a Wratten 80) gives the image a cooler cast, a green filter gives the image a greenish cast, and so on.

However, if you use those filters in conjunction with the Auto white balance setting, they won't have the same effect. The Auto white balance feature detects the color cast from the filter and does its best to counteract the color cast and render the scene in neutral colors. Sometimes the Auto white balance feature successfully compensates for the filter and sometimes it doesn't. The results are unpredictable, and might even include a color shift in the opposite direction from the filter. As a result, you should avoid using Auto white balance with filters.

If you want to use filters in a situation where you need to set the white balance from a gray card, doing so is usually not a problem. Just be sure to set the white balance *without* the filter in place. Then, after you establish the white balance, you can add a filter to the lens to shift the color whatever way you want.

WHAT'S YOUR EXPOSURE

If you already know all about the interrelationships of aperture, shutter speed, and sensitivity, and you routinely calculate equivalent exposures in your head, then you can skip or skim this chapter. But if you're a typical photographer who relies on your camera's automatic exposure system for most of your photographs, then you're probably a little fuzzy about some of the details of what the exposure system is telling you, and perhaps a bit reluctant to step in and override the camera's automation to achieve a desired effect. If your understanding of the elements of exposure is somewhat rusty, this chapter should help.

WHAT IS AN EXPOSURE?

In photographic terms, *exposure* means to allow light (presumably, light that is being focused through a lens) to strike the film or image sensor, thereby recording the image. However, a great deal more happens during exposure than just haphazardly exposing the image sensor to light. You must precisely control the amount of light that reaches the image sensor if you want to get the proper exposure — one that reflects the photographer's vision of the scene with the proper range of tonality and good detail in highlights, midtones, and shadows. You, or your camera's automatic exposure system, adjust the camera's aperture, shutter speed, and ISO (sensitivity) settings, collectively called the *elements of exposure,* to adapt to variations in the brightness of the light being reflected from the scene and control how much of it reaches the sensor in order to achieve the proper exposure.

Sometimes, getting a good exposure is relatively simple. The brightness of the mid-day sun is constant and predictable, so you don't need fancy light meters and exposure programs in your camera to get a good exposure of a scenic subject in full sun, as figure 3-1 shows. Well-established exposure guidelines, such as the *sunny-16 rule,* work as well as the most sophisticated automatic exposure system under such predictable lighting situations.

3-1
Photo courtesy PDPhoto.org

X-REF

See Chapter 4 for more exposure guidelines.

If you took pictures only in full sun at mid-day, your camera wouldn't need much in the way of exposure controls. However, when you are indoors, or in situations in which the sun is filtered and reflected in unpredictable ways, the brightness of the light varies dramatically and so do the exposure settings you need to use to achieve the correct exposure.

Modern digital cameras employ built-in light meters and sophisticated automatic exposure systems to help you get good exposures under almost any lighting conditions you're likely to encounter. But there's more to good photographic exposure than just getting the right amount of light on the image sensor. Different combinations of aperture, shutter speed, and sensitivity can create different effects in your image. To produce images like figure 3-2, with its flowing water in the softly reflected light at the bottom of a canyon, you need to understand the relationship of aperture, shutter speed, and sensitivity, so you can make an informed decision about the optimum combination to produce the effect you want.

3-2
Photo courtesy PDPhoto.org

Over and Under Exposure

Exposing the image sensor in your camera to light reflected from a scene that you want to photograph usually results in something getting recorded, no matter what exposure settings you use. The trick is to get a good exposure that produces a good-quality image.

Figure 3-3 shows a good exposure of a test subject, with a good balance between highlights, midtones, and shadows. The result is a natural-looking rendition of the scene. You can see detail in the highlights, good color in the midtones, and detail in the shadows. The black velour background goes totally black, as I intended.

3-3

Recognizing Under Exposure

If you don't let enough light from the scene get to the image sensor, the result is an under-exposed image. For example, figure 3-4 shows the test subject from

figure 3-3 under exposed by two stops. The image looks dark overall. The lightest tones, such as the end of the large shell, don't look too bad, but midtones, such as the colors of the toy and the vase, are muted and dull. Shadow areas, such as the butcher block base, are very dark and lack detail, particularly toward the back edge and around the base of the wine glass.

3-4

Under exposure seriously degrades the quality of an image. Even if you try to compensate for the under exposure by adjusting the overall brightness and contrast in an image editor, the lack of detail in the shadow areas is still apparent. Figure 3-5 shows a close-up section of the under exposed image after processing in Photoshop. Notice that the color noise creates almost a posterized effect in the wood. Compare that to the same section of the properly exposed image in figure 3-6. Notice the smoother shading and more natural tones in the properly exposed image.

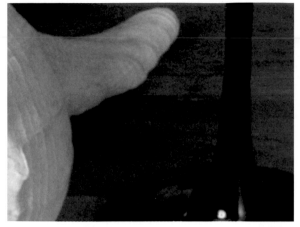

3-5

3-6

3-7

RECOGNIZING OVER EXPOSURE

Letting too much light reach the camera's image sensor is just as bad, if not worse. Figure 3-7 shows the same test subject with two stops over exposure. Now plenty of detail can be seen in the shadow areas, but the colors of the toy are a little washed out, and the highlights, such as the hat and the end of the large shell, are blown out— they're white, with almost no detail at all.

As you can see in figure 3-8, attempting to compensate for over exposure by darkening the image in Photoshop doesn't help much. The detail in the end of the shell is gone, and so is most of the detail in the wheels of the toy. All the colors are exaggerated, garish, and unreal. That may be an interesting effect, but it's not a realistic rendering of the scene. Figure 3-9 shows a comparison with the same section of the properly exposed image.

PRO TIP

The preview image you see on the camera's display immediately after taking a photograph may make the image look significantly lighter or darker than what the camera actually recorded. Don't base your exposure judgments solely on the appearance of the preview. Your camera's histogram display provides more reliable exposure information.

3-8

3-9

WHAT'S THE CORRECT EXPOSURE

Ideally, the correct exposure is the one that captures all the tones and values from the original scene and records them accurately. Unfortunately, photographers don't live or take pictures in an ideal world, so they must adjust exposures to adapt to a range of challenging conditions.

Like film before it, the image sensor in a digital camera is capable of reproducing a limited brightness range. An image with an 8-bit color depth, such as a standard JPEG image file, can record brightness

values from 0 to 255 in each of the three color channels, which is a ratio of 256:1, or a range of eight stops. This range is often called *exposure latitude*.

Being able to record a brightness range of 256:1 sounds pretty good until you consider that typical photographic scenes often have brightness ranges of 1000:1 or more. In direct sun, the range can easily exceed 20,000:1. Therefore, the brightness range of the scene you are trying to photograph is likely to exceed the brightness range you can record as a digital image.

If you are fortunate enough to be taking a picture in fairly flat lighting, such as the foggy scene in figure 3-10, the brightness range of the original scene may fit easily within the range that you can record in an image file. In that case, the correct exposure is the one that captures all the values from the scene, and you should be able to record good detail in highlights, midtones, and shadows.

However, when the brightness range of the scene is greater than you can record in an image file, there's no way to capture all the values from the scene. Inevitably you're going to lose some of the lightest or darkest values. If you adjust your exposure to retain detail in the brightest highlights, the darker shadows will go black, and if you adjust your exposure to retain shadow detail, the highlights burn out.

When faced with a scene with an excessive brightness range, such as the sunlit landscape in figure 3-11, you have to modify the definition of what constitutes a good exposure. Because it's not possible to retain detail throughout the entire range of highlights, midtones, and shadows, you have to determine what detail is most important and bias your exposure to record it. Therefore, the correct exposure is the one that records all the important detail while sacrificing the least detail at one or both ends of the brightness range. In figure 3-11, the photographer sacrificed some at both ends in order to achieve a realistic rendering of the sunlit foliage and a nice reflection in the

3-10
Photo by Tony Guffy

3-11
Photo courtesy PDPhoto.org

lake water. You hardly notice the loss of subtle shading in the snow on the distant mountaintops, but the exaggerated darkness of the foreground trees and shadowed foliage across the lake is more apparent. The overall effect is to focus your attention on the properly exposed portions of the scene.

READING A HISTOGRAM

The *histogram* is one of the most important and useful tools that a digital photographer has available for evaluating exposure. It plots the distribution of tones in an image, with the range of values from dark to light going from left to right along the base of the chart and the prevalence of a given value represented as height.

Almost all digital SLR cameras (and many of the better point-and-shoot cameras) include an option to display a histogram of your images as you shoot. The histogram in figure 3-12 is superimposed on the preview image. The histogram may also appear on a

separate screen that you can select, but whatever the format, it provides valuable information about the image. Film photographers would have to wait for their film to be developed, and then take a tedious series of densitometer readings and plot the results in order to get information comparable to the histogram that digital photographers can see within seconds of clicking the shutter.

Histograms are very useful, but they require some interpretation.

Theoretically, an average scene would produce a histogram shaped like the classic bell curve — a large hump, centered in the chart, and tapering evenly on both ends. In real life, you seldom see such a histogram. The histogram in figure 3-13 is about as close as they come. This histogram is from the Levels dialog box in Photoshop. (It's essentially the same information as the histogram displayed on a camera's preview screen, but it's easier to see on these pages.)

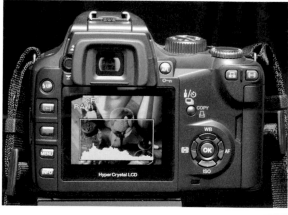

3-12

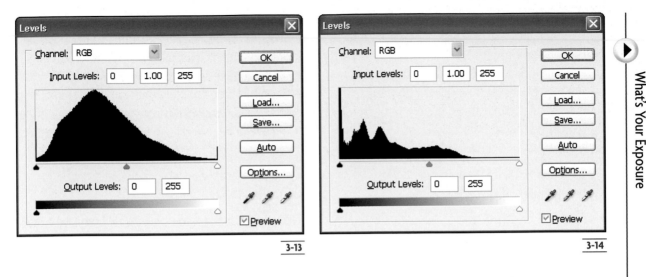

3-13

3-14

The tonal distribution is well contained within the chart, without any spikes at either end. At the same time, the tones are distributed along almost the full value range. Together, this indicates a good exposure. The center of the hump is a little off center, which simply indicates a slight predominance of darker mid-tones in the scene, not an exposure problem. There may be one or more humps or peaks in a histogram. Their position doesn't have any implication for the overall exposure as long as they correspond to the distribution of tones in the subject. A dark subject shows peaks on the left side of the histogram and a light subject has peaks on the right.

Figures 3-14 and 3-15, on the other hand, are histograms from under and over exposed images. Notice how the tones are shifted toward one side of the chart, with a large spike at one end and a distribution that ends before reaching the other end of the value range. Compare the histograms of the under exposed image in figure 3-14 and the over exposed image in figure 3-15 to the histogram of a properly exposed image in figure 3-13.

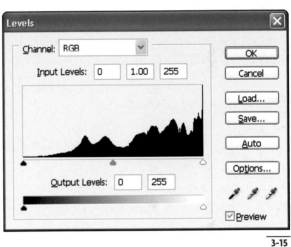

3-15

APERTURE, TIME, AND SENSITIVITY

The goal is to deliver just enough light to the camera's image sensor to get the optimum exposure — one that has good detail in highlights, shadows, and midtones and records as much as possible of the full brightness range of the original scene.

The amount of light required to record such an image on the sensor falls within a fairly limited range. The range of brightness of the light reflected from different photographic subjects varies tremendously, going from the dim light of a single candle flame to the blinding brilliance of direct sunlight. To control the light reaching the sensor and ensure good exposures in a variety of lighting conditions, you need to balance three factors:

> **Aperture:** Controls how much light can pass through the lens at any given moment. In telescope and binocular lenses, the aperture is a fixed value determined by the maximum diameter of the lenses and their optical design. In camera lenses, the aperture is adjustable by means of a diaphragm that you can partially close to reduce the effective diameter of the lens, thus restricting the amount of light that can pass through. Apertures are expressed as *f*-numbers (commonly called *stops*), with the smaller numbers (*f*-4) designating a wider aperture opening and smaller numbers (*f*-22) designating narrower aperture openings.

The Digital Image Sensor Is Like a Sponge

To help visualize the relationship of these three exposure elements, a mentor of mine offered the following analogy. Think of the film (or digital image sensor) as a sponge and the light as water. The sponge soaks up the water you pour onto it, up to a point. Your goal is to saturate the sponge with water without overfilling it and having excess water spilling out.

In this analogy, the ISO rating is based on the thickness of the sponge, and indicates how much water it will hold. So, if the sponge is rated to hold one gallon of water, you need to fetch a one-gallon bucket full of water and pour it on the sponge to achieve a good exposure.

However, you can't just dump the entire bucket contents on the sponge all at once. (That would splash water everywhere and make a mess.) The water needs to reach the sponge in a controlled flow through a hole in the bottom of the bucket. The controlled flow is analogous to focusing the light through a lens.

You can control the size of the hole in the bottom of the bucket, which is analogous to the lens aperture. The time it takes for the one gallon of water (your exposure) to flow through that hole and onto the sponge is analogous to the camera shutter speed. If you make a small hole in the bucket, it takes more time to empty the bucket than if you make a larger hole. The point is that whether it's a small hole for a longer time or a bigger hole for a shorter time, you're still delivering the same amount of water to the sponge.

The water bucket exposure analogy works well to help visualize the relationship of aperture, shutter speed, and ISO rating, but it doesn't account for another factor that affects exposure settings, and that's the brightness of the scene. However, it isn't too hard to extend the analogy to cover that. Just replace the bucket with a hose. The hole in the bucket (the aperture) becomes a nozzle on the hose and the time factor (the shutter speed) is regulated with a shut-off valve. Now you can visualize scene brightness as pressure on the hose. A bright sunny day is like a fully pressurized fire hose. It pushes the maximum flow of water through the nozzle in the minimum time. A dimly lit subject that reflects less light is like reducing the flow of water in the hose to a trickle. At the reduced pressure, there's not as much water rushing through the nozzle and you need to enlarge the opening and/or leave the valve open longer to allow the same total amount of water to flow through.

> **Time:** Controls how long the image sensor is exposed to the light coming through the lens. In the early days of photography, exposures were measured in seconds or minutes (sometimes hours) and controlled by removing and replacing a cover over the lens. Nowadays, exposures are measured in fractions of a second and controlled by an electronically controlled shutter in the camera. For convenience, camera controls normally list only the denominator of the fraction, so a shutter speed of 500 is really 1/500 of a second. For shutter speeds of one second and longer, camera displays typically add a suffix, such as 2s for two seconds.

> **Sensitivity:** A numerical value that indicates how sensitive the photographic recording medium is to light. In film-based photography, different film stocks require different amounts of light for a good exposure, and the sensitivity rating provides you with the information on which to base your exposure settings. The image sensor of a digital camera has a similar sensitivity rating. The sensitivity rating is expressed as the *ISO* (International Standards Organization) number, which takes its name from the organization responsible for the rating system. Higher numbers indicate increased sensitivity. The default sensitivity for most digital camera image sensors is ISO 100.

Film sensitivity can be adjusted somewhat with special processing, but it's not practical to change the sensitivity rating within a roll of film. Digital cameras, on the other hand, give you more control over the ISO setting. The image sensor is electronically controlled, and you can amplify its signal to boost the sensitivity at any time. As a result, the ISO setting on a digital camera becomes an effective exposure control tool instead of a fixed parameter.

EQUIVALENT EXPOSURES

The water bucket exposure analogy makes the point that you can empty the bucket by letting the water flow through a small hole for a longer time, or a larger hole for a shorter time. The total amount of water in the bucket (the total exposure) is the same either way.

The concept of *equivalent exposures* states that there are multiple combinations of aperture, shutter speed, and ISO that all produce the same exposure. A larger aperture paired with a faster shutter speed can deliver the same total amount of light to the image sensor as a smaller aperture paired with a slower shutter speed.

NOTE

Equivalent exposures are also referred to as the principle of *reciprocity*. I prefer the term equivalent exposure because it's more descriptive. Some other books use reciprocity. It means the same thing.

Aperture, shutter speed, and ISO ratings have different numbering systems, but each has the same proportional effect on exposure. Everything works in EV (Exposure Value) units. An increment of one EV increases or decreases the light by factor of two, so an increase of one EV doubles the exposure, and a decrease of one EV cuts it in half. For example:

> Each full *f*-stop of change in aperture is one EV. For example, the difference between f8 and f11.

> Each time you double or halve the shutter speed, that's one EV. For example, the difference between 1/250 and 1/500.

> Each time you double or halve the ISO rating, that's one EV also. For example, the difference between ISO 200 and ISO 400.

So, suppose that you start with the standard exposure for an average subject in direct sunlight at midday. According to the sunny-16 rule, that's *f*-16 at 1/100 with ISO 100. If you open up the aperture one stop to *f*-11, cut the shutter speed in half to 1/200, and leave the ISO setting the same, the overall exposure is exactly the same. They're equivalent exposures. Table 3-1 shows a more extensive listing of the equivalent exposures for the same common lighting situation. As you can see, you have lots of choices for combinations of aperture, shutter speed, and ISO that all deliver the same amount of light to the digital image sensor in your camera.

X-REF

See Chapter 7 for more information on depth of field and aperture selection.

Table 3-1: Equivalent Exposures for a Sunny Day

Shutter Speed	ISO				
	100	200	400	800	1600
1/6400	f2	f2.8	f4	f5.6	f8
1/3200	f2.8	f4	f5.6	f8	f11
1/1600	f4	f5.6	f8	f11	f16
1/800	f5.6	f8	f11	f16	f22
1/400	f8	f11	f16	f22	f32
1/200	f11	f16	f22	f32	f45
1/100	f16	f22	f32	f45	f64
1/50	f22	f32	f45	f64	
1/25	f32	f45	f64		
1/12	f45	f64			
1/6	f64				

ONE BEST EXPOSURE

For any given light level, there are lots of different equivalent exposures that all deliver the appropriate amount of light to the digital image sensor for a correct exposure. But that doesn't mean that all the equivalent exposures are exactly the same. The total exposure may be the same, but aperture, shutter speed, and ISO each affect your images in other ways besides controlling the exposure. Consider the following:

> Aperture affects depth of field, causing objects that are closer to or farther from the camera to appear more or less blurred.

> Shutter speed controls both subject motion and camera shake.

> Increasing the ISO increases the appearance of digital noise in your image — sometimes dramatically. Noise degrades the quality of your image, so

it's almost never a desirable thing, but it's often acceptable in small amounts. However, some image sensors are prone to sudden sharp increases in noise at certain ISO levels, and high noise levels can render an image unacceptable.

Depending on what effect you're going for in a given photograph, certain apertures, shutter speeds, and ISO settings may work better or worse than others. As a result, one combination of aperture, shutter speed, and ISO is optimum for the situation. Out of all the equivalent exposures, there's just one *best* exposure that delivers precisely the right amount of light to the digital image sensor and also gives the best possible balance between depth of field, motion control, digital noise, and all the other factors.

X-REF

See Chapter 6 for more information on controlling motion with shutter speed selection.

BRACKETING FOR EXPOSURE INSURANCE

Getting precisely the right exposure is critically important to producing excellent quality photographs. But, even the best light meters and exposure systems can be fooled by difficult lighting situations, and the preview image you see on your computer's display after each shot isn't always a reliable indication that you got the best exposure. So what can you do to ensure a good exposure?

The answer is to shoot the scene at several different exposures and choose the best one later. The technique is called *bracketing* because you shoot a bracket of alternate exposures over and under the presumed good exposure. Ideally, you end up with a set of images like those in figure 3-16. They range from under exposure, through correct exposure, to over exposure, and the best exposure is the one in the middle. However, the beauty of a bracket is that if your base exposure wasn't exactly right, one of the other steps in the bracket will probably be properly exposed and you have a perfectly exposed image to work with instead of having to try to salvage an image that's too light or too dark.

Obviously, bracketing works best with static subjects that sit still while you shoot multiple frames that are

3-16
Photo courtesy PDPhoto.org

identical except for minor changes in exposure settings. To be effective, the bracket needs to include a wide enough range of under and over exposure to cover any likely variation of the actual good exposure from the expected norm. The minimum bracket is usually three steps: one under exposed, one properly exposed, and one over exposed. For more uncertain lighting, a five-step bracket may be called for.

Another factor in a bracket is the exposure increment between the steps. They must be large enough to cover a good range in a reasonable number of steps and small enough to ensure that the optimum exposure doesn't fall in between the steps. In most cases, I find that bracketing in increments of two-thirds of a stop is about right, but half-stop or full stop increments may work better for you.

The most straightforward way to shoot an exposure bracket is to use your camera's exposure compensation feature to apply the exposure adjustment to each step of the bracket. Here's the procedure for shooting a simple three-step bracket in two-thirds stop increments.

1. Prepare to take the picture normally. Select aperture-priority or shutter-priority automatic exposure as appropriate. Select average, spot, or matrix metering pattern as appropriate. Frame and focus the picture.

2. Adjust the exposure compensation to feature to −2/3 EV using whatever combination of buttons and dials are appropriate for your camera. Then, fine-tune the framing and focus as needed and press the shutter release to shoot the first step of the bracket. Exposure compensation instructs the camera's automatic exposure system to reduce the exposure by the specified amount. You don't have to do any exposure calculations yourself.

3. Adjust the exposure compensation to 0 EV and then shoot the middle step of the bracket.

4. Adjust the exposure compensation to +2/3 EV and shoot the final step of the bracket.

You can easily adapt this procedure to add steps to the bracket or change the exposure increment of the steps. The exposure compensation feature is available on most digital cameras and it's usually convenient and easy to use. Not only that, it works with the standard auto exposure modes. It may also work with programmed scene exposure modes on some cameras.

Some cameras have an automatic bracketing feature that makes the process even easier. On an Olympus E-500, you activate the AE (auto exposure) bracket feature and set the exposure increment using the camera's menu system; then the camera makes all the adjustments for you as you shoot. In single-frame shooting mode, you press the shutter release three times to shoot the bracket — once for each step of the bracket. In continuous shooting mode, you just press and hold the shutter release. The camera fires off a three-shot burst, adjusting the exposure automatically for each shot.

NOTE

Some cameras offer an automated bracketing feature for flash exposures and for white balance, in addition to normal exposures. It's the same idea of shooting a set of frames of the same subject using slightly different settings when you're not sure what the optimum setting might be. For flash bracketing, the variation is in flash output and usually works only with the camera's built-in flash or a dedicated flash unit made specifically for your camera model. For white balance bracketing, the variation is in the color temperature setting.

Q&A

What's the sunny-16 rule you mentioned at the beginning of the chapter?

The sunny-16 rule is a standard exposure guideline that photographers have been using for decades. It states that the correct exposure for an average subject lit by the direct light of the mid-day sun is *f*-16 at the shutter speed equal to the reciprocal of the ISO rating of the film or digital image sensor. Therefore, when the ISO setting is 100, the correct exposure for an average scene in mid-day sunlight is *f*-16 at 1/100 second; if the ISO is 200, the exposure is *f*-16 at 1/200; and so on. Of course, you don't have to use *f*-16 as your aperture to follow the sunny-16 rule. Any equivalent exposure, such as *f*-8 at 1/400 for ISO 100, works equally well.

How reliable is the sunny-16 rule in determining correct exposure?

There is no more reliable light source than the sun. In fact, I often use the sunny-16 rule to test a light meter or a camera's exposure system. If the meter doesn't produce a reading that comes very close to the sunny-16 guideline when reading an average scene (or gray card) in mid-day sunlight, then I assume that there's something wrong with the meter and send it in for repair.

What about the camera's programmed exposure modes? You haven't mentioned them.

Programmed exposure modes, or scenes as they are sometimes called, preset the camera's automatic exposure mode (aperture priority or shutter priority), ISO setting, and sometimes the white balance to what the camera manufacturer deems appropriate for a given general photographic subject. The default program selection is often labeled "Program" and there may be several additional selections such as scenery, portraits, or sports action. Each program may also include rules to give priority to a faster shutter speed to stop action in sports mode, or a larger aperture for a soft-focus background in portrait mode.

Programmed exposure modes were developed to aid beginning photographers who are unfamiliar with aperture or shutter speed. They don't have to understand the elements of exposure or make an informed decision about what exposure settings to use. Instead, they can just select the program for the general type of subject and let the camera do the rest. Programmed exposure modes work reasonably well for subjects and lighting conditions that are a good match for what the camera maker envisioned when they created the programs, but the programs often fail to give good results when you try to use them in unusual situations.

Frankly, I don't use programmed exposure modes, and I don't know any experienced photographers who do. I'm not comfortable being a passive observer of what exposure settings the camera is selecting for me. I simply don't want to surrender that much creative control over my images to the camera. Besides, with just a little knowledge and experience, most photographers can do a better job of evaluating the scene and selecting the appropriate exposure than the arbitrary rules of the programmed exposure mode.

Chapter 4

MEASURING YOUR EXPOSURE

A camera produces a picture by capturing light reflected from a subject and recording it on the camera's photosensitive recording media — whether it's film in a traditional camera or the combination of a digital image sensor and storage device in a digital camera. That photosensitive media must be exposed to a precisely controlled amount of light in order to render the subject appropriately.

If you take photographs only of average subjects with standard illumination, the camera could be preset to deliver the proper amount of light to the image sensor each time you press the shutter release, without any manual or automatic adjustment ever being needed. In fact, that's exactly the premise behind disposable cameras. Everything is preset for a typical snapshot, either a typical outdoor scene in direct sunlight or an indoor subject about five feet from the camera's built-in flash. Such a camera is inexpensive to manufacture because it's simple — there's no focusing mechanism and no exposure adjustments. However, these cameras cannot adapt to changing lighting conditions. The

camera takes successful pictures only when the subject and lighting conditions match its preset exposure parameters. Other pictures "don't come out" because of "subject failure," which means that the subject didn't conform to the very limited conditions for which the camera was designed.

In the real world, photographic subjects and light levels vary tremendously, and photographers want to take successful pictures in conditions ranging from brilliant sunlight (figure 4-1) to dim indoor scenes (figure 4-2). To accommodate that need, most higher-end digital cameras have extensive exposure controls that allow you to adapt to widely varying lighting conditions and still deliver that precisely controlled amount of light to the image sensor. The aperture and shutter speed allow you to control how much light passes through the lens and how long it's allowed to strike the image sensor. The ISO setting lets you adjust the sensitivity of the image sensor.

In order to adjust the exposure settings properly, you (or your camera) need to know exactly how bright or

4-1

4-2
Photo by Fred D. Reaves

dim the light illuminating the scene really is. The human eye is an unreliable tool for evaluating brightness levels because it automatically adapts to such a wide range of light conditions.

MEASURING THE LIGHT

A *light meter* is an instrument for measuring the brightness of light. Light meters are used by architects to test light levels in buildings; by engineers to test the lights themselves; by lighting directors to set lighting on film and stage sets; and of course, by photographers to determine the correct exposure settings for photography.

Light meters provide an objective, quantitative measurement of light levels. The meters used by engineers typically display their measurements in *lux,* which is a standard unit of measure for illuminance. Photographic light meters, on the other hand, normally translate that scientific measurement into EV (Exposure Value) units, and also provide a direct readout in *f*-stop

and shutter speed for a given ISO number. (See figure 4-3.)

For generations, photographers used separate hand-held light meters to measure light levels, and then manually adjusted their camera's exposure settings based on the information from the meter. Most modern cameras have built-in light meters that are an integral part of their automatic exposure systems. The camera automatically adjusts the aperture and shutter speed in response to input from the built-in light meter. The process is faster and easier, but the light meter's role in determining the brightness of light in the scene is still the same.

4-3

REFLECTED VERSUS INCIDENT METERS

There are two basic types of photographic light meters. *Incident* light meters measure the light falling on the subject. *Reflected* light meters measure the light reflected *from* the subject. Incident light meters read the illumination level of the scene directly, and reflected light meters take an indirect approach by measuring the reflected light and inferring the illumination level from that measurement.

INCIDENT LIGHT METERS

Incident meters, such as the one in figure 4-4, are usually separate, hand-held units distinguished by the white diffuser dome or disk over the light sensor. The typical diffuser looks like half of a small ping pong ball.

4-4

Because an incident light meter measures the light falling on the subject, its readings aren't influenced by variations in subject reflectance. This tends to make incident light readings more reliable than a reflected light meter.

However, an incident light meter is sometimes less convenient to use because the meter must be positioned at the subject to take a reading. That's not usually a problem in the studio, but it's a major issue in sports and wildlife photography, and in other areas where the subject is inaccessible.

REFLECTED LIGHT METERS

Reflected light meters come in various shapes, sizes, and configurations. They range from separate hand-held units, such as the one in figure 4-5, to totally integrated components of a camera body. Some take an overall reading of light reflected from an entire scene, some take a spot reading from a small portion of the scene, and some take multiple readings and

4-5

then calculate an exposure for the range of light levels in the samples. Some allow you to select from any of those metering modes.

Because this type of meter reads light reflected from the scene (and presumably, towards the camera), you can take readings from the camera position. This is generally more convenient for the photographer, especially when the meter is built into the camera. Also, because you don't need to position the meter at the subject, problems rarely occur with inaccessible subjects. In fact, with a telephoto lens and a meter built into the camera, you can get light readings from subjects that are hundreds of yards away as easily as you can a subject that is within arm's reach.

One drawback of reflected light meters is that the light level reading is strongly influenced by the reflectance of the subject. If your subject is significantly more or less reflective (lighter or darker) than the hypothetical average for which the meter is calibrated, then you must adjust the indicated exposure settings to compensate for that difference if you want a good exposure that accurately renders the scene.

THE MYTH OF AVERAGE REFLECTANCE

Reflected light meters attempt to determine the illumination level of a scene by measuring how much light is reflected from that scene, and then calculating the proper exposure for the light level that is presumed to have produced the measured light reflection. The calculations are based on the assumption that the typical photographic subject reflects an average of 18 percent of the light that strikes it, which is the equivalent of a middle gray.

The assumptions work reasonably well for an average photographic subject, such as figure 4-6. For a typical subject, the lights, darks, and midtones all average out to the equivalent of a middle gray. When the subject reflectance matches to this expected average, the exposure reading from a reflected light meter is essentially the same as the reading from an incident

4-6

light meter (which measures the amount of light falling on the scene).

The problem is that not all photographic subjects conform to the assumed average reflectance. High key subjects (figure 4-7), with their predominance of light tones, reflect a much higher percentage of the light. Low key subjects, which are composed of mostly dark tones, reflect much less light than the hypothetical average. Backlit subjects may include large overwhelmingly bright areas, and so on.

A reflected light meter doesn't know whether it is reading light reflected from a white snow bank or a black pile of coal. It always interprets differences in reflected light level as if they were corresponding differences in the scene's illumination level. The

amount of light reflected from a snow scene is the same as the light reflected from an average subject in much brighter light, so a reflected light meter calculates an exposure that renders both scenes as the same medium gray.

USING A GRAY CARD

As long as your subject conforms to the expected norms by reflecting about 18 percent of the light illuminating the scene, a reflected light meter provides accurate and reliable exposure readings. But the exposure settings indicated by a reflected light meter get seriously skewed when a subject reflects significantly more or less light than that standard.

The most straightforward way to deal with this problem is to always try to determine your exposure by metering a subject that is reasonably consistent with the reflectance standard. But what do you do when the subject you want to photograph doesn't meet the standard reflectance that the meter expects? Well, one solution is to temporarily replace the problem subject with one that does match the reflectance standard, and use the standard subject to determine the correct exposure.

Photographic supply stores sell a variety of standardized reference targets that you can use to give your camera's light meter a reliable basis for determining the correct exposure in most any lighting situation. The traditional 18 percent gray card, is simply an 8 x 10 inch card with a solid matte gray surface on one or both sides. It's inexpensive and very effective. Some photographers prefer the convenience of a collapsible gray fabric disc instead of a rigid card. The spring-loaded disc stores in a small pouch, and pops open to provide a larger metering target than a typical gray card. There are also larger and smaller gray cards, some made of cardboard, some made of plastic, some fold, some don't.

4-7
© Charlotte K. Lowrie | wordsandphotos.org

The technique for using a gray card (or disc, or other standard target) to determine the correct exposure is simple and straightforward. Just follow these steps:

1. Set up your shot normally, with the background, subject, and lighting you want to use for the finished image. Then take a moment to evaluate the scene to see if it contains an average distribution of lights, darks, and midtones. If the overall scene or the main subject is noticeably lighter or darker than average, the reflected light meter in the camera will misinterpret the disproportionate reflectance as a different illumination level and give you the wrong exposure. For a high-key subject such as the one in figure 4-8, the result is underexposure — unless you give the camera's meter a better target to use for its exposure calculations.

4-8

2. Place a gray card into the scene to serve as a metering target, as in figure 4-9. Be sure to position the card where it receives the same light as the main subject you want to photograph, and make sure that the card's surface is free of shadows or glare.

3. Take an exposure reading from the gray card and lock the settings. If your camera has a spot metering mode, use that to read the exposure for the gray card without including any of its surroundings. If your camera doesn't offer a spot metering mode, you can zoom in on the gray card and/or move closer so that the gray card fills the viewfinder before you take the exposure reading. (Make sure you don't cast a shadow on the gray card when you get up close.) To lock in the exposure setting from

4-9

4-10

the gray card, use the camera's exposure lock feature if it has one. (You probably don't want to hold the exposure by half-pressing the shutter release because that typically locks the focus as well as exposure.) If your camera doesn't offer an exposure lock, note the exposure settings indicated for the gray card, and how much they differ from the settings indicated for the overall scene.

4. Remove the gray card from the scene and reframe the shot with your original subject in place.

5. Take the picture using the exposure settings from the gray card. If you were able to lock those settings in step 3, all you need to do is press the shutter release. If your camera doesn't offer an exposure lock feature, you can either manually set the aperture and shutter speed to match the settings that the camera's light meter indicated for the gray card, or use exposure compensation to adjust the auto exposure to those same settings. Using the gray card exposure gives you a much more natural rendition of the scene as shown in figure 4-10.

USING SEPARATE LIGHT METERS

In the days of cameras with built-in light meters and sophisticated exposure systems, separate light meters may seem like an anachronism. Although separate light meters are no longer an essential piece of photographic gear found in every photographer's bag, they remain a useful supplemental tool. They're compact, easy to use, and come in handy in numerous situations, such as:

> Reading the illumination level of a scene directly with an incident light meter. You generally get a more reliable reading than you can with the camera's built-in reflected light meter readings because incident light meters aren't influenced by variations in subject reflectance.

> Checking the light levels in a scene before unpacking your camera. That way, you know in

advance whether there's enough available light for hand-held shots, or you need to set up lights, tripod, or the big shoe-mount flash.

> Checking light levels frequently as you set up lights or observe changes in natural lighting. It's faster and easier with a hand-held meter, and you don't waste camera batteries just checking the scene.

> Testing lighting ratios. You can do it with an in-camera meter in spot metering mode, but a hand-held meter is more convenient.

> Using a flash meter to determine exposure settings to use with studio flash lighting or other off-camera flash units.

> Using a spot meter for ultra precise readings. Hand-held spot meters usually have a smaller angle of view than most camera's spot metering mode.

> Metering extreme situations that the camera's built-in meter may not handle well. Separate light meters often have a greater sensitivity range than the built-in meter in some cameras.

The actual operation of most hand-held light meters is pretty much the same. After you turn the meter on, taking a light reading is usually a quick one-button operation. On some older models, you may need to adjust dials and align numbers to get the reading, but most newer models have a digital display. You normally preset the ISO and either the shutter speed or aperture. Then, when you take the reading, the meter supplies the missing exposure setting. Some meters may add optional displays and additional features, such as the ability to save readings in memory and compare them, but the basic operation is generally very similar from meter to meter.

REFLECTIVE LIGHT METER

A plain, hand-held reflected light meter is probably the easiest of all light meters to use, but it's the least accurate. To use it, you just point the meter toward the scene, press the button, and then read the exposure settings from the display.

Meters such as the one in figure 4-11 are good for overall readings of average subjects, but the wide angle of view of the meter's sensor makes it difficult to know how much of the scene is included in the reading. (This particular model includes a small incident dome accessory, but the normal reflected light sensor is located just to the right of the sliding white dome.) Also, like all reflected light meters, their accuracy is heavily influenced by variations in subject reflectance.

PRO TIP

You may be able to use your subject's skin (or your own) as a substitute gray card. Typical Caucasian skin reflects approximately twice as much light as a standard gray card. In other words, it's one stop brighter than middle gray. Knowing that, you can take a reflected meter reading from the skin (a spot meter reading from your hand works well), and then open up one stop to compensate for the difference in reflectance between skin and a gray card. Darker-skinned people may need different amounts of exposure compensation. You'll need to test to see how your skin color relates to middle gray, but once you do, you'll never be without a handy reference for light meter readings.

4-11

Spot Meter

A *spot* meter is a special type of reflected light meter with a lens and viewfinder that enable you to select and meter a small portion of the scene. The biggest advantage of the spot meter is that you know exactly what portion of the scene you're metering because you can see it, clearly marked in the viewfinder. The light level reading comes from that portion of the scene and nowhere else. A spot meter is useful in situations such as getting a good exposure reading from the front surface of a backlit subject without the bright backlight affecting the reading.

X-REF

Spot meters are particularly well suited to working with the Zone System because they enable you to measure the range of brightness of various portions of the scene. See Chapter 5 for more information on the Zone System.

4-12

A spot attachment for a general-purpose light meter might have an angle of view of 5-10 degrees, which is equivalent to a telephoto lens. Special-purpose spot meters, such as the one in figure 4-12, usually have an angle of view of only 1 degree, which enables you to be very precise in selecting what part of the scene you're metering.

You can try a few basic approaches when you use a spot meter.

> Select a portion of the scene that should render as a midtone, equivalent to middle gray, and measure that area only. Use the indicated exposure settings as is.

> Select the most important part of the subject and meter that area with the spot meter. Adjust the indicated exposure settings as needed to compensate for any difference in reflectance between the metered area and middle gray. For example, if you're shooting a portrait of someone with typical Caucasian skin and meter the highlighted side of the face, you need to increase the indicated exposure by one stop to compensate for the lighter skin tone compared to the 18 percent gray standard.

> Select and read several areas of the scene, including the brightest highlight areas and the darkest shadow areas in which you want to retain detail. Note the range of brightness between the extremes and make sure it doesn't exceed the exposure latitude of your camera (usually five to seven stops for a JPEG image, and nine stops or more for Camera Raw). Set your exposure to the midpoint between the exposures indicated for the brightness extremes.

Incident Light Meter

An incident light meter reads scene illumination by sampling the light falling on the subject. This is the most accurate and reliable kind of exposure reading you can get for most subjects, and it's generally available only with a separate hand-held light meter. Some reflected light meters have an accessory diffusion dome attachment that allows them to take incident light readings, but I prefer using a meter like the one in figure 4-13, which is designed primarily for incident readings. The larger diffusion dome does a better job of gathering a good light sample from multiple lights, and the swivel head makes it easier to position the dome next to your subject.

To take an exposure reading with an incident light meter, you position the meter at your subject location so that it is in the same light as your subject and point the meter's diffusion dome towards the camera lens. The diffusion dome collects light from a full 180-degree field, and the meter calculates the exposure based on the brightness of the light striking the dome. The indicated exposure setting from a good incident light meter is normally very accurate without any need to compensate for subject reflectance, backlights, or anything of the sort.

Incident light meters are also a handy tool for testing lighting ratios — the ratio of brightness in the highlights (lit by the main light) and the shadows (lit by the fill light). To measure lighting ratios you just need to modify your incident light metering technique slightly.

1. Measure the brightness of the light on the highlight side of the subject in much the same way you would take a base exposure reading, but instead of pointing the dome toward the camera lens, point it half way between the lens and the main light source. Note the exposure indicated by the meter.

2. Reposition the meter to read the brightness of the light on the shadow side of the subject by positioning the meter's diffusion dome so that it's lit by the fill light, but not the main light. Usually, all you need to do is pivot the diffuser to point it toward

the fill light and use your other hand to shade it from the main light. Take another reading in that position and note the results.

3. Calculate the difference in the two readings, expressed as a ratio. A one-stop difference means that the highlight side is twice as bright, which is a 2:1 ratio, and so on.

FLASH METER

The duration of the short burst of high-intensity light from a photographic flash is too brief to register on a standard light meter. A flash meter is a special purpose light meter that can accurately read the brightness of the light from studio flash.

Flash meters can be reflective, spot, or incident style meters, but the incident style is most common. Flash

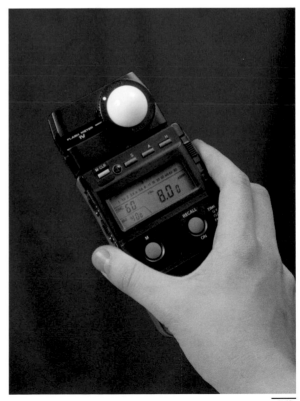

4-13

meters typically have an ambient light reading mode in addition to flash mode, so the same meter can read both flash and continuous light. Some high-end models are true multipurpose light meters, combining both spot and incident reading styles with the ability to take both flash and ambient light readings.

In use, the only difference between a regular light meter and a flash meter is that you need to sync the meter with the flash in order to take a light reading. You typically do that in one of two ways:

> In cord mode, you connect the sync cord from the flash to a PC socket on the flash meter as shown in figure 4-14. Pressing the button to take a meter reading triggers the flash, just like pressing the shutter release on the camera.

> In non-cord mode, there is no direct connection between the meter and the flash unit. You select

non-cord mode and press the button on the meter to prepare to take a reading. The flash meter goes into a sort of stand-by mode, waiting for the flash. Then you trigger the flash separately with a test fire button or remote control. The flash meter detects the sudden pulse of light and records its intensity.

Using an In-Camera Meter

These days, cameras normally have light meters built into the camera body as part of the camera's automatic exposure system. The built-in light meter is what enables the camera to detect the light level of the scene and automatically adjust the exposure settings accordingly. In many point-and-shoot cameras, the entire process is completely automated, leaving the photographer with very little knowledge of, or control over, the exposure settings. In contrast, most digital SLRs and high-end consumer cameras display full exposure information in the viewfinder and give the photographer at least some measure of control over the exposure settings.

The key to effective use of an in-camera meter (and the rest of the camera's automatic exposure system), is to understand a couple of facts about the metering system in your camera and its strengths and limitations.

> Virtually all in-camera exposure meters are reflective light meters, which means that they attempt to calculate the scene illumination level (and thus the proper exposure settings) from the amount of light reflected from that scene. The accuracy of that calculation is heavily influenced by differences in subject reflectance. If the subject reflects significantly more or less light than the standard 18 percent reflectance, you must adjust the exposure indicated by the meter to compensate for that difference.

> Most of the better cameras offer the option of using different metering modes that take light readings from different parts of the viewfinder as

4-14

the basis for their exposure calculations. The secret to getting the best results from your camera's light meter and exposure system is to select the best metering mode for the shooting situation and use its strengths to your advantage.

AVERAGE METERING

The simplest form of in-camera light metering is *average metering*. As the name implies, it reads light levels across the entire viewfinder and calculates an exposure based on the overall average. It works well for average scenes such as figure 4-15 with its equal amounts of lights, darks, and midtones. However, average metering mode is easily fooled by any scene

that doesn't average out to the standard 18 percent reflectance.

Center-weighted average metering is a popular variation on average metering mode that gives the brightness of objects in the central portion of the viewfinder more weight in the exposure calculation than objects around the outer edges of the frame. The assumption is that the object of main interest is likely to be near the center of the frame and it should get exposure preference over peripheral objects. This helps keep a strip of bright sky across the top of the frame from skewing the exposure for a flower or a person's face in the center. Although center-weighted metering helps in some situations, it actually makes the metering

4-15

system more susceptible to variations in subject reflectance within that central metering area.

SPOT METERING

Spot metering mode is the polar opposite of average metering. Instead of calculating exposure based on the average brightness of the entire viewfinder, spot metering samples the brightness of a small screen area and ignores the rest. The spot metering zone is usually a small area in the center of the screen. Some cameras offer multiple, selectable spot metering zones. Sometimes, the spot metering zones correspond to the camera's autofocus points, and the active zone selection moves in tandem with the autofocus point selection.

Spot metering mode allows you to select the exact portion of the scene on which you want to base your exposure. It's very useful for situations where large areas of very light or dark tones would create an exposure bias that would detract from the central subject, such as backlighting, high key, or low key scenes. For example, to shoot the backlit portrait in

figure 4-16, the photographer used spot metering to base his exposure on the model's face, which allowed the bright background to be overexposed. A different metering mode would have biased the exposure towards the large bright background, resulting in an underexposed face.

Working in spot metering mode allows you to be very precise in your metering, but it usually requires a more deliberate shooting technique that consciously separates the light metering step from the actual exposure. The process goes something like this:

1. Evaluate the scene to determine what portion will make a good basis for the exposure reading. Ideally, you select a midtone with about 18 percent reflectance, but you can also select a lighter or darker tone and set the exposure compensation to adjust the exposure accordingly.

2. Frame the shot to position the active spot metering zone on the selected area. Note that the framing for the spot exposure reading is usually *not* the way you want to frame the final shot.

4-16
Photo by Ramon Rodriguez

3. Take an exposure reading and lock it in. If your camera has an exposure lock feature, use it to lock in the exposure settings. Holding the exposure settings by half-pressing the shutter release isn't usually a viable option because that typically locks the focus as well as exposure, and you probably need to refocus after reframing the shot. If your camera doesn't offer an exposure lock, make a mental note of the exposure settings indicated for the spot reading, and then switch to manual exposure mode and set those aperture and shutter speed values manually.

4. Frame and focus the shot for your final composition and take the picture using the exposure settings from step 3.

MATRIX METERING

Camera manufacturers use names like Evaluative Metering, 3D Matrix, and Digital ESP to describe a metering mode that samples light levels at dozens of locations across the frame and then uses sophisticated algorithms to compute an exposure to balance the range of brightness it finds. This metering mode is a huge improvement over the traditional averaged reflected light reading.

Matrix metering is much less susceptible to differences in subject reflectance. The exposure is based on a large number of samples that include a range of lights and darks as well as the standard 18 percent reflectance midtone. It's more tolerant of light or dark areas within the frame, such as the sky behind the model in figure 4-17.

Matrix metering mode is a good choice for general photography. It delivers good exposures across an impressively wide range of lighting situations. However, it's not totally immune to exposure errors due to differences in subject reflectance. Matrix metering can still be fooled by any kind of extreme lighting, such as strong backlight or a high key or low

key subject without a normal range of tones anywhere in the frame.

SELECTING THE METERING MODE

Most of the better digital cameras offer more than one metering mode and allow the photographer to select which mode to use for a given photograph. That selection is an important part of the creative process. The camera doesn't know whether you're photographing a typical landscape or a snow scene, so it's up to you to evaluate the scene and select the most appropriate metering mode (and exposure compensation).

Selecting the metering mode is usually fairly simple to do. The details of the selection process vary from

4-17
Photo by Alicia McGinnis

camera to camera, but the following steps for changing metering modes on an Olympus E-500 is a typical example:

1. Press the Metering button (the left arrow button) on the back of the camera. The meter selection menu appears on the LCD display (see figure 4-18).

2. Use the selection wheel to move the highlight to the icon for the metering mode you want to select.

3. Press the OK button on the back of the camera to activate the highlighted metering mode.

In addition to the menu selection for metering mode, some cameras enable you to quickly switch metering modes while the camera is at eye-level by using some combination of buttons and dials.

4-18

4-19

LOCK/HOLD EXPOSURE

When you press the shutter release to take a picture with most digital cameras, a whole series of events unfolds. As you press the shutter release button half way down, the camera focuses the lens, meters the light level, adjusts the exposure settings according to the scene brightness detected by the light meter, and displays that information in the viewfinder. Then, when you press the shutter release button down the rest of the way, the camera actually takes the picture (which is a multistep process of its own).

Normally, this entire process takes place in a fraction of a second with the picture framed up just as you want the finished image to look. However, most cameras lock the focus and exposure settings and hold them as long as you keep the shutter release half-pressed. This feature allows you to frame the picture initially to place an autofocus point or spot metering zone at an advantageous location, half-press the shutter release to hold the focus and exposure settings, and then reframe the shot slightly before taking the picture. Many photographers get into the habit of pausing momentarily with the shutter release half-pressed, even if they don't plan to reframe the shot. It's an opportunity to take stock of the situation and check the automatic focus and exposure settings before committing the image to memory by pressing the shutter release fully.

Sometimes you may want to further separate the exposure determination from the other shooting steps — usually because you need to insert a gray card into the scene as a target for the light meter reading. That's when the exposure lock feature comes in handy (if your camera has one). The exposure lock is usually a separate button (see figure 4-19) that you can press to lock down the current exposure settings and prevent them from changing as you reframe and refocus the shot. On this camera, it's labeled AEL for auto exposure lock.

For most cameras that offer the feature, the procedure for using the exposure lock goes something like this:

1. Aim the camera at the target you want to use for exposure determination (usually a gray card), and half-press the shutter release button to take the light reading and calculate the exposure.

2. With the shutter release still half-pressed, press the exposure lock button to freeze the exposure settings. Then you can let go of the shutter release button.

3. Remove the gray card from the scene, reframe the shot, and make whatever other adjustments you need to make. The exposure lock keeps the exposure settings from changing, even if you walk away from the camera for several seconds.

4. When you're ready, take the shot by pressing the shutter release all the way down in one motion. As long as you don't pause at the half-press stage, the camera will use the locked exposure settings instead of recalculating the exposure.

EXPOSURE COMPENSATION

Exposure compensation (sometimes called exposure bias) is a very useful — and often overlooked — camera feature. It enables you to increase or decrease the exposure that the camera calculates from the light meter reading, without resorting to manually setting the aperture and shutter speed yourself. The camera continues to function in automatic exposure mode, automatically responding to changes in light levels, but with the exposure adjustment you specify applied to each exposure the camera calculates.

You most often use the feature to adjust the exposure to compensate for differences in subject reflectance, such as a highly reflective snow scene that the camera would misinterpret as a scene with exceptionally bright illumination and underexpose if you don't override the normal exposure.

Exposure compensation is usually displayed in EV (exposure value) units, and shown as positive or negative values relative to the camera's normal automatic exposure calculation. So, +1 EV is one stop more exposure than the base exposure as indicated by the light meter reading, and -1 EV is one stop less exposure than the base. Most cameras allow you to apply exposure compensation in one-third or one-half EV units for reasonably precise adjustments.

The actual procedure for making exposure compensation adjustments varies. On the Olympus E-500, you use the feature by pressing the exposure compensation button (which is located near the shutter release button) and turn the selector wheel to dial in the amount of exposure compensation desired. The camera displays the exposure compensation setting in the viewfinder and in the information screen on the display screen on the back of the camera (see figure 4-20).

METERING SPECIAL SITUATIONS

Reflected light meters, including the meter in your camera's automatic exposure system, rely heavily on the assumption that a typical photographic subject reflects an average of about 18 percent of the light

4-20

illuminating the scene. The exposure settings indicated by the meter and auto-exposure system are calculated based on that assumption. Although this approach works well for most average subjects, there are several photographic situations where the scene illumination and/or subject reflectance vary from the norm enough to cause the meter to give erroneous exposure readings.

When that happens, you need to use your judgment to override the meter and adjust the exposure settings in order to get a good exposure. Let's take a look at a few of the more common situations where that is necessary.

BACK LIGHT

One of the classic exposure problems is backlighting, where the subject is lit from behind or surrounded by a very bright background. It could be a person silhouetted against a bright sky, or subject with a background of brilliantly lit snow or sand that is much brighter than the light on the main subject. If the subject casts a shadow towards the camera, you have a backlight situation.

When you try to photograph a backlit subject, the overwhelming brightness of the background dominates the light meter's reading, causing the foreground subject to be significantly underexposed. Figure 4-21 simulates the kind of results you can expect from shooting a backlit subject with typical auto-exposure settings.

The solution is to use your camera's spot metering mode to selectively read the brightness of the main

4-21
Original photo by Alicia McGinnis, edited to simulate exposure difference

4-22
Photo by Alicia McGinnis

subject and omit the overly bright background from the light level reading. The result is a good exposure for the main subject (as shown in figure 4-22), although it usually means that the background is somewhat overexposed. Also, if the part of the scene where you took the spot reading is significantly more or less reflective than the 18 percent gray standard, you may need to apply the appropriate exposure compensation for that difference.

HIGH KEY OR HIGHLY REFLECTIVE SUBJECT

A high key subject is one that is composed primarily of white or light colors with only small areas of darker shades. A snow scene is a high key subject, as is a portrait of a person wearing a white shirt and posed on a white background.

High key subjects are almost guaranteed to fool any reflected light meter because the meter assumes average subject reflectance even though the light-colored

subject is reflecting much more light. The high levels of reflected light make the meter think the illumination level is much brighter than it really is, so the indicated exposure settings underexpose the shot. Figure 4-23 is a simulation of a snow scene shot with exposure settings as indicated by a normal meter reading. In this case, the underexposure doesn't look too bad on its own, but it isn't a very good representation of the scene as the photographer

PRO TIP

If your camera doesn't have a spot metering mode that allows you to selectively meter a small portion of the scene from your normal camera position, you can zoom in and/or move closer to fill the frame with the area you want to meter as the basis for your exposure. Use the exposure lock feature (or manually exposure settings) to set your exposure based on that reading. Then you can return to your normal shooting position, reframe the shot, and fire away.

4-23

experienced it. Figure 4-24 shows a more natural rendering of the scene, which required plus one EV exposure compensation to counteract the meter's underexposure.

Average, spot, and matrix metering modes all fall into the same trap when faced with this kind of situation. The matrix mode may do a little better job than the other two if there are a few dark areas in the scene to help establish the lower end of the value range. The best way to get a good exposure of a high key subject is to take an incident light reading with a hand-held light meter. The next best solution is to use spot metering mode and either select a naturally occurring area of average reflectance, or use the gray card technique to supply your own metering target. If that's not convenient, you can just use exposure compensation

to counteract the meter's tendency toward underexposure by adding a stop or two.

LOW KEY SUBJECT

A low-key subject consists of predominantly black or dark colors with relatively small areas of lighter shades. Reflected light meters misinterpret the low light levels from the low-reflectance subject as low illumination levels and indicate exposure settings that overexpose the image.

Figure 4-25 simulates the result of shooting a low key subject with the exposure settings indicated by a normal meter. There's good detail in the model's dark hair and jacket, but the skin tones are washed out and the image lacks the dramatic effect that the photographer intended. Figure 4-26 shows the result of basing the

4-24

exposure on the model's skin and letting the dark areas go nearly black.

BRIGHT LIGHT IN THE FRAME

Another common exposure problem is a light source or other bright object appearing in the frame. This often occurs in interior scenes where a lamp or large window is in the picture. Outdoors, you can have the problem if the sun is in the frame, either directly or as a reflection off a glass or metal surface. The problem is that the light meter assumes that it's reading all reflected light, and the higher intensity of the direct light source overwhelms the rest of the scene, making it seem brighter than it really is. As a result, the meter underexposes the rest of the scene.

4-25
Original photo by Alicia McGinnis, edited to simulate exposure changes

4-26
Photo by Alicia McGinnis

Figure 4-27 simulates this kind of situation with the bright windows behind the model causing a normal meter reading to underexpose the main subject. In contrast, figure 4-28 shows the corrected exposure. Adding about a stop to the exposure produced better skin tones and more detail in the model's jacket.

This problem is very similar to the high key subject problem in many ways. The cause is different, but the result is the same (underexposure) and so are the solutions (incident readings, spot metering, or exposure compensation of plus one or two EV).

A sunset such as figure 4-29 is the ultimate case of a light source in the frame. You're usually shooting straight into the setting sun, which puts the brightest

of all lights right in the center of the image. That will definitely skew normal light meter readings.

The way to deal with this situation is to remember that the sunset effect is from the clouds, not the sun. Therefore, you need to base your exposure on the clouds and eliminate the sun from the exposure calculations. The easiest way to do that is to use spot metering mode to read the light level of some clouds.

PRO TIP

For richly colored sunsets, try deliberately under exposing with an exposure compensation of minus 1 or 2 EV. It's not the most accurate rendition of the scene, but it sure looks nice.

4-27
Original photo by Alicia McGinnis, edited to simulate exposure changes

4-28
Photo by Alicia McGinnis

Frame the shot to position the spot metering zone on a cloud with a nice medium tone, lock the exposure setting, then reframe the shot, and take the picture.

EXPOSURE RULES OF THUMB

In the days before in-camera meters and automatic exposure systems, photographers learned about proper exposure from experience and developed exposure guidelines for many common situations. You may no longer need to rely on these rules of thumb for your primary exposure determination, but they can still be very useful to know. Familiarity with some of the time-honored guidelines, such as the following, can provide a reference point to help you recognize problem situations where your camera's auto exposure system is giving you the wrong information, and provide clues to how you can compensate for the error.

> **Sunny day:** The sunny-16 rule is probably the best known exposure guideline — and the easiest to remember. It also establishes the exposure baseline on which other guidelines depend. It states that the proper exposure for an average subject in direct mid-day (10am to 4pm) sun is *f*-16 at the shutter speed equivalent to the reciprocal of the ISO setting. So, for ISO 100, the sunny-16 exposure is *f*-16 at 1/100 second.

> **Open shade:** The lighting condition where your subject is in the shade, not direct sun, but is lit by large expanse of open sky. For example, a subject that is on the shadow side of a hill or in the shade of a building on a sunny day is in open shade. Open up two stops (plus two EV) over the sunny-16 exposure.

> **Cloudy day:** For a typical cloudy day — a light overcast or when the sun goes behind a cloud — open up three stops (plus three EV) over the sunny-16 exposure. For heavy cloud cover or a stormy sky, you may need to open up four stops or more.

> **Snow, sand, and water:** Snow, sand, and water all reflect lots of light back into a scene, effectively making it brighter than it would be from the direct illumination alone. As a result, you need to stop

4-29
Photo by Tony Guffy

down one stop (minus one EV) to compensate for all that extra light bouncing around. Stop down two stops if you're photographing the snow or beach itself rather than a person or other subject in the scene. A bright scene *will* fool your meter, so read the scene (or start with the sunny-16, open shade, or cloudy day guidelines), then apply compensation to achieve the correct exposure.

> **Office interior:** Lighting levels vary in offices, but most offices with bright overhead fluorescent lighting fall into a general range. Typical exposures are around *f*-2.8 at 1/60 with ISO 400 (plus or minus a stop or two).

> **Home interior:** Residential interiors are usually dimmer than offices and vary a lot. A typical exposure for average home lighting at night is around *f*-2.8 at 1/15 with ISO 400, but dimmer rooms may require as much as five stops more exposure.

> **City streets at night:** A typical exposure for subjects lit by streetlights is about *f*-2.8 at 1/8 with ISO 400. If there's a lot of extra light from signs,

cars, store windows and the like, the exposure might be closer to *f*-2.8 at 1/60 with ISO 400.

> **School and church auditoriums:** The lighting level is often pretty close to average home lighting, and the exposure is around *f*-2.8 at 1/15 with ISO 400.

> **Gymnasiums:** A typical exposure for an indoor sports venue is *f*-2.8 at 1/60 with ISO 400.

> **Stage shows:** The lighting can vary tremendously for music performances and other acts with a lot of lighting effects. For a play, the lighting is usually more predictable — somewhere around *f*-2.8 at 1/60 with ISO 400.

> **Outdoor sports stadiums:** During the day, you can use the sunny-16 rule, adjusted for shade or clouds as needed. At night, under the lights, the exposure is usually in the neighborhood of *f*-2.8 at 1/125 with ISO 400.

Use these guidelines as a starting point for an initial test exposure, and then evaluate your results with your camera's preview image and histogram display; adjust your settings as needed to improve subsequent exposures.

Q&A

What's the proper exposure for a scene lit by firelight, candle light, oil lamps, and the like?

The light given off by an individual candle is fairly predictable, so you can calculate an exposure. (An exposure of *f*-2.8 at 1 second with ISO 400 should be about right for a subject one foot from a single candle.) The illumination from firelight, on the other hand, varies significantly depending on the size of the fire, as does the light from oil lamps and groups of candles. When you're shooting a firelight scene, the light source (the fire) is usually included in the frame, along with the subject and a lot of dark background. The best way to meter this kind of scene is to take a spot reading off the subject and ignore both the bright light of the fire and the dark background. Don't forget to adjust the exposure if the subject you're metering is lighter or darker than the 18 percent reflectance standard. For Caucasian skin, the exposure compensation is plus one stop.

What's the best exposure for fireworks and lightning against a night sky?

Fireworks and lightning are both relatively small, bright light sources that travel across the black background of the night sky. The combination of extreme high contrast and the brief duration of the light make them almost impossible to meter properly. Manual exposure based on a guideline derived from experience is the only way to go.

What's the correct exposure for a full moon in the night sky?

Most people think it takes a long time exposure to photograph the moon — after all, you're shooting at night and it's dark outside. However, that's not the case at all. The surface of the moon is illuminated by direct sunlight. It's a bright sunny day on the moon, and you need to set your exposure accordingly if you expect to retain the surface detail. Theoretically, you should get good results with a sunny-16 exposure of *f*-16 at 1/100 with ISO 100, or an equivalent exposure, such as 1/400 at *f*-8. That exposure might actually work on a clear, dry night at high altitude, but at lower altitudes, you may need to open up a stop or two to compensate for light lost to atmospheric haze. Still, your exposure is going to be a lot closer to a sunny day than your darkened surroundings lead you to expect.

Chapter 5

MAKING CREATIVE EXPOSURE CHOICES

Although much of the creativity involved in making a photograph is in subject selection, composition, and lighting, exposure also has an important role to play as a creative tool. Much more goes into exposure than the perfunctory process of properly recording the creative masterpiece you see in the viewfinder.

In this chapter, you find out why you may not want to let the camera do the work and why it's often better to take matters into your own hands. By exercising creative control over exposure, you can control subject motion and depth of field. More importantly, you can use exposure to control how values are rendered in your photograph. You can render the scene as accurately as possible, with a full tonal range, or you can elect to shift the natural values lighter or darker for creative effect. For example, in figure 5-1, the photographer deliberately chose to underexpose the image compared to the metered exposure, thus making the image darker, which accentuated the sky and reduced the trees to a silhouette.

SELECTING THE BEST EXPOSURE

The multi-area metering modes (sometimes called *matrix* or *evaluative* metering) that are available in most modern cameras are very good at determining the nominally correct exposure value for most scenes. As a result, you can often use the camera's automatic exposure system to capture a reasonably faithful rendering of the scene with good detail in the shadows, midtones, and lighter tones — no manual overrides required. You can get good results a surprisingly large portion of the time. However, certain situations can fool even the best metering systems (see Chapter 4), and you may want to diverge from the metered exposure for creative effect.

X-REF

See Chapter 4 for more information on metering modes and common photographic situations that cause meters to give erroneous readings.

5-1
Photo by Rob Sheppard

LET THE CAMERA DO THE WORK

Modern digital cameras typically include a number of programmed exposure modes that are capable of totally automating the process of determining and setting the exposure. There's usually a default program for general photography (which may be labeled Auto, Program, or Normal), plus several additional programs for situations such as landscapes, portraits, sports, children, sunsets, night scenes, and so on. All you have to do is select the program mode (or scene, as they are sometimes called) that matches the kind of subject you're photographing, and the camera does the rest, leaving you free to concentrate on your subject. The results can be very effective, as shown in figure 5-2, in which the camera's default Normal program mode automatically selected a very reasonable exposure of f-5 at 1/160.

However, if you elect to use one of the camera's built-in programmed exposure modes, you surrender direct exposure control to the program. The camera's meter senses the light level and then the program sets the aperture, shutter speed, ISO, and white balance, according to a set of criteria that gives priority to different exposure elements depending on the program selected. For example, the Sport program mode usually gives priority to a high shutter speed to stop subject motion, while the Portrait mode aims for a blurred background by giving priority to a large aperture for shallow depth of field. The better cameras display the aperture and shutter speed selected by the program in the viewfinder, but it's an informational display only. The camera is in control of the exposure settings, not you.

Programmed exposure modes are just another tool in the photographer's arsenal, and like other tools, you can learn to use them effectively and creatively. They can be very useful in fast changing situations such as a child that runs from sun to shade and back again. The program can quickly adapt to the drastic changes in light levels— a task that would challenge the most experienced and nimble photographer.

The secret to mastering programmed exposure modes is understanding how each program prioritizes the exposure elements of shutter speed, aperture, and sensitivity, as well as what other camera settings are changed by each program. (Some programmed exposure modes change color rendering and auto-focus modes in addition to exposure settings.) Developing that understanding takes some work, because you won't find the detailed information you need in the camera's menu system. You need to read the program descriptions in the manual, and then do some testing to discover how the general program goals translate into specific aperture/shutter speed combinations under various conditions.

After you develop a thorough understanding of how each programmed exposure mode operates, you can make an informed decision about which program to use in each shooting situation, instead basing your

5-2
Photo courtesy of Erin O'Mara

PRO TIP

Personally, I'm not a big fan of programmed exposure modes. Although they're convenient and useful for beginners, using them makes me feel like I'm abdicating some of the responsibility for selecting exposure settings. And that doesn't sit well with an admitted control freak.

selection of a scene name and a vague description on the camera's menu screen. You're still delegating exposure control to the program that you select, but you do so knowing that the program will operate within predictable guidelines. Still, you must carefully monitor the aperture and shutter speed selected by the program in the viewfinder, so you can switch to another shooting mode and override those settings if you disagree with the camera's exposure settings.

X-REF

In Chapter 3, I discuss selecting the one best exposure from the multiple aperture/shutter speed combinations that all deliver the same amount of light to the image sensor in your camera.

5-3
© Charlotte K. Lowrie | wordsandphotos.org

CONTROLLING AN AUTOMATIC EXPOSURE

In addition to programmed exposure modes, nearly all digital cameras have two other automatic exposure modes: aperture-priority mode and shutter-priority mode. They both provide the convenience of automatic exposure while affording the photographer substantially more creative control.

When using aperture-priority exposure mode, you select the ISO and aperture and the camera automatically adjusts the shutter speed to obtain the proper exposure as determined by the built-in meter. Shutter-priority mode works the same way, except that you set the shutter speed, and the camera adjust the aperture automatically.

The aperture-priority and shutter-priority exposure modes allow you to choose which exposure element is more important and take direct control of that aspect of the exposure. Then, when you select the aperture or shutter speed, you're selecting the dominant half of that best exposure combination. The camera automatically sets the other half of the aperture/shutter speed pairing based on the light level and ISO setting. You get control without giving up the convenience and shooting speed of auto-exposure. This is an excellent way to work as long as the subject and lighting conditions are such that the camera's built-in meter can deliver a good exposure, which is most of the time.

Figure 5-3 shows aperture-priority exposure mode in operation. The photographer selected the aperture

X-REF

See Chapter 7 for more information on aperture and depth of field.

(*f*-8) to obtain enough depth of field to keep the flower petals sharp while allowing the background to blur out of focus. The camera's auto-exposure system set the shutter speed to 1/180. Controlling depth of field is a good example of a situation in which setting the aperture takes priority and the shutter and sensitivity are variables that can be adjusted as needed.

In contrast, Figure 5-4 shows an example of an exposure using shutter-priority mode. In this case, the photographer selected the shutter speed needed to stop the sports action (1/500) and allowed the camera to set the aperture for the light conditions.

DELIBERATE EXPOSURE DEVIATION

Creative exposure can also be deliberate deviation from the metered exposure as indicated by your camera's built-in meter. Sometimes you need to depart from the indicated exposure because the combination of subject and lighting creates a situation that fools the meter into giving an incorrect reading. Usually, that happens when the subject is composed of predominantly light or dark values instead of an average distribution of dark, light, and middle tones.

Figure 5-5 shows just such a situation. The meter doesn't know that the subject is actually a white onion

X-REF

See Chapter 6 for more information on controlling motion with shutter speed.

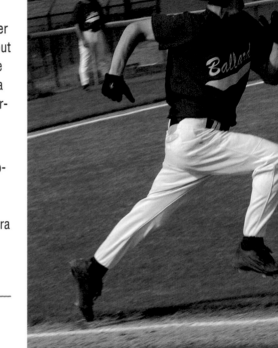

5-4
Photo by Tony Guffy

5-5

on a white background and assumes that the light is being reflected from an average scene. Therefore, the metered exposure renders the onion as gray on gray instead of white on white. To accurately render the subject (figure 5-6), I needed to increase the exposure by a couple of stops. In this case, I manually set the aperture and shutter speed for the desired exposure,

5-6

but you can achieve the same effect by using the camera's exposure bias setting to shift the metered exposure by a couple of EV units.

Sometimes you need to override the metered exposure to compensate for erroneous readings and achieve a natural rendering of an unusually light or dark subject. Other times, the goal isn't to produce a natural rendition of the scene at all. Instead, you may want to exaggerate some tones and subdue others by using exposure to shift all the values in a picture darker or lighter.

For example, figure 5-7 simulates the metered exposure of sunlight from a window creating highlights on some pews. It's a natural rendering of the scene, but the light, washed out highlights on the bland midtones of the surrounding pews don't have a lot of visual impact. In figure 5-8, the photographer emphasized the warm sunlight highlighting the pews by deliberately underexposing the image so that the highlights are a richly colored midtones contrasting against dark surroundings.

5-7
Original photo by Charlotte Lowrie, edited to simulate exposure change

There are a few different ways to achieve this kind of exposure effect. They all accomplish the same thing, but take different paths to reach the goal.

> **Manual exposure:** The most direct technique for overriding the camera's metered exposure is to switch to manual exposure mode and set the aperture and shutter speed yourself.

> **Exposure compensation:** You can also use your camera's exposure compensation (also called exposure bias) feature to adjust the normal metered exposure up or down by a selected amount. In this case, you'd need to reduce the exposure by about three EV.

> **Spot metering:** Finally, you can switch to spot metering mode and set the exposure with the metering spot pointed at the highlight on the back of the pew. By using the brightest part of the scene instead of a middle tone as the basis for your exposure, you're telling the camera you want to make that the new midtone and everything

else in the scene should be darker, which effectively creates a low-key image from what could be a normal scene.

GETTING INTO THE ZONE SYSTEM

One of the challenges facing photographers is how to visualize the effect of exposure changes on the values in the finished photographic image.

The Zone System, made famous by Ansel Adams, was originally designed for black and white photography, using sheet film that was exposed and developed one sheet at a time and printed onto single-contrast graded photographic paper. Photographs are rarely produced that way nowadays. Although photographic production technologies have changed, the basic visualization elements of the Zone System remain as applicable to photography today as they were in Adams' day. It's an excellent tool to help photographers develop a better understanding of the interrelationship of exposure and tonal range, which in turn makes it easier to predictably produce properly

5-8
© Charlotte K. Lowrie | wordsandphotos.org

exposed images like figure 5-9 that capture the huge brightness range of a sunlit scene within the limited tonal range of a normal image.

5-9
Photo by Rob Sheppard

REDUCING A WIDE TONAL RANGE TO ZONES

The world around us is composed of a wide range of colors and brightness. To help visualize how that immense brightness range translates into tonal values in a photograph, Adams' Zone System breaks the gray scale into 11 discrete steps, called zones.

The zones progress from absolute black to pure white, with each zone being twice as bright as the next darker step. Thus, the zones are arranged in increments that correspond to one stop of exposure (one EV).

Adams numbered the steps of the Zone Scale with roman numerals, starting with black at 0 and progressing to white at X (10). Zone V (5) is middle gray, which corresponds to the 18 percent reflectance that is the standard target for all photographic light meters. Figure 5-10 shows a representation of the zone scale compared to a continuous gray scale. (Some of the steps may not be visible on the printed page of this book.)

The following list briefly describes the zones and some of the objects that commonly have the corresponding tonal value:

> **Zone 0:** Pure black, no tone or texture whatsoever — absolute darkness, or its photographic equivalent

> **Zone I:** Near black, barely discernable tone, no texture — deepest shadows and silhouettes — *dark end of the dynamic range*

Ansel Adams and the Zone System

The great Ansel Adams was a consummate master of the techniques required to capture an image of a natural landscape and create a beautiful photographic print that appears to have a full tonal range, even though the photographic paper is not capable of reproducing the entire brightness range of the original scene. Adams carefully cultivated the ability to analyze a scene and to predict and control how the brightness range of the original scene would translate into film density on the negative and then to the tonal values of the finished print.

Ansel Adams, along with Fred Archer, developed the Zone System in 1940 as a tool to teach some of those skills to students at the California School of Fine Arts in San Francisco (now the San Francisco Art Institute). Adams continued to use the Zone System in his classes and in his own work throughout his career.

> **Zone II:** Textured black, very dark but showing a hint of textural detail — deep shadows on dark hair or cloth — *dark end of the texture range*

> **Zone III:** Dark gray, shows distinct tone and textural detail — detailed shadows such as the dark bark on the shaded side of a tree

> **Zone IV:** Medium-dark gray, an open dark gray with excellent textural detail — open shadows such as the shadowed side of a sunlit building or a strongly lit portrait, dark green foliage

> **Zone V:** Middle gray, the tone of a standard 18 percent gray card — a luminous shadow such as the shadowed side of a low-contrast portrait, weathered wood, or dark stone — *the standard target value for light meters*

> **Zone VI:** Medium-light gray, a bright midtone showing sharp details — average Caucasian skin in good lighting, a concrete or stone building

> **Zone VII:** Lightest gray, the brightest tone that still shows good textural detail — gray hair, light-colored cloth

> **Zone VIII:** Textured white, very light but showing a hint of textural detail — highlights on light skin, textured snow or white sand — *light end of the texture range*

> **Zone IX:** Near white, barely discernable tone, no texture — highlights on white or light colored objects such as an egg shell or teacup — *light end of the dynamic range*

> **Zone X:** Pure white, no tone or texture — specular highlights and light sources

Note that zones 0 and X are each five stops from the exposure for middle gray. These are extremes that are beyond the effective range of most photographic mediums, whether film or digital. Values don't get any darker or lighter by exceeding the extremes.

Zones I through IX are called the *dynamic range* because they approximate the maximum effective tonal range of photographic media such as negative films and top-quality digital sensors. (Contrasting slide film and some digital sensors have a significantly shorter range.)

Zones II through VIII (middle gray plus and minus three stops) are called the *texture range* because they represent the working limits of the tonal range that is capable of showing any texture or detail. Most important image information in a photograph will fall into zones III through VII (middle gray plus or minus two stops).

USING THE ZONE SYSTEM MANUALLY

The best way to work with the Zone System is to use your camera's built-in light meter in spot metering mode. Doing this enables you to selectively meter different areas of the scene you want to photograph and visualize where those areas fall on the zone scale. After you take meter readings from a few key areas of the scene, you can calculate the correct exposure based on those readings and then set the exposure manually. Here's how it works:

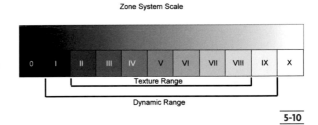

Zone System Scale

5-10

PRO TIP

To get the maximum tonal range and quality out of the digital sensor in your camera, you need to shoot and store your images in camera Raw format. Camera Raw gives you an extended dynamic range that better matches with the zones of the Zone System. If you shoot JPEG format, you need to adjust the zone scale by omitting zones 0 and X and moving everything else in one step from the ends. This shortens the entire range to nine steps (I thru IX), the dynamic range to seven steps (II thru VIII), and the texture range to five steps (III thru VII).

1. Select an area of the scene and mentally "place" it's brightness on the zone scale. For example, you might place a Caucasian flesh tone at zone VI or a textured shadow at zone III or IV, depending on how dark the shadow is.

2. Use your camera's spot meter to read the exposure for the selected area and note the exposure settings the meter recommends.

3. Mentally adjust the metered exposure by the number of steps between the selected zone and middle gray. For example, zone VI is one stop brighter than zone V, so you decrease the indicated exposure by one stop. Zone III is two stops darker, so you increase the metered exposure by two stops to reach zone V. If you're reading zone V, no adjustment is necessary.

4. Repeat steps 1, 2, and 3 for other important tonal areas. If you properly place each area in the appropriate zone, the adjusted exposure settings in step 3 should be the same.

5. Manually set your camera for the exposure you calculated in step 3 and take the picture.

Figure 5-11 is an example of a scene that would be difficult to meter normally. The scene is composed almost entirely of dark and light tones with very few midtones, and there's significantly more light than dark, so it doesn't average out to a normal exposure. But despite the challenging situation, the zone system enables you to calculate the correct exposure easily.

Meter the foliage on the mountainside and place it in zone III. Meter some of the darker cloud areas and place them in zones VI and VII. Meter the lighter cloud tops and place them in zone VIII. Adjust the metered exposure settings to the equivalent of zone V and take the picture. The result is a properly exposed photograph with a natural-looking tonal range and without the burned out highlights or muddy black shadows that come with over- or under-exposure.

ADJUSTING THE EXPOSURE WITH A SLIDING ZONE SCALE

Part of the power of the Zone System is its ability to predict the impact of exposure changes on the tonal values of an image. The zones of the Zone System scale are arranged in one stop increments, so changing the exposure one stop moves all the image values up or down the scale by one zone. Therefore, after you meter various areas of a scene and place them on the zone scale relative to a given zone V exposure, you can easily imagine the changes in tonal values if you increase or decrease the exposure.

For example, in figure 5-12, the side of the house is zone VIII and the dark strip of grass across the foreground is zone II. The middle of the grassy field and the darker gray of the clouds are both zone V. Reducing the exposure one stop slides all the zones down one step (as simulated in figure 5-13). This gives the side

5-11
Photo by Rob Sheppard

5-12

5-13

Original photo by Charlotte Lowrie, edited to simulate exposure change

of the house more color by moving it to zone VII. Making the clouds and the lighter grass a little darker doesn't hurt anything. However, that same exposure changes the dark grass to zone I, which transforms it from a dark textured green to a near black with little or no texture.

It takes some practice to develop the ability to visualize the effects of exposure on your images and to anticipate how changing the exposure will alter an image. Until you master that skill, bracketing your exposures is the best way to ensure that you always get an optimum exposure, even if it's not the one you (or your camera's automatic exposure system) thought was correct. As an added bonus, analyzing the alternate exposures of the bracket is an excellent way to learn how exposure changes impact the image. The value of the Zone System is that it provides a tool for structuring your observations and then for applying what you observe to future shooting situations.

USING A QUICK AUTO ZONE V EXPOSURE

The Zone System works best when you take the time to carefully meter several areas of the scene and then set the exposure manually. However, you often can use a modified form of Zone System metering with your camera in auto-exposure mode when you need to work quickly in changing lighting conditions.

The trick is to use spot metering mode instead of the more common multi-area metering and to select something in the scene that you want to place at zone V. The camera's meter and auto-exposure system are designed to produce the proper exposure for middle gray, so that matches perfectly with zone V on the zone scale. You control the exposure by metering a zone V area of the scene and let the camera automatically control the actual exposure settings. Here's how it's done:

1. Make sure your camera is set for spot metering mode and your preferred auto-exposure mode. Either aperture-priority or shutter-priority auto-exposure generally works best, but you can use this technique with most programmed exposure modes as well. Set the appropriate aperture or shutter speed if you choose aperture-priority or shutter-priority mode.

2. Scan the scene and select an area that you want to place at zone V.

3. Train the spot meter dot on the zone V area in the scene. Press the auto-exposure lock to lock that exposure into the camera.

4. Reframe the image and take the photograph.

X-REF

See Chapter 3 for information on exposure bracketing.

5

Making Creative Exposure Choices

This technique is fast and easy to use — and all it requires is that the scene contain something in zone V that you can use as the metering target. It's especially useful in a situation such as Figure 5-14 that has a relatively small area of interest surrounded by a large dark (or light) background that's likely to confuse a standard metering pattern. In this case, spot metering the column behind the seated lady (or the lady's hat) yields the correct exposure for the sunlit subject and allows the rest of the scene to go dark.

CREATING EXPOSURE EFFECTS

There are many potential situations in which you might want to exercise your creative control and override your camera's indicated exposure settings. The most common examples are high-key and low-key images in which the overwhelming predominance of light or dark tones create an impossible situation for normal metering. The exposure indicated by the meter renders the image with an average value of middle gray. For a light, high-key subject, that's a gross under exposure, making the image look much too dark. For a dark, low-key subject, the metered exposure is an over exposure that makes the image too light.

Therefore, to get a natural rendering of a high-key scene such as figure 5-15, you must override the exposure as indicated by the meter. Undoubtedly, the best way to do that is to use the Zone System to calculate the exposure and set it manually as described earlier.

However, you can also use a rough rule of thumb for high-key subjects and simply open up two stops from the metered exposure. If your camera has an exposure compensation feature, use it to increase exposure by two EV. Otherwise, just set the exposure manually. Since this is just a rough guideline and the actual exposure compensation will vary depending on how bright your subject is, you should either bracket around the new base exposure, or shoot a test image and then make further exposure adjustments based on its histogram.

5-14

© Charlotte K. Lowrie | wordsandphotos.org

Another way to get a good exposure of a high-key subject is to use the Quick Auto Zone V technique. It usually works because even a high-key subject typically has some zone V areas on which to base your exposure. In figure 5-15, that's the under side of the lower-right petal.

Low-key scenes, such as figure 5-16, have exactly the same exposure issues as high-key scenes, except in reverse. The normal metered exposure for a low-key scene creates an image that is too light, and to correct the problem, you need to reduce the indicated exposure.

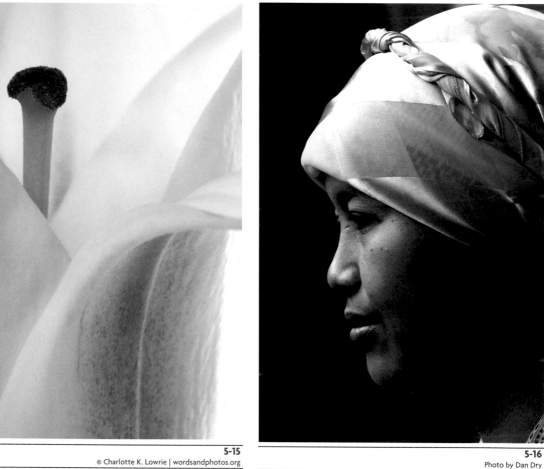

5-15
© Charlotte K. Lowrie | wordsandphotos.org

5-16
Photo by Dan Dry

Q&A

What does "expose for the shadows, develop for the highlights" mean?

That's a famous saying from Ansel Adams that refers to the custom film development component of his Zone System process. It advises the photographer to always give the film enough exposure to ensure good textural detail in the darker tones (zones II, III, and IV), then adjust the chemical processing of the film to control the density of the highlight areas (zones VI, VII, and VIII). If the lighting of the original scene exceeded the normal range, causing the highlight areas to be too bright, Adams could shorten the development time to reduce contrast in the negative and decrease the density of those highlight areas by as much as two zones. Similarly, extending the development time of the negative could increase contrast, and push the highlights into a higher zone. The goal was to produce a negative with appropriate tonal range to print on a standard photographic paper grade.

As digital photographers, we no longer use negative film with chemical development, so this specific advice no longer applies in a literal sense. However, a modified version of the saying does have some validity.

Considering that digital image sensors tend to lose highlight detail abruptly when overexposed, and given the opportunities you have for adjusting image tonalities during processing of Raw files, the digital photographer's version of this saying might be: "expose for the highlights, process for the balance." In other words, make sure your original camera exposure is correct for the upper midtones and highlights. Record their full brightness, but be very careful not to overexpose them. Then use the Camera Raw processing controls to adjust the black and white points and the midtone brightness to bring them into line with the highlight tones. Actually, when you get the upper midtones right, the rest of the Camera Raw settings seldom needs anything more than minor adjustments.

Why not just spot meter the most important part of the scene in a high-key or low-key image?

Using your camera's spot metering mode to meter the most "important" part of the scene doesn't always produce a good exposure — particularly with high-key or low-key subjects. The camera's meter is calibrated for an average middle gray and calculates exposure settings based on the assumption that the subject reflectance matches that standard. If the most important part of the scene is a midtone, then spot metering that area produces a good exposure. However, when the most important part of the scene is lighter or darker than middle gray, as is usually the case in high-key and low-key scenes, then spot metering such an area produces an erroneous exposure reading. If the target area is lighter than middle gray, the result is under-exposure. If it's darker, the result is over-exposure. You may be able to find a suitable spot metering target somewhere in the scene, but it's not usually the central, dominant subject in a high-key or low-key image.

Chapter 6

CONTROLLING MOTION WITH SHUTTER SPEED

Shutter speed is the exposure element that controls how long your camera's sensor is exposed to light. It's the time-based factor of exposure, and as such, it

X-REF

See Chapter 5 for an overview of the relationships between shutter speed, aperture, and sensitivity.

6-1
Photo by Dan Dry

becomes the critical exposure element when you must control motion in a photograph.

Most photographers think of shutter speed primarily in terms of freezing subject motion, such as that of the horse and rider in figure 6-1. That's an important consideration, but there's more to shutter speed selection than just picking a fast enough speed to stop the motion of a moving subject. In fact, the shutter speed selection can be just as important when shooting an unmoving subject or when your goal is to accentuate the motion instead of stopping it.

UNDERSTANDING SHUTTER SPEED'S EFFECT ON EXPOSURE

Shutter speed is one of the three basic elements of exposure. Because the goal is to balance all three elements to achieve the correct exposure for a given light level, changes that you make in shutter speed necessarily affect one or both of the other exposure elements, aperture and sensitivity (ISO).

Selecting a slower shutter speed increases exposure by allowing light to strike the camera's sensor for a longer time, which lightens the image or allows you to maintain the same overall exposure while using a smaller aperture to increase depth of field or lower ISO setting to reduce the effect of noise. Conversely, selecting a faster shutter speed for a given light level reduces exposure, which darkens the image or requires you to compensate by selecting a wider aperture (which reduces depth of field) or a higher ISO (which increases noise) in order to maintain the same equivalent exposure. The trick is to find the optimum balance point between them.

It's essential to understand how changes in shutter speed relate to changes in aperture and sensitivity.

The three different exposure elements use different numbering schemes (fractions of a second for shutter speed, *f*-stops for aperture, and ISO numbers for sensitivity), but they all relate back to exposure, which is measured in EV units (which most photographers call a *stop*). A change of one EV (one stop) changes the exposure by a factor of two, halving or doubling the base exposure.

Historically, shutter speed settings always changed in one EV increments, with each step of the shutter speed selector on such a camera representing a full stop increase or decrease in the exposure. Smaller exposure adjustments were handled by aperture selection, not shutter speed. Table 6-1 shows the traditional standard shutter speeds and also the standard *f*-stops, all in full stop (one EV) increments. (The aperture and shutter speed pairings in this table would be appropriate for ISO 100 on a cloudy day.)

Table 6-1: Standard Shutter Speeds & *f*-stops

Standard Shutter Speeds	Standard f-stops
1 second	f-64
1/2	f-45
1/4	f-32
1/8	f-22
1/15	f-16
1/30	f-11
1/60	f-8
1/125	f-5.6
1/250	f-4
1/500	f-2.8
1/1000	f-2
1/2000	f-1.4
1/4000	f-1

PRO TIP

If you use more than one camera, try to set the EV increment the same on all the cameras. If one click of the dial or press of the button always has the same effect on your exposure, you'll be able to make quick exposure adjustments by feel. It really pays off when you need to react quickly to changing conditions.

Most cameras today have abandoned the traditional full-stop shutter speed increments in favor of finer adjustments that give the photographer more precise control. On most digital SLR cameras, each "click" of the shutter speed dial is typically one-third or one-half stop and you end up with a lot of intermediate shutter speeds (such as 1/350 and 1/650) in addition to the standard speeds shown in Table 6-1. On some cameras, you can select your preferred shutter speed increment — usually as part of an EV increment setting that applies to shutter speed, aperture, and ISO.

One advantage of the full-stop shutter speed increments is that you can envision how your shutter speed adjustments affect exposure. Each click of the shutter speed dial represents one stop, or one EV. With the smaller increments, you may need to move the shutter speed dial or button two or three steps to make the same change in your exposure.

Having to do so is not really a problem because the aperture and ISO adjustments on most cameras move in the same size increments as shutter speed, so you can increase one and decrease the other in predictable steps. But you have to get used to how big (or small) a change in exposure you get with each step of increase or decrease in shutter speed on the camera you're using at the moment. And smaller increments make it a little easier to lose track of how far you've moved from your starting point when making manual exposure adjustments.

SHUTTER SPEED AND SUBJECT MOTION

When figuring out the best shutter speed to use, your first consideration is usually subject motion. You need to think about whether and how the subject is moving, and how you want to represent that motion.

If the subject and camera are both stationary, you can base your exposure decisions on the aperture and ISO you want to use without regard for whether the shutter speed is fast or slow. But when the subject is moving, you have to consider how much movement may occur while the shutter is open and what effect that will have on your finished image.

A slow shutter speed allows the image of a moving object to move across the sensor during exposure, resulting in a blurred image, even if the image was sharply focused. In figure 6-2, you can see the path of the soccer ball during the 1/4 second that the shutter was open. Conversely, figure 6-3 shows how a fast shutter speed can freeze motion and capture a sharp image of fast moving soccer players because the subject doesn't have time to move significantly during the brief instant that the shutter is open.

Proper shutter speed selection depends first on whether your goal is to freeze the action or allow the moving object to blur. Then you need to analyze the speed and direction of the moving object to determine just how fast or slow the shutter speed needs to be to achieve the desired effect.

X-REF

See Chapter 12 for more information on shooting action.

6-2
Photo by Rob Sheppard

STOPPING ACTION

Generally, most photographers want to avoid blurred images, so stopping the action is the name of the game whenever the subject is moving. That means shooting at a fast enough shutter speed to minimize, if not totally eliminate, any blurring due to subject motion.

How fast is fast enough to freeze motion? The answer is that it depends on how fast the subject is moving and in what direction. In figure 6-4, the photographer used a shutter speed of 1/1250 to freeze every hoof splash and whip flick, although a slightly slower speed might have been sufficient.

Obviously, a race car speeding around the track is moving faster than a running human, and you'd

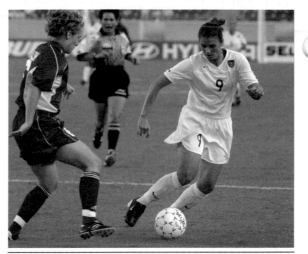

6-3
Photo by Tony Guffy

6-4
Photo by Dan Dry

expect to need a faster shutter speed to freeze the motion of the faster-moving object. However, the sheer speed of the subject isn't the only factor. The direction of motion relative to the camera position also makes a difference. Freezing motion across the frame requires a faster shutter speed than movement straight toward or away from the camera. So both speed and direction are significant.

IMPLYING MOTION

Normally, you want to avoid blur from a moving subject, but sometimes, deliberate blur can imply speed and motion in a way that a normal photo cannot. Sometimes the effect is subtle, as in figure 6-5, where the blurring of the spokes of the bicycle wheels are just enough to imply that the rider is moving forward and not just balancing in place. The effect works

because the spokes are moving faster than the rider and bicycle as a whole, and the shutter speed is just fast enough to stop the rider's motion but not the spokes in the spinning wheels.

Figure 6-6 combines a slower shutter speed and a faster-moving subject to create a photo in which the blurred image conveys a feeling of speed and energy. In order to shoot at the slow shutter speed (1/6) required to produce this effect on a bright sunny day, the photographer selected an aperture of f-32.

Figure 6-7 shows another variation on subject motion blur. In this case, the blur of the moving subject contrasts with the relative sharpness of its static surroundings. Using a tripod and a shutter speed of 1/10 second keeps the background sharp but blurs the walking man moving through the scene.

6-5

6-6
© Charlotte K. Lowrie | wordsandphotos.org

6-7
© Charlotte K. Lowrie | wordsandphotos.org

SHUTTER SPEED AND CAMERA MOTION

The subject isn't the only thing in motion in most photographs —the camera often moves, too.

Most shots are hand held, and a living, breathing human body isn't the most stable camera platform. So unless you use a tripod or other camera support, you need to consider camera motion in addition to subject motion when selecting the most appropriate shutter speed.

STOPPING CAMERA SHAKE

For an image to be sharp, there must be no significant movement of the image on the sensor while the shutter is open. Any movement of the image during exposure creates a blur. The most obvious source of movement in the image is a moving subject, and you control it by selecting a fast shutter speed. The other source of image movement is camera movement, which can cause just as much image blur as subject movement. The cure for camera movement is the same as for subject movement: a faster shutter speed.

Figures 6-8 and 6-9 show the effect of shutter speed on the blur from camera movement. Figure 6-8 is noticeably blurred as a result of hand holding the camera at a slow shutter speed of 1/4 second. In comparison, figure 6-9 is also a hand-held shot, but the 1/500 second shutter speed effectively stopped all camera shake and produced a sharp image.

Select a relatively fast shutter speed to stop camera shake in hand held shots. The shutter speed required to control camera shake depends on a number of factors, including the focal length of the lens and the photographer's skill at holding the camera steady.

Longer focal length lenses magnify the image and also magnify the effect of any camera movement. Therefore, longer focal lengths require faster shutter

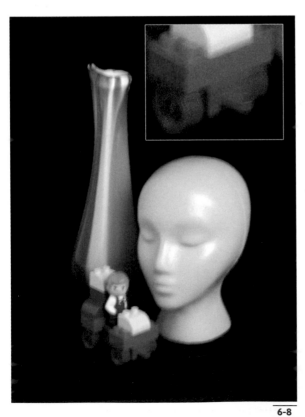

6-8

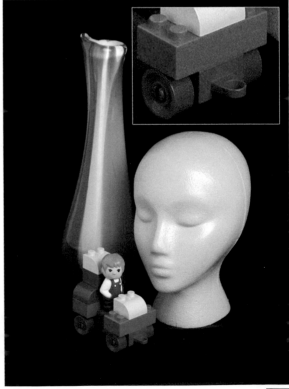

6-9

speeds to effectively control camera shake. Most photographers can get acceptably sharp images when hand holding wide angle and normal lenses at moderate shutter speeds (around 1/60 or 1/125). With practice and good technique, you might get by with slightly slower speeds (down to about 1/30) with wide-angle lenses. Hand holding a moderate telephoto lens usually requires a little faster shutter speed such as 1/250 or 1/500. For a really long telephoto lens, a very fast shutter speed or a tripod is essential.

PANNING WITH THE MOTION

Camera motion can actually be used to reduce the blur caused by subject motion. The technique is called panning and it produces images such as figure 6-10 in which a moving subject appears relatively sharp against a blurred background. The background blur adds to the feeling of motion in the photograph.

Panning is a tricky technique to master. It involves moving the camera to track the subject movement during an exposure with a moderately slow shutter speed. The camera movement offsets the subject movement so that the image of the main subject remains stable on the image sensor during the exposure. At the same time, the camera movement causes the static background objects to blur. Doing it right takes good eye-hand coordination, practice, and no small amount of luck. Here's the general procedure:

1. Prefocus your camera on the spot where the subject will be when you want to take the picture. Half-press the shutter release to lock and hold that focus point (or use whatever focus lock or manual focus feature your particular camera offers).

2. Start tracking the subject in the viewfinder well before it reaches the spot where you want to take the picture. The success of the panning technique depends on keeping the subject in a stable position in the frame as it moves across the background, and you need to establish the subject position and the pace of the panning motion early so you can continue the pan smoothly throughout the shot.

6-10
Photo by Dean Lavenson

Shutter Speeds for Flash Synchronization

You need to be aware of some special considerations when selecting the correct shutter speed for flash photography. You generally don't have to worry about flash/shutter synchronization as long as you're using the camera's built-in flash or a dedicated on-camera flash unit from the camera manufacturer. The camera takes care of synchronization for you automatically in most shooting modes and warns you if you attempt to use inappropriate settings in manual mode. However, flash synchronization speed becomes an issue when you work with an external flash, whether it's a non-dedicated on-camera flash or a studio strobe system.

The typical SLR camera shutter is composed of two curtains. When you trip the shutter release, a curtain, which had been covering the sensor, opens to start exposing the sensor to light coming in through the lens. Then, a fraction of a second later, a second curtain follows the first across the sensor, shutting off the exposure. At slower shutter speeds, the sequence is open, expose, close. At higher speeds, the

second curtain starts to close even before the first curtain gets all the way across the sensor opening. As a result, the entire sensor opening isn't exposed all at once. Instead, the two curtains create a slit that moves across the sensor during the exposure.

This traveling slit exposure that occurs at higher shutter speeds is a problem for flash photography because the flash duration is usually much shorter than the fastest shutter speed. The flash exposure works properly as long as the light from the flash can reach the entire image sensor at the same time, which means the flash must fire after the first curtain opens completely and before the second curtain starts to close the sensor opening. That usually occurs at speeds of 1/125 or 1/60 and slower, but it can be as fast as 1/500 on some cameras. If you select a faster shutter speed than your camera supports for flash synchronization, the entire sensor opening won't be open when the flash fires and only a portion of the frame will be properly exposed as shown in the figure below.

3. When the subject reaches the target zone, gently press the shutter release while continuing the panning motion. Remember that the viewfinder of most SLRs go black during the exposure and the subject disappears momentarily. You must be prepared for that and continue to pan smoothly, following the subject even when you can't see it. Keep both eyes open during the entire pan so you can use your peripheral vision to keep yourself oriented during the viewfinder blackout.

4. Continue the panning motion to follow the subject after the exposure. When the subject returns to the viewfinder, it should be in the same position in the frame as before. This follow through is essential to maintaining a smooth panning motion during the exposure.

5. Check your results on your camera's preview screen. If your camera has a zoom feature, use it to see just how well you kept the subject sharp and just how much blur there is in the background.. Evaluate the results and try again. If there's not enough blur in the background, try a slower shutter speed. If there's too much blur, try a faster shutter speed. If the subject bounced or blurred too much, just try again, and again, and again. Be persistent. It usually takes many attempts to get one good panning shot.

SPECIAL CONSIDERATIONS FOR LONG EXPOSURES

The sensors in digital cameras, like the film that preceded them, are designed to record images in a fraction of a second at light levels that you typically find outdoors in daylight. As light levels drop, you can use larger apertures and slower shutter speeds to deliver the necessary amount of light to the sensor for a successful exposure — up to a point. The kind of

time exposures required to shoot night scenes such as the one in figure 6-11 stretches most current image sensors to their limits.

The sensors in most digital cameras respond as expected to changes in shutter speed, as long as you're working within the normal shutter speed range

X-REF

See Chapter 8 for more information on ISO settings and digital noise.

6-11
Photo by Dan Dry

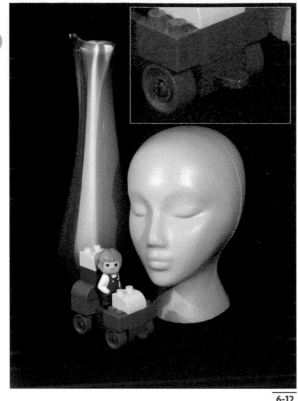

6-12

(1/4 second or faster). However, despite the fact that many digital SLRs have shutter speeds that go as high as 30 seconds, most image sensors do not perform well at shutter speeds over 1 second. Sensors may exhibit reciprocity failure (require disproportionately greater exposure time at low light levels), excessive noise, or both.

Digital noise can be especially troublesome in long exposures. The random bright pixels scattered throughout the image often become more numerous and brighter as the exposure time increases. Figure 6-12 shows the noise resulting from the combination of a slow shutter speed (2 seconds) and high ISO (1600). The noise is more visible in the enlarged section of the shadow area in a long time exposure. In extreme cases, the noise can be so bad that it renders the image unusable.

Q&A

How fast does my shutter speed have to be to freeze most action?

As a general rule, a shutter speed of 1/500 is sufficient to stop most human and animal actions. You may need to use a faster shutter speed if your subject is a speeding race car or an arrow in flight. On the other hand, you can often get by with somewhat slower shutter speeds (1/250 or 1/125) if you capture the relative pause at the peak of a motion, or if the subject just isn't moving very fast to begin with.

Remember that the motion of the subject, and therefore, the shutter speed you need to use to freeze that motion, isn't affected by light levels. A group of bicyclists can pedal just as fast in the dim light of dusk as they can in the bright light of mid-day sun. However, your ability to get a sharp photograph of that moving subject is dependent on having enough light available to support the fast shutter speeds you need to freeze the action. Shooting a fast-moving subject at 1/500 is easy on a sunny day, but shooting the same subject at dusk can be a real challenge. Even with your lens aperture wide open and a high ISO setting, there may not be enough light to get a good exposure at such a fast shutter speed. You may have no choice but to use a slower shutter speed and accept some motion blur, or try to catch a pause in the motion.

What's the slowest safe shutter speed for hand held shots?

That depends on the focal length of the lens and the skill of the photographer. If you practice good technique (solid stance, good camera grip with elbows close to the body, controlled breathing), you can minimize camera shake and get good results at much slower shutter speeds than if you try to shoot on the run with an unstable stance and a shaky hold on the camera.

Assuming good technique, the other factor that most influences safe hand holding shutter speed is lens focal length. Shorter wide angle lenses tend to minimize camera motion and longer telephoto lenses magnify camera motion, so the longer the focal length, the faster the shutter speed needs to be if you want a sharp hand held shot.

The rule of thumb for most photographers is that the slowest safe shutter speed for hand held shots is equal to the inverse of the lens focal length. So for hand holding a 50mm lens, you need to use a shutter speed of 1/50 second or faster. For a 30mm wide-angle lens, the safe hand holding shutter speed is about 1/30, and for a 200mm telephoto lens, it's 1/200, and so on.

The rule was developed for 35mm cameras, and for most digital SLRs, you need to apply the appropriate conversion factor to the lens focal length to find its 35mm equivalent. For example, if you're using a 40mm lens on a digital camera with a lens conversion factor of 1.5, the lens is equivalent to a 60mm lens on a traditional 35mm camera and the safe hand holding speed is 1/60 second.

Of course, you can shoot at much slower shutter speeds without encountering problems from camera shake if you use some form of camera support. The best portable camera support is a good sturdy tripod. A monopod is much less cumbersome to carry and set up and still provides reasonably good support. If you forgot your tripod, you can use any stable object as a makeshift camera support. Hold the camera against a doorframe or set it on the roof of a parked car for support. Brace yourself against the trunk of a tree or plant your elbows on a countertop. Anything you can do to minimize camera movement will help ensure that your pictures come out a little sharper.

What are some typical shutter speeds for panning subjects on a sunny day?

It depends entirely on the subject's speed and how much background blur you want in the finished image. It doesn't matter whether you're shooting on a sunny day or under heavy rain clouds — it matters only how fast the subject is moving across the frame relative to its background. Actually, the background blur is created by the movement of the camera, not the subject, but the technique is based on panning the camera to track subject movement in perfect synchronization, so it's the speed of the subject that dictates everything else.

If you're panning the camera to follow an Indy race car as it zooms around the track at nearly 200mph, you might get noticeable background blurring with shutter speeds as fast as 1/250. For a kid on a bicycle, you might get a similar effect at 1/30. For a given panning speed, a slower shutter speed produces a more pronounced blurring effect in the background. For the bicyclist, you might try 1/30 for a slightly blurred background, 1/15 for a prominent blur, and 1/8 or 1/4 to reduce the background to streaks. You might use a shutter speed of 1 second or more for a panning effect with a slow-moving subject.

Chapter 7

TAKING CONTROL OF APERTURE SELECTION

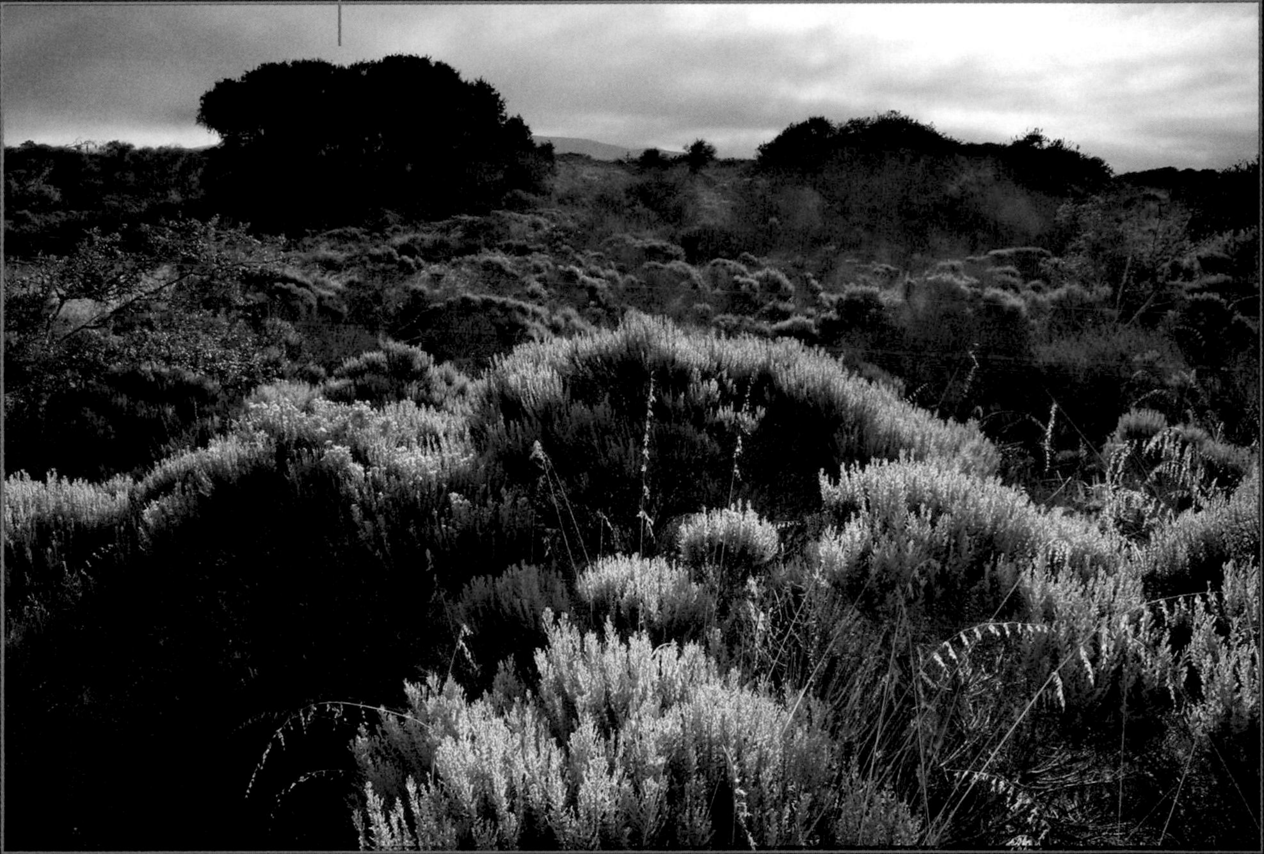

In photography, the lens aperture functions like the iris of the human eye, opening and closing to adapt to changing light levels. The aperture opens wide to admit more light in low-light situations and closes down to a pinhole when the light gets bright.

With older cameras, the photographer often had to adjust the aperture setting manually for each shot. However, modern, auto-exposure, digital cameras typically set the aperture automatically to produce the correct exposure as indicated by the camera's built-in light meter. As a result, digital photographers seldom need to deal with aperture selection — unless they really want to.

But just because you don't have to actively manipulate aperture settings for each shot in order to get successful exposures, doesn't mean that you should ignore the aperture component of your exposures completely. This chapter explores some of the ways in which aperture selection can have a significant effect on other aspects of your finished image besides the exposure. For example, the selective-focus effect that blurs the distracting background foliage in figure 7-1, is the result of selecting a large aperture to minimize depth of field.

This is just one example of a situation where you want to exercise creative control over the aperture setting, instead of letting the camera make that decision for you. Fortunately, all digital SLRs, and most higher-end consumer point-and-shoot cameras, give you the option to control the aperture by providing an aperture-priority shooting mode in addition to a manual exposure mode.

UNDERSTANDING APERTURE'S EFFECT ON EXPOSURE

As one of the three basic factors of every photographic exposure, the aperture setting controls the amount of light passing through the lens by adjusting the size of an opening in a diaphragm positioned between (or behind) the lens elements. Opening the diaphragm wider (selecting a larger aperture setting) allows more light to pass through the lens and strike the image sensor. Conversely, reducing the size of the diaphragm opening (selecting a smaller aperture setting) restricts the light going through the lens to the image sensor.

Aperture normally serves as the counterpoint to the time factor in the exposure. For a given light level and ISO (sensitivity) setting, a larger aperture coupled with a faster shutter speed produces the same equivalent exposure as the combination of a smaller aperture and a slower shutter speed. At a given light level, any one of a series of aperture and shutter speed combinations delivers the same total amount of light to the image sensor in your camera.

You can use a fast shutter speed with a large aperture to stop motion in an action shot, such as the one in figure 7-2. When shooting action, selecting a fast

7-1
Photo by Rob Sheppard

X-REF

See Chapter 3 for more about the elements of exposure.

7-2
Photo by Dan Dry

shutter speed usually takes priority over aperture selection. In this case, the exposure was 1/500 at *f*-4.

Figures 7-3 and 7-4 show the effect of selecting different aperture/shutter speed combinations to photograph the same scene. The exposure for figure 7-3 was 1/80 at *f*-2.8, which is a typical exposure for the conditions. In figure 7-4, the photographer elected to use a slower shutter speed at a smaller aperture (0.8 seconds at *f*-22) to get a different motion effect while maintaining the same overall exposure. Motion effects are controlled by shooting at specific shutter speeds, which relegates aperture selection to whatever is needed for proper exposure.

Of the three factors in an exposure — aperture, time, and sensitivity — aperture gets the lowest priority in

most shooting situations. You (or your camera's auto-exposure programming) typically select the sensitivity and time settings first and leave the aperture to last, adjusting the aperture to whatever value is necessary to produce a correct exposure for the light level. However, if the aperture reaches the end of its range, the photographer must adjust the shutter speed or ISO in order to get the correct exposure. This behavior is actually very understandable, because it mimics the way humans all ignore the automatic adjustments of the irises of our eyes unless exceptionally bright or dim light forces us to reach for sunglasses or a flashlight.

7-3
Photo by Dan Dry

7-4
Photo by Dan Dry

BALANCING EXPOSURE AND DEPTH OF FIELD

When you are thinking only about exposure, you can think of the aperture as a simple regulator that controls the flow of light through the lens. If your goal is to allow a certain amount of light to reach the imaging sensor in the camera, whether you set the regulator for maximum flow for a very short time, or much smaller flow for a longer time does not affect the image, as long as the total is the same.

However, the aperture has other effects on your image besides regulating the amount of light that passes through the lens during an exposure. Aperture also controls *depth of field,* and changes in depth of field can cause dramatic changes in your images.

As you may remember from Photography 101 or your other reading, depth of field is the area in a lens' field of view where objects appear acceptably sharp.

NOTE

Theoretically, all aperture/shutter speed/ISO combinations that produce equivalent exposures should produce images of the same quality. In practice, slow shutter speeds and high ISO settings both introduce digital noise that degrades the image. So, selecting a small aperture that requires a very slow shutter speed can affect the image in the real world. See Chapter 8 for more information on digital noise.

Objects within the depth of field zone appear sharp, while objects outside the depth of field appear visibly blurred. Depth of field extends some distance in front of and behind the vertical plane that represents the actual focus point of the lens — and aperture controls just how shallow or deep this zone of acceptable sharpness is. Smaller apertures produce greater depth of field and larger apertures produce shallower depth of field.

In order to control depth of field in your photograph, you must control the aperture. Therefore, aperture selection becomes a balancing act between exposure and depth of field considerations. Aperture is not just an exposure regulator anymore.

PRO TIP

Photographic joke: The *circle of confusion* is a bunch of photographers sitting around discussing the exact definition of depth of field.

Exactly What Is Depth of Field?

Depth of field doesn't describe what part of the scene is precisely in focus. Instead, the term describes an area of *acceptable* sharpness.

A lens that is focused on a point of light produces an image of a single point on the film or sensor in the camera. Points of light that are closer or farther away than the focus point are blurred into disk shapes instead of single points. The edge of such a disk is known as the *circle of confusion.* Depth of field is the zone where the diameter of the disk (the circle of confusion) is small enough that the average human eye can't perceive the difference between the disk and a single point.

The size of the film or image sensor, the focal length of the lens, and the magnification of the final print, in addition to the aperture, all affect depth of field. However, aperture is the only variable that the photographer normally controls at the time of exposure.

KEEPING EVERYTHING SHARP

Perhaps the most common concern that most photographers have about depth of field is how to maximize it to make as much of the scene as possible appear acceptably sharp. You may want to maximize depth of field in a product shot where the entire product must be sharp, or in a scenic shot such as figure 7-5. Or perhaps you're shooting people or pets whose positions are changing rapidly and you need plenty of depth of field to make up for not having time to focus carefully and accurately.

Because smaller apertures produce greater depth of field, maximizing depth of field means using the smallest aperture you can possibly manage. Try f-16, or the smallest aperture available on your lens. Obviously, selecting the aperture means using an exposure mode (manual mode, or aperture-priority auto) that allows you to control that setting.

Of course, to get an equivalent exposure with a smaller aperture, you need to use a slower shutter speed. Unless you're shooting in very bright light conditions, the shutter speeds that combine with those small apertures to produce the correct exposure are sometimes too slow to allow hand-holding the camera, so a tripod or other camera support essential.

ADJUST THE HYPERFOCAL DISTANCE

One of the best ways to maximize depth of field is to focus your camera to the *hyperfocal distance* for your lens. The hyperfocal distance is the focus point at which the farthest reaches of depth of field extends to infinity. Focusing at the hyperfocal distance allows objects to appear sharp from some relatively near point all the way out to infinity, as you can see in figure 7-6.

Because changing the aperture changes the depth of field, it also changes the hyperfocal distance. Smaller apertures increase depth of field and move the hyperfocal distance closer to the camera. Larger apertures decrease depth of field and move the hyperfocal

7-5
Photo by Rob Sheppard

7-6
Photo by Rob Sheppard

distance farther away. There are tables and charts available in books and from various Web sites that show the hyperfocal distance for various combinations of lens focal length and aperture. However, I never seem to have the tables handy when I need them, or I'm using a lens or zoom setting that isn't included in the tables, so I usually employ one of the techniques in the following sections to determine hyperfocal distance.

USING MANUAL FOCUS LENSES

Finding the hyperfocal distance for a given lens and aperture can be a little tricky, but the results can be impressive.

Manual-focus lenses (or lenses that have manual focus capability) usually have a distance scale and depth of field indicators (pairs of hash marks for each *f*-stop arrayed on either side of the central focus mark) engraved on the lens barrel, as shown in figure 7-7. To find the hyperfocal distance, you rotate the focus ring to align the infinity mark of the distance

scale with the distant depth of field indicator for your chosen shooting aperture (in this case, *f*-8). The central focus mark indicates the hyperfocal distance (10 feet), and the other depth of field indicator shows the near limit of acceptable sharpness (5 feet). The lens barrel markings are often small, which makes precise adjustments challenging, but this technique can get you close to the hyperfocal distance.

7-7

If the lens has a focus distance scale and depth of field indicators marked on the lens barrel, you can follow these steps:

1. Focus on the closest portion of the subject that needs to be sharp — for example, the foreground bush in figure 7-7. Note the distance on the focus distance scale.

2. Rotate the focus ring so that the infinity mark is aligned with the depth of field indicator for a given aperture and the close focus distance (from step 1) is aligned with the corresponding depth of field indicator on the opposite side of the central focus point. Leave the lens focused at that point and note the aperture that allows the depth of field indicators to encompass the desired range from close to infinity.

3. Set the aperture to the *f*-stop noted in step 2, or smaller.

4. Frame your shot and shoot, being careful not to change the focus distance or aperture.

Using Auto-Focus Lenses

The real challenge comes with some newer auto-focus lenses that don't have a distance scale or depth of field markings on the lens barrel. The lens still has a hyperfocal distance, but there is no easy way to find it. You just have to make an educated guess at where in the scene the hyperfocal distance should be and focus on that point. Then, if your camera features a depth of field preview button, you can use it to see if your focus point and aperture setting produce the zone of acceptable sharpness that you expect. Here's the step-by-step technique:

1. Focus on the closest portion of the subject that needs to be sharp. Make a mental note of its distance from the camera.

2. Focus on a distant point beyond which the lens doesn't need to change focus any more as the distance to the subject increases. For typical lenses, the infinity focus point is about 50-100 feet, but it may be closer for some wide angle lenses.

3. Mentally divide the space between the points you found in steps 1 and 2 into thirds. Look for an object near the boundary of the first and second thirds behind the close focus point — one-third of the way back toward the distant point. Focus on that point and lock focus.

4. Set the aperture to the smallest opening that the light level and other exposure elements allow. If your camera has a depth of field preview button, use it to test the aperture setting to see if it allows enough depth of field to cover the desired range.

5. Frame your shot and shoot without changing the focus or aperture. You can use your camera's focus lock and/or exposure lock features to keep the camera from changing your settings.

Selective Focus

Controlling depth of field doesn't always entail using small apertures to maximize how much of the subject appears to be sharp. Sometimes your goal is just the opposite — to create a shallow depth of field that isolates a sharp-focused subject against an out-of-focus background or blurs a distracting foreground object. For example, the background behind the foreground flower in figure 7-8 would be busy and

PRO TIP

About one-third of the depth of field is in front of the focus point (nearer to the camera) and two-thirds of the depth of field extends behind the focus point (farther from the camera).

distracting if it were in crisp focus, but the out of focus blur caused by the photographer's use of shallow depth of field creates a pleasingly soft backdrop.

Just as smaller apertures increase depth of field, wider apertures decrease depth of field. So, creating selective focus effects with shallow depth of field usually entails large aperture settings (f-4.0 or wider).

Distance from the lens to the subject also affects depth of field. The closer the subject is to the lens, the shallower the depth of field becomes. Therefore, a close-up subject (such as the flower in figure 7-7) combined with a large aperture often creates a depth of field that measures only fractions of an inch.

APERTURES AND IMAGE QUALITY

Most lenses offer a range of aperture settings, and you can use any aperture in the range to get a correct exposure. However, just because you can get an equivalent exposure at every available aperture by combining it with the appropriate shutter speed and ISO settings, doesn't mean that you get equivalent image quality at *all* apertures.

Most lens designs produce optimum results at a specific aperture or within a limited range of apertures. To make the lens usable in a wider variety of situations, lens designers frequently must compromise image quality in order to expand the aperture range. This is especially true of zoom lenses.

The lens produces the best results when you shoot at or near the optimum aperture. For most lenses, the optimum aperture is somewhere toward the middle of the available range, although some lenses are at their best when stopped down. Apertures toward the extremes of the range often tend to exhibit somewhat less sharpness and more distortion. For example, the building on the left side of the frame in figure 7-9 displays noticeable barrel distortion (bowing out from

7-8
Photo by Rob Sheppard

PRO TIP

Most pros try to avoid shooting with their lens aperture "wide open" because most lenses exhibit the most distortion and lack of sharpness at maximum aperture.

the center of the frame). This type of distortion is typical of wide angle lenses, and is often exaggerated at the largest aperture. Telephoto lenses often exhibit the opposite distortion effect (pinching in toward the center of the frame), called pincushion distortion.

USING APERTURE-PRIORITY EXPOSURE

Most auto-exposure cameras default to shutter-priority or programmed exposure modes, but an aperture-priority mode is usually available as an option. You can use aperture-priority mode for those times when controlling depth of field by specifying the shooting aperture is more important than specifying the shutter speed.

7-9
Photo by Randy McCaffery

7-10
Photo by Rob Sheppard

Figure 7-10 shows how a carefully selected depth of field (shooting at *f*-5.6) keeps all the facial features and clothing sharp while allowing the background to blur. The result is a clear separation between foreground and background, despite some bright spots in the background that would be very distracting if they were sharper.

In aperture-priority mode, you select the aperture and let the camera adjust the shutter speed automatically to achieve the correct exposure. The procedure sounds simple, and it is, but using aperture-priority mode effectively requires you to pay careful attention to the shutter speed that the camera selects.

When shooting at small apertures, it's all too easy to end up with blurred pictures caused by camera shake because the shutter speed was a little too slow. Attempts to improve picture sharpness by increasing depth of field often have the opposite effect. You can avoid that particular pitfall by monitoring the automatically set shutter speed and using a tripod when the speed dips too low.

Shooting at large apertures to create shallow depth of field can cause problems with shutter speeds. It's surprisingly easy to select an aperture that needs a faster shutter speed than most cameras have available. For example, suppose you're shooting a close-up of a flower on a sunny day and want to use shallow depth of field to blur the background. You set the ISO to 100, choose aperture-priority mode, and select f-2.8 as the shooting aperture. According to the sunny-16 rule, the correct exposure at ISO 100 is f-16 at 1/100, and the equivalent exposure at f-2.8 is 1/3200. But only a few cameras have that shutter speed available — many top out at about 1/1000. You could reduce the ISO setting if your camera has a lower setting available, but many do not. So, either you have to select a smaller aperture and accept the increased depth of field, or you need to add a neutral density filter to the lens, or wait for a cloud to pass over the sun and decrease the light level.

■ **Are there specific aperture settings I should avoid because image distortion is more apparent?**

Perhaps so. The optimum aperture is different for each lens, and the amount and kind of aberrations that appear at sub-optimum apertures vary. Some lenses deliver excellent results throughout their entire aperture range. Other lenses do produce noticeably different results at different apertures, and some of those results may be unacceptable under certain circumstances. Test each of your lenses at every aperture setting to become familiar with their weak points.

Most of all, what constitutes unacceptable sharpness or distortion varies significantly with the subject you're shooting. If you're trying to capture expressions on people's faces at medium distances, a slight soft focus or pincushion distortion probably won't even be noticeable. However, the same amount of soft focus and distortion could be quite objectionable on an architectural subject or a product photograph for a catalog.

How can I maximize depth of field when I also need to use a faster shutter speed to stop subject motion?

You normally control exposure by manipulating aperture and shutter speed, and when you increase one, you must decrease the other to maintain an equivalent exposure. If subject motion dictates that you use a relatively fast shutter speed, doing so naturally limits your aperture selection to some of the wider settings, leaving you stuck with fairly shallow depth of field. To maximize depth of field, you need to select the slowest shutter speed that will stop the subject motion. If you're photographing a toddler at play, you can get by with a slower shutter speed than if you're shooting a stock car race. Selecting the slowest possible shutter speed allows you to shoot at the smallest possible aperture. If that doesn't give you enough depth of field, you can adjust the third exposure element — the ISO setting. Setting the ISO higher increases the sensitivity of the image sensor and allows you to stop your aperture down. Starting from a typical default ISO setting, you can usually increase it two or three stops (EV), and sometimes more. But beware of increased digital noise at higher ISO settings.

Another trick is to select your focus point to make best use of the depth of field you get from any given aperture setting. Remember that depth of field extends both in front of and behind the focal point. Therefore, focusing about one-third of the way into the object uses both the front and rear depth of field, whereas focusing on the leading edge uses only the depth of field beyond the focal point and waste the portion that is closer to the lens.

Chapter 8

DEALING WITH DIGITAL FILM

You could shoot images like those shown in figures 8-1 and 8-2 with either traditional film or digital photography — the results are essentially the same. It's unlikely that you could tell the difference between the film and digital images if they are both printed the same way, on the same paper, at the same size, and so on.

(In fact, one of these images was shot digitally and the other was shot on film and then scanned to create the image file used to layout this page. Can you tell which is which?)

It may be hard to tell the difference between film and digital when you look at the printed results, but there are significant differences in the way you work with film and digital photography mediums. Some of the differences are immediately evident, such as recording the image on a digital image sensor instead of film, and viewing and printing it with a computer instead of developing and printing it in a photo lab. No doubt, you're familiar with the obvious differences between film and digital, so this chapter skips the big stuff and focuses on some of the details of the digital photography medium that may not be apparent at first glance, but are important to understand if you want to master the medium and exercise creative control over your photographs.

8-1
Photo by Alicia McGinnis

8-2
Photo by Alicia McGinnis

Image Preview & Analysis

Perhaps the biggest single difference between film and digital photography is the time it takes to see the image. With film, you usually finish shooting a whole roll of film before taking it to a lab for chemical processing, which takes hours, sometimes days. In contrast, most digital cameras display the image on the camera's LCD screen within seconds. Digital photographers know immediately whether they got the shot or not. No more waiting for days wondering whether or not the flash fired or if the ball was in front of Junior's face.

Being able to view a digital image immediately is a revolutionary advantage, but the small size and limited brightness of the camera's LCD screen severely restricts the photographer's ability to analyze the quality of that image. (See figure 8-3.) As a result, many digital photographers barely glance at the post-shot image on the camera's LCD or they turn off the display completely — and that's a serious mistake. Most higher-end digital cameras include several features that make the image display much more useful, despite its diminutive size. Using these tools can help you to evaluate the accuracy of your exposure.

To partially compensate for the small size of the preview screen, most of the better digital cameras include zoom and pan features that enable you to get a closer look at portions of the image. It's not an ideal way to perform a critical evaluation of each image, but it's sufficient for a quick check to confirm the focus or to see if your portrait subject blinked just as you pressed the shutter.

Most digital cameras have even more features to help you evaluate exposure.

The brightness of the image preview isn't a reliable indication of correct exposure because its apparent brightness varies dramatically depending on the ambient light levels. A preview image that looks too light when viewed in a dark room might be too dark to see clearly in bright sunlight. Consequently, you need to use a more objective tool to determine whether or not you got a good exposure.

The first, and most important, tool for evaluating exposure is the histogram — an area chart showing the distribution of tonal values in the image. The base of the histogram represents a grayscale going from black on the left to white on the right. The relative number of pixels of the various brightness levels is plotted as height on the chart.

The histogram is usually superimposed over the image as shown in figure 8-4, although some cameras display the histogram separately and some even display

8-3

8-4

8-5

8-6

separate red, green, and blue histograms. The histogram tells you at a glance whether or not your exposure falls within the image sensor's range.

A good exposure of an average subject shows a tonal distribution that extends from left to right across nearly the full width of the histogram, but avoiding major spikes at either end. If the histogram shows a big peak at the left side of the chart, tapers out toward the middle, and shows nothing toward the right side, this indicates an underexposure (or a subject that is all dark gray to black). Conversely, a big peak on the right side of the histogram and little or nothing on the left indicates overexposure (or a subject that's nearly all white).

In addition to the histogram display, most digital SLR and better point-and-shoot digital cameras also offer optional displays that indicate highlight and shadow clipping. These displays alert you to possible exposure problems by showing you what portions of your image exceed the image sensor's range. These are the areas that will reproduce as bright white or solid black, with little or no textural detail.

The highlight clipping display, seen in figure 8-5, typically uses flashing black spots to indicate areas that are at or near the upper limit of the image sensor's exposure range. Highlight clipping that extends beyond a few small specular highlights, such as the reflection of the sun off a chrome bumper or water ripples, almost always indicates serious overexposure that should be corrected. Unless corrected, the overexposed areas will be blown out, totally lacking textural detail. And that's not something you can fix in Photoshop.

The shadow clipping display (figure 8-6) uses flashing white spots to indicate the darkest shadow areas — the parts of the image that are so dim that they

PRO TIP

To correct overexposure as indicated by highlight clipping, try reshooting with an exposure compensation of -1 EV or an equivalent change to your manual exposure settings. If the highlight clipping is extensive, you may need to make an even larger exposure adjustment.

reproduce as black. As a general rule, it's acceptable, even desirable to have some areas of solid black in an image, so a modest amount of shadow clipping doesn't necessarily indicate a bad exposure. However, if the shadow clipping is excessive, you can compensate by increasing the exposure some.

ISO Settings and Digital Noise

The image sensors in digital cameras produce optimal results at a certain sensitivity level, which usually corresponds to the lowest available ISO setting. To expand the camera's useful working exposure range, the sensitivity of the image sensor can be adjusted by amplifying its signal. However, increasing the sensitivity also increases the noise that is recorded along with the image data.

Digital noise is a random pattern of colored dots that end up being embedded into the image. It looks very similar to the "grain" effect that is characteristic of higher-speed photographic films.

When working at their optimum ISO settings, the best digital cameras produce images that are almost totally

noise-free. But as the ISO setting goes up, so does the visible noise in the images.

To demonstrate the effect of digital noise resulting from changes in ISO settings, I shot the series of test shots shown in figures 8-7 through 8-12. Figure 8-7 shows the full frame test subject with a small red rectangle indicating the portion of the image that is enlarged in the other figures. The ISO setting in figure 8-8 is 100; in figure 8-9, it's 200; in figure 8-10, it's 400; in figure 8-11, it's 800; and in figure 8-12, it's 1600. Hopefully, the book printing will retain enough detail for you to see the modest increase in noise from 8-8 to 8-10, and the more dramatic increase in 8-12.

Increasing the ISO always involves a tradeoff. Consider whether increasing the ISO in order to get an acceptable exposure at a lower light level is worth whatever negative impact the increased noise will have on the quality of your images. When increasing the ISO means the difference between getting the shot or missing it altogether, then it's probably worth most any amount of noise. Otherwise, you can minimize noise by working at the lowest possible ISO setting that allows you to get decent exposures at a given light level.

All digital cameras available today exhibit some increase in noise at higher ISO settings. However, some image sensors are noisier than others. Some sensors show a gradual noise increase as ISO levels increase, while others show an abrupt jump in noise levels at certain ISO settings. The only way to be sure how much noise your particular camera model produces at various ISO settings is to test it. Here's how:

1. Set up a test target consisting primarily of a solid-color background. It doesn't have to be a standard gray card like I used, but it'll be easier to see the noise on a fairly neutral color of a midtone value — not too dark, not too light, not too strong a color, and definitely not patterned or strongly textured. Add some small objects for contrast and to provide a sense of scale.

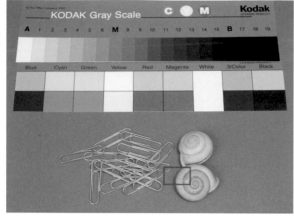

8-7

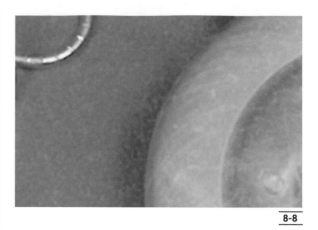

8-8

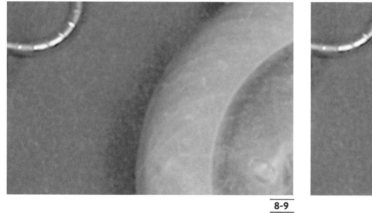

8-9

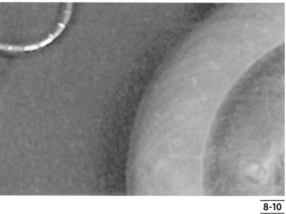

8-10

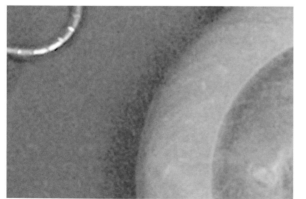

8-11

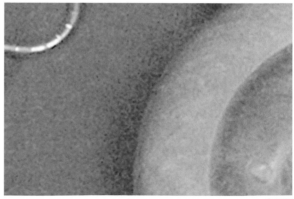

8-12

2. Light the test target. Use uniform lighting of medium intensity. If the light is too bright (such as direct sunlight) you may not be able to test your highest ISO settings without overexposing. If the light is too dim, you may not be able to test the lowest ISO settings without underexposing or using excessively long shutter speeds, which introduce their own problems.

3. Set the camera on a tripod and focus on the test target.

4. Set your camera for aperture-priority automatic exposure and select the highest available ISO setting. Then select the widest aperture that allows the automatically selected shutter speed to remain within the normal range without overexposing. Shoot the first test frame.

5. Change the ISO setting to the next lower value and shoot the next test frame, allowing the auto exposure system to adjust the shutter speed.

6. Repeat step 5 as needed to test all the available ISO settings your camera offers. Make sure that the shutter speed for the lowest ISO settings is less than 1 second. If necessary, adjust the aperture to keep the shutter speed faster than 1 second.

7. After you shoot tests at all the ISO settings, transfer the test images to your computer and open them in Photoshop or your favorite image editor. To see the noise clearly, zoom in to 100% or greater magnification. Try to examine and compare the same spot on the solid-color background of each image so you're seeing the difference in noise, not shadows or other variations in the image.

TIME FOR TIME EXPOSURES

The problem of increased digital noise at higher ISO settings is generally associated with taking pictures at low light levels. That's because low-light photography is the situation in which you typically need the extra sensitivity of higher ISO settings in order to

enable you to use shutter speeds fast enough for hand-held shots without excessive camera shake. You might think you can avoid the noise issue completely when you have a static subject and a tripod-mounted camera by sticking with a lower ISO setting and using a longer shutter speed to get the required exposure. The concept works, up to a point. However, exceptionally slow shutter speeds create their own problems with a different kind of digital noise.

The longer you leave the image sensor powered up and actively recording an image, the more likely it is to develop hot spots — random bright pixels that look like stars in a night sky (see figure 8-13). Hot spots are the result of heat build-up in the image sensor, and the longer the shutter is open and the image sensor under power, the bigger, brighter, and more numerous the hot spots become. Higher ISO settings generate more heat faster, so that tends to make hot spots worse, as does higher ambient operating temperatures.

NOTE

Figure 8-13 was created by shooting a 20-second time exposure in a darkened room with the lens cap on — essentially shooting total darkness so that only the sensor anomalies were recorded. The resulting hot spots were clearly visible when viewing the dark frame in Photoshop. However, they were too small to survive the translation to the printed page in this book, so I exaggerated the hot spots slightly in hopes of creating a useful illustration.

8-13

PRO TIP

If your camera doesn't include an automatic noise reduction feature, you can do the same thing manually by shooting a dark frame at a matching shutter speed and then converting it to an inverse image and combining it with your primary image in your image editor.

Hot spots are seldom much of a problem at shutter speeds of one second or faster. However, as you move into the time exposure realm, hot spots rapidly make their presence known. The severity of the problem varies with ISO setting, ambient temperature, the characteristics of each camera model and the sensor

it contains, how much time the sensor has to cool down between shots, and of course, shutter speed. A 15-second exposure with most cameras contains enough hot spots to require a great deal of retouching, especially if the subject contains large solid areas of black or dark colors that provide stark contrast for the bright hot spots. At 30 seconds, a glow may appear at one corner of the image, as if there were a light source at the edge of the frame.

The best way to deal with hot spots is to avoid shooting the long time exposures that produce them, so keep your time exposures as short as possible.

Some cameras have a noise reduction mode that attempts to counteract the effect of hot spots. When activated, the process is usually completely automated, but it goes something like this:

1. You press the shutter release to shoot the image, which is usually a time exposure. The camera opens the shutter, times the exposure, closes the shutter, and records the image.

2. After the shutter closes, the camera records a second image of equal duration while the shutter remains closed. This creates a dark frame containing just the hot spots from the sensor, much like figure 8-13.

3. The camera's built-in image processing software combines the two frames so that the hot spots from the dark frame are reversed and added back to the main image, which cancels out most of the hot spot effect.

The good thing about this feature (if your camera has it) is that it's automatic and it works reasonably well for problems like cleaning up the dark backgrounds in night shots. The bad thing is that it's a time consuming process. If you take a 30-second time exposure, you have to wait while the camera makes a second 30-second exposure before you can do anything else with the camera.

IN-CAMERA IMAGE PROCESSING

Another difference between film and digital photography is the image processing that occurs in a digital camera. This is one area where film is faster. Here's what happens inside a film camera:

1. Opening the shutter to expose the film creates an instantaneous chemical reaction between the photosensitive components in the film emulsion and the light energy focused onto it by the lens.

2. The instant the shutter closes, ending the exposure, the latent image is securely stored on the film. Of course, the film requires chemical processing to develop that latent image, but the development process is a separate operation that is done later. The design of the camera and film cassette protects the film from accidental exposure to light until it can be processed.

3. To get ready for the next shot, the camera must advance the film to the next frame and re-cock the shutter, but that can be done in a tiny fraction of a second. Consequently, professional film SLRs can attain sequence shooting speeds of about 10 frames per second and maintain that speed through an entire roll of film.

In a digital camera, the process is a little different.

1. Like a film camera, the exposure starts when the shutter opens allowing light from the lens to strike the camera's image sensor. The reaction between the light energy and the photosensitive surfaces of the sensor is analogous to what happens with film.

2. That part of the exposure stops when the shutter closes, but that's where the similarity to film stops. In a digital camera, the light energy is converted to electrical energy and then to digital data instead of being chemically stored in the film emulsion.

3. The camera collects the data from the image sensor and stores it temporarily in the camera's buffer memory. While that is happening, the camera also resets the shutter and other mechanical parts.

4. The camera's built-in image processing software then goes to work on the image data, applying color correction and other adjustments to the image and converting it into a standard file format for storage. At the same time, the camera usually displays the image on its LCD screen for review by the photographer.

5. Finally, after the processing is complete, the camera writes the file to removable storage media such as a Compact Flash memory card. The files from modern multi-megapixel cameras are large, so writing the file to storage typically takes several seconds.

All the steps and processing that goes on in a digital camera takes several seconds from start to finish. Fortunately, you don't have to wait for the entire process to be completed before you and your camera can start the next exposure. The camera includes a memory buffer that has room for multiple images, and you start the next exposure as soon as the image data gets transferred from the sensor to that buffer. Still, it takes time, so a digital SLR that can shoot 5 frames per second is considered reasonably fast, and few of them can shoot more than 10 frames at that speed before filling the buffer.

FILE FORMATS

The electrical impulses generated by light striking a digital camera's image sensor start out as meaningless gibberish. The camera's built-in image processing circuitry and software processes the image data and transforms it into a usable digital image. Then the image data is saved in one of several file formats and resolutions.

Some cameras support only one file format (usually JPEG) for all images, but most cameras let you choose one of several formats.

CAMERA RAW

Camera Raw isn't really a single file format. Instead, it's one of several proprietary file formats linked to specific camera manufacturers. In general, each manufacturer creates and maintains its own Raw format, such as the NEF (Nikon), CRW and CR2 (Canon), and ORF (Olympus) formats. Most digital SLRs and higher-end consumer zoom cameras offer the option to save images in Raw format, but each one supports only their own Raw variant with no interplay between them.

Raw files get minimal processing in the camera, preserving as much raw data from the image sensor as possible. Many of the better image sensors record either 12-bit or 16-bit images, which enable them to capture more image information than can be stored in standard 8-bit image formats, such as JPEG. This gives Raw images greater exposure latitude and a much longer tonal scale.

The Raw format provides a way to bypass most automatic in-camera image processing, such as color balance, brightness and contrast, sharpening, and condensing the image into an 8-bit format, and move those operations to a separate program where the photographer has the opportunity to intervene. However, the proprietary nature of Raw files means that they require additional processing with special software to convert them to another format for general use. Each camera manufacturer supplies its own Raw processing software, but the Adobe Camera Raw plug-in for Photoshop, which can read and process Raw files from most of the popular digital cameras, is by far the most popular Raw processing program.

Most Raw file formats feature some form of lossless data compression to achieve smaller file sizes than uncompressed TIFF files without sacrificing image quality or introducing compression artifacts like JPEG compression does. However, the compression isn't as efficient as JPEG, so Raw files tend to be much larger.

Figure 8-14 shows an image saved as a Camera Raw file and then tweaked in Adobe Camera Raw before saving it in another format for publication. This afforded me the opportunity to adjust the color balance slightly instead of accepting the color balance preset that the camera imposed when it made the file conversions that follow.

TIFF

The TIFF file format usually produces the largest image files of any of the common image file formats due to its lack of compression. For example, the image file used to produce figure 8-15 is roughly twice the size of a JPEG file of the same resolution and about 15 percent larger than a Raw file. Oddly, the TIFF file format is a widely accepted standard that includes provisions for lossless compression, but the compression option isn't normally implemented by the in-camera image processing software. The lack of compression means that there are no JPEG-like compression artifacts or lack of sharpness and detail. However, the in-camera processing does convert to an 8-bit image and applies the camera's preset color balance, contrast, and sharpening adjustments. Notice the difference in color between the TIFF image in figure 8-15, which uses the camera's preset white balance, and the slightly warmer custom color balance of the Raw image in 8-14.

TIFF files were once the high-quality alternative to JPEGs for digital camera images, but that role has been mostly taken over by Raw files. Consequently, TIFF files are not as common as they once were, but the option is still available on a lot of digital cameras.

JPEG

Most digital cameras offer several different JPEG file format options, giving you a choice of different

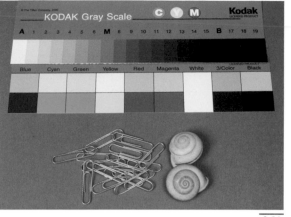

8-14

8-15

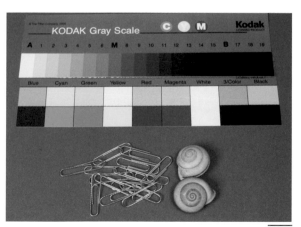

8-16

8-17

8-18

resolutions and compression settings. The JPEG format is a universal standard for image files, so saving your image as a JPEG file enables you to read, open, edit, print, or share the file with just about anyone anywhere.

Like TIFF files, JPEGs get the same in-camera processing to convert the camera's raw image data to an 8-bit image and apply the camera's preset color balance, contrast, and sharpening adjustments.

The JPEG format features very efficient compression to minimize file sizes, and the compression ratios are adjustable. Even with minimal compression, the file size of a typical JPEG image file saved from a camera is barely more than half the size of a comparable TIFF file. Smaller file sizes mean you can store many more files on the same size memory card and writing those files to memory is faster.

A typical JPEG image file with a minimal compression setting (figure 8-16), shows no obvious loss of quality compared to a comparable TIFF file (figure 8-15) — at least not in the initial file version.

However, the JPEG file compression scheme does degrade image quality as the compression ratios get higher. Figure 8-17 shows an enlarged section of the full JPEG file in figure 8-16. Compare that to figure 8-18, which shows the same section of another JPEG

8-19

file saved from the camera with slightly higher compression settings. The file size is about a fourth smaller, and the image still looks pretty good although there is a detectable loss of subtle shading in the spirals of the shell.

Now compare that to figure 8-19, which shows the same section of a JPEG file saved from the camera at a lower resolution and with a more aggressive compression ratio. All the more subtle textures on the shell are gone and there are ugly compression artifacts visible surrounding the paperclips. Ugh!

PRO TIP

One of the problems with JPEG compression is that the data loss and artifacts are compounded if you open, edit, and resave JPEG files. If you save your digital camera files in the JPEG format and plan to edit them, open the file in your editor and immediately save it in the editor's native file format (PSD for Photoshop) or some other lossless or uncompressed format (such as TIFF). Do your edits on that file and save it. Then you can convert the edited file back to JPEG if you want. By using a lossless file format as an intermediary for your edits, you'll minimize the compression-artifact-compounding effect of resaving directly from the JPEG file.

Q&A

▶ **Which is the best file format for saving digital images in my camera?**

There is no one file format that is "best" in all circumstances. All but the very simplest digital cameras give you multiple file format options to choose from. Each file format has its advantages and disadvantages, and you need to select the one that best matches your particular needs.

> Use the JPEG format for snapshots, where convenience is more important than the subtleties of the absolute best image quality. JPEG is a universal image file format that you can open, edit, and print with just about any computer software.

> Use the JPEG format for maximum working speed. JPEG files are smaller, so the camera can write the files to the storage medium (memory card) faster. This is a significant consideration for cameras that must finish writing one image before you can take the next shot. It's less of an issue for higher-end dSLRs with buffer memory capable of holding several images. However, when that buffer is full, you can't take another picture until the camera clears space in its working memory by writing the image to the storage card. The smaller JPEG files mean that you're less likely to fill the buffer faster than the camera can clear it, and if you do, you won't have to wait as long before you can take the next shot.

> Use the JPEG format combined with a lower resolution and higher compression when you need to maximize the number of images you can store on a memory card. The best way to make sure you can shoot lots of images is to have several spare memory cards available. However, if you're caught without a spare and need to maximize the number of images you can fit onto a card, selecting a lower resolution JPEG file format can allow you to keep shooting long after you would have run out of room for larger image files. You can save dozens of compressed JPEG images in the space required for just one Raw image file.

> Use your camera's Raw file format for studio shots and other images where the utmost quality and control are essential.

> Use the Raw format for difficult lighting situations such as high contrast or high dynamic range lighting. The Raw format retains more exposure data, which gives you more options manipulating the image later.

> Use the Raw format for critical color balance control. Instead of having to commit to a white balance setting before you shoot, you can adjust the color after the shot, when you process the Raw file.

> Use TIFF if you need to maintain maximum image quality in a standard file format that you can open and use in other programs without first processing the image in dedicated Raw software. TIFF is preferable to JPEG if you plan to open, edit, and resave the image repeatedly.

> Use the Raw + JPEG combination (if your camera offers it) to record two image files of each shot. This gives you the convenience of the universal JPEG file format that you can open, view, print, and share anywhere; and also the Raw file if you need to go back to it to fine-tune the color balance or brightness range, or wto generate a higher-resolution version of the JPEG file. This the best of both worlds, but you pay for it with storage space. You're saving two files of each image, so you can't fit as many shots onto a memory card.

Which of the two pictures at the beginning of the chapter is the digital image and which one was shot on film?

If you can't tell the difference, it doesn't really matter. Both images were taken by the same photographer and neither one is significantly better or worse because it was shot on film or digital.

If you really must know, figure 8-2 is the digital image. Figure 8-1 is a scan from a color transparency. Ordinarily, you might expect the film image to have a slight advantage in overall resolution and sharpness. However, in this case, the 12-megapixel digital image from a high-end professional dSLR outperforms the medium-speed 35mm slide film slightly — not that it makes a visible difference after both images go through the four-color book printing process.

PUT A LITTLE LIGHT ON THE SUBJECT

Chapter 9

LIGHTING TOOLS AND APPROACHES

In many situations, the natural light on a subject is beautiful. In figure 9-1, lovely sunset light acted like a spotlight to bring out this blossom's color and texture. To create such a photograph, all you need to do is capture the image with your camera. Of course, you need an eye for good framing, focus, and composition, and you need to make sure you get a good exposure, too. The natural light itself needs no embellishment.

However, natural lighting isn't always available in sufficient quantity and quality to produce the kind of images a photographer envisions. When that's the case, the photographer must go beyond simply adjusting exposure settings to record the image with the camera and take an active role in controlling the light that illuminates the subject. Fortunately, a large assortment of lighting tools is available that enable the photographer to add light to the scene and to modify and manipulate both natural and artificial light to achieve the desired results.

The range of lighting tools available to photographers is as varied as the different lighting approaches that photographers can envision. From the keep-it-simple approach of supplementing window light with an inexpensive reflector panel, to the complex approach of building a lighting scheme from scratch in a studio equipped with multiple strobes, diffusers, gobos, softboxes, and strip lights, the vision of the digital photographer today is limited only by imagination and budget.

In this chapter, you find out how lighting tools can help you achieve the look you want in your images. Although most of the tools are typically found in the context of a photographic studio, many of them are equally useful outside the studio to supplement and enhance the ambient lighting on location.

LIGHTING TOOLS

The options for lighting in the studio open up a world of new and exciting opportunities for photographers. Unlike outdoor and most ambient-light scenes, the studio affords photographers the ability to control light and get predictable and reproducible results, whether shooting table-top and product

9-1
© Charlotte K. Lowrie | wordsandphotos.org

photography, fashion and glamour, or portraits, such as the one in figure 9-2.

There are two basic categories of photographic lighting: continuous light systems and strobe or flash systems. As the name implies, continuous lights stay on continuously during a shooting session. Strobes, by contrast, emit a brief flash of light when activated. The technology is the same as the built-in flash unit in most cameras, but it's available on a larger scale.

The ultimate choice of system is yours, and it's best to check the latest systems and features at a local or online dealer before making a decision. Some dealers include setups of various lighting systems so that you can test-drive them before buying.

CONTINUOUS-LIGHT SYSTEMS

Historically, a lot of photographic lighting equipment (see figure 9-3) was adapted from equipment developed for use in stage lighting, and in the film and television industries where the lights must stay on continuously throughout a scene. Stage, film, television, and still photography share the same need for bright, controllable lights with predictable color, so it's no surprise that some of the equipment is the same. Over the years, several different kinds of lights have been adopted for use in stage, film, and photography, including incandescent lights (called hot lights), fluorescent lights (called cool lights), HMI lights, and even carbon arc lights (which are rarely used in a still photography studio).

As a group, continuous lights have several advantages and disadvantages when compared to strobes:

> Because the light stays on continuously at full brightness, there's no difference between the light

9-2
© Charlotte K. Lowrie | wordsandphotos.org

9-3
Image provided by Dreamstime.com

you see as you set up the shot and the light the camera sees during the exposure. This allows the photographer to make accurate assessments of light and shadow without worrying that the quality of the light might be different during the brief burst of light from a strobe system.

> Your camera's onboard reflective meter and automatic exposure systems work normally with continuous lights. Unlike strobe systems, you don't need a separate flash meter or trial-and-error testing to determine the proper exposure.

> You can use the same continuous lights for both still photography and film or video. (The momentary flash of light from a strobe is totally unsuitable for lighting several seconds of continuous action for video.)

> You cannot conveniently vary the intensity of light output from a given lighting instrument. If you need a brighter light, you must generally switch to another light with a higher wattage bulb. For a dimmer light, you can add an accessory scrim or switch to a lower wattage lamp. In contrast, many strobes allow you to adjust the light output with a simple switch or dial. A few continuous lights have a similar feature, but most do not.

> The light output of typical continuous lights tends to be less than that of strobes, so the range of available shooting apertures and shutter speeds is more limited.

> It is more difficult to freeze subject motion with continuous light than it is with the brief flash of strobe light.

> Continuous lights put a larger drain on the studio electrical system than strobes of comparable light output. The continuous lights must constantly convert electrical power into light, whereas strobe systems require much less electricity to recharge between their brief bursts of bright light.

Hot lights

Hot light systems are the most common form of continuous lights. They typically use incandescent lamps (tungsten or quartz-halogen) that are mostly bigger, brighter versions of common household lighting. Incandescent lights continually convert electrical power into light *and heat* — hence the term "hot" lights because over time, the lights, as well as the subjects, can become very hot.

Hot lights have been around for a long time, and they come in a wide variety of sizes, shapes, brands, and configurations. They can range from small units that

9-4

use 100-watt bulbs up to huge 10,000-watt monsters, although 500-watt to 1000-watt bulbs are the typical range in a still photography studio.

Many of the hot light systems are small and light-weight and can be easily transported for location shooting. Some come in kits that offer an economical entry point for photographers who want to set up a small home studio without making a major investment.

Perhaps the simplest form of hot light is the photoflood (shown in figure 9-4 beside a regular light bulb). As you can see, it looks like an oversized version of a standard household bulb. It will even fit into a standard screw-in lamp socket, (although it's not a good idea to do so because normal household lighting sockets aren't built to withstand the heat generated by the high-wattage photoflood bulbs). Other than size and wattage, the main difference between a photoflood and the bulb in the table lamp beside your couch is that the photoflood is designed to emit light at a standardized color temperature of about 3400 kelvin.

Lights that use photoflood bulbs are usually simple and inexpensive, which makes them popular for low-end starter lighting kits. However, the bulbs themselves tend to be bulky, fragile, and short-lived, so they're not the best choice for serious use where compact size and durability matter.

Most photographic hot lights use quartz-halogen bulbs. They're much more compact and durable than photofloods and they're available in higher wattages for higher light output. The lamps come in a variety of sizes and configurations. Some are bulb-shaped, like the one in figure 9-5, and others are tube-shaped, like the one in the light in figure 9-6.

The lighting instruments that contain quartz-halogen bulbs also come in a wide variety of sizes and shapes. A tube-shaped bulb in a wide, shallow reflector, such as the one in figure 9-6 emits light over a wide area,

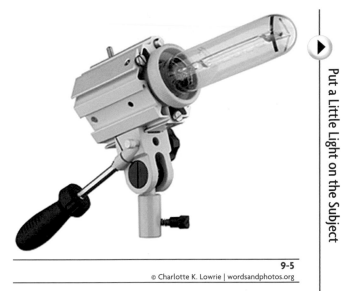

9-5
© Charlotte K. Lowrie | wordsandphotos.org

9-6
Photo by David Shawley | Dreamstime.com

and it's commonly referred to as a *broad light*. Figure 9-7 shows a different kind of light, called a *fresnel* (pronounced fur-nell), with a round reflector behind the bulb and a lens composed of concentric circles that help to focus the light into a spot and also soften it slightly.

There are many more different lighting instruments than can be shown on these pages. They go by a variety of names. Some of the names (such as scoop and ellipsoid) describe the shape of the reflector, and other names (such as Mole, Klieg, Omni, Tota, and Red-Head) are manufacturers and brand names that have come to be associated with a particular style of light.

Here are some of the advantages and disadvantages of hot light systems:

> Hot lights tend to be more economical than strobe systems for small-scale starter kits. You can get a photoflood-based multi-light outfit that is adequate for lighting a small tabletop or headshot for less than the cost of a single small studio strobe head. However, as you get into bigger lights for more light output, the pricing is much closer.

> Hot lights are available in a staggering variety of different configurations, including many specialty

lights and accessories that aren't available for strobes. Hot lights benefit from generations of innovation in the stage, film, and video industries as well as their long use in still photography.

> Hot lights get hot! This means a potentially less comfortable and safe shooting environment. You also must be careful to ensure that all the reflectors, umbrellas, softboxes, and other light modifiers that you use with hot lights are made from heat-resistant materials to avoid scorching.

> Hot lights are the least efficient of the commonly used photographic lights at converting electrical power into light, so they put a larger drain on your electrical system than strobes and other lighting systems of comparable light output. A typical home or office electrical circuit can handle no more than one or two average hot lights. The more powerful lights require high-capacity electrical circuits.

Cool lights

Cool lights are fluorescent lights that are specially color balanced to provide acceptable color rendition for photography and video lighting. They're available in both daylight and tungsten color balance. Photographic fluorescent lights are called cool lights because they are a continuous light source that generates much less heat than hot lights, so the lights, the studio, and the subject all stay much cooler.

Like all fluorescent lights, cool lights use a ballast to create a rapidly pulsed light instead of a true continuously radiant light like a tungsten filament lamp, but the lights are engineered to minimize flicker, so it's not usually a problem.

The smallest cool lights are compact fluorescent lamps with a standard Edison screw-in base. Their small size and ability to fit into a standard light socket make them inexpensive and convenient, but they aren't very powerful. Often, two or more lamps must

9-7
Image provided by Dreamstime.com

be ganged together as shown in figure 9-8 to create the light output comparable to a small photoflood. Other cool lights are long tubes, like standard office lighting. A large rectangular light containing a bank of several cool light tubes can create a large soft light with a respectable light output.

Here are some of the other advantages and disadvantages of cool lights.

> Cool lights are more efficient at converting electricity into light than hot lights, so they consume less power and generate less heat than an incandescent light of comparable light output. In other words, you get about 2.5 times more light per watt of electricity.

> Cool lights are light weight and relatively inexpensive, partially because their components don't need to be as heat-resistant or carry as much electrical current as hot lights. They last much longer than incandescent lamps.

> Cool lights offer relatively low light intensity compared to other light sources. Therefore, light levels are low and exposure times are long.

> Cool lights tend to be very bulky, and they are available in only a relatively limited range of sizes, powers, and configurations.

HMI lights

Hydrargyrum Medium arc Iodide lights are commonly referred to simply as *HMI lights*. They are high-performance, continuous output lights with daylight color balance that were developed for the film and video industries. HMI lights have two to four times the light output of quartz or tungsten lights of comparable wattage, and generate less heat. They use a transformer and ballast similar to a fluorescent light, and because of that, early HMI lights had a pulsed flicker that created a problem for movie and video cameras at certain speeds and for some digital cameras with high-resolution scanning image sensors.

However, newer flicker-free electronic ballasts have pretty much eliminated the problems.

The quality of the light put out by an HMI light is beautiful, but they're very expensive and require long warm-up times to reach full working output. Because of their high cost, you're not likely to see HMI lights in a photography studio. However, you might encounter them on a movie set or in a television studio. If you see a big bright light that looks like artificial sunlight rather than the orange light of a normal incandescent lamp, set your camera for daylight color balance and shoot away. Enjoy the opportunity, and be glad that someone else is footing the bill.

9-8
Photo by Marzanna Syncerz | Dreamstime.com

FLASH AND STROBE LIGHT SYSTEMS

Unlike continuous lights, which radiate light continuously (or in a virtually continuous series of pulses), strobe lights emit a single brilliant flash of light that is synchronized to fire at the exact instant that the camera shutter opens to make the exposure. Everyone is familiar with the small onboard flash that is built into most cameras. Other photographic strobes and flashes are simply variations on that same technology. They range from small, battery-powered flash units that attach to the camera, to slightly larger AC-powered flash units, to large studio strobes such as the one shown in figure 9-9. The larger studio strobes have the power to light whole room sets and accept all sorts of accessories and light modifiers.

Flash and strobe lights store electrical power in a capacitor and then discharge the stored energy into a gas-filled tube to create the flash of light that exposes the image. The flash provides a brief (1/1000 second or faster), predictable, and adjustable burst of light at a predictable color temperature, usually in the range of 5500 to 5600K. The flash tube doesn't waste energy emitting light in between exposures, which makes it very efficient at converting electrical energy into light that is actually used to create an image in the camera. However, it also means that the photographer can't see the light from the flash prior to the exposure.

Because the flash of light from a strobe light must synchronize exactly with the opening of the camera's shutter, there must be an electronic control connection between the camera and the flash. For the camera's built-in flash, the controls are all internal, but an external flash connects to the camera through connections in the camera's hot shoe or through a PC sync cable that plugs into a socket on the camera body or lens.

Here are some of the advantages and disadvantages of flash and strobe lights in general:

> Strobe and flash systems are generally much smaller and lighter than continuous lights of comparable light output. You get very high light output from a small package.

> The power required to recharge the capacitor between flashes is low enough to allow some flash units to be powered by batteries, and an entire studio strobe system with enough power to light a room set can operate on a single, standard household electrical circuit.

> The brief duration of the flash (often 1/2000 second or faster) can effectively freeze subject motion.

9-9
© Charlotte K. Lowrie | wordsandphotos.org

> The effective light output of a flash or strobe can be varied by adjusting the duration of the flash, and the adjustment doesn't alter the quality or color temperature of the light. This allows studio strobes to be built with variable light output and portable flash units to work with automatic exposure systems.

> Strobes stay cool because they flash only for a fraction of a second. When the flash tube fires, it emits heat along with light, but the duration of the flash is so short that there is usually no significant heat buildup. As a result, the lighting equipment and subject stay cool and there is little need to ensure that lighting accessories are heat resistant.

> The inability to see the effect of the light prior to the exposure can make it very difficult to work with flash or strobe for critical lighting tasks. Most studio strobes include modeling lights to assist the photographer in previewing the lighting effect, but the modeling lights don't always accurately represent the light of the strobe, and modeling lights aren't available on most portable flash units. As a result, photographers who work with strobe must work to develop their visualization skills from experience with their equipment.

> The time required to recharge strobe units between flashes makes them unsuitable for video and also for rapid-fire sequences of still images.

> Standard light meters can't measure the short duration of the light from a flash. You need a special flash meter for accurate exposure readings. Because the camera's normal auto-exposure system is based on readings from its built-in reflective light meter, that doesn't work with most flash units either. Although many cameras are capable of automatic exposure control with flash, the feature works only with special dedicated flash units that are engineered to work with the specific camera models.

> The need to synchronize the flash with the camera's shutter means that the camera must be connected to the flash via the camera's hot shoe, a cable, or one of several kinds of optical slave or wireless remote control. If the connection is interrupted, the flash doesn't fire and you miss the shot.

> Flash units must be synchronized to ensure that the flash fires while the shutter is fully open during an exposure. This can restrict your choice of shutter speeds. Typically, the sync speed is 1/125 or slower, although some camera/flash combinations can sync at faster shutter speeds. Shooting with flash at a higher shutter speed can leave part of the image dark, or unexposed.

> The brief, intense flash of light can startle and distract human and animal subjects. It can cause portrait and snapshot subjects to blink, and disrupt wedding ceremonies and other events. A flash can even be dangerous if it momentarily blinds or disorients a subject.

Portable flash

The portable flash unit is one of the handiest of all lighting tools. Whether it's built into the camera body or an accessory flash (hot-shoe mounted or handheld unit), most portable flash units operate on battery power. In the case of a built-in flash, such as the

NOTE

Flash and *strobe* are two different terms for the same technology. Although the terms can be used interchangeably, most photographers tend to use *flash* to refer to small, battery-powered, portable flash units such as the camera's built-in flash and accessory flash units that can be mounted on the camera's hot shoe. The term *strobe* typically refers to larger, more powerful, studio lighting instruments that are normally plugged into a wall outlet for AC power.

one pictured in figure 9-10, the flash is powered by the camera battery. Hot-shoe-mounted flash units and hand-held flash units are powered by batteries in the flash unit, or by a separate power pack. Some portable flash units can also operate on AC power to conserve battery power when you're working within range of a wall outlet.

Most portable flash units include some sort of automatic exposure control system that adjusts the light output of the flash as needed to achieve proper exposure. The specifics of the exposure control mechanisms vary in the different brands and models of cameras and flash units, but most of them fall within the following general categories:

> **Built-in flash:** The camera's built-in flash is integrated with the camera's own automatic focus and automatic exposure systems, which work together

X-REF

See Chapter 10 for more information on using portable flash and examples of some flash techniques.

9-10
© Charlotte K. Lowrie | wordsandphotos.org

to control the flash output for proper exposure of the primary subject (the one the camera is focused upon). In low light conditions, the camera may fire a series of preflashes that not only helps reduce red-eye in subjects, but also helps the camera determine distance and focusing information. Some camera models offer features such as flash exposure compensation, flash exposure bracketing, and automatic balancing of flash and ambient exposure.

> **Non-Dedicated flash:** This is a separate accessory flash unit that is designed to work on a variety of different camera models. It is usually significantly more powerful than the camera's built-in flash, and it typically offers features such as a tilt and swivel head to facilitate bounce flash techniques. The flash unit connects to the camera via the camera's hot shoe or a simple PC sync cable. The flash unit typically contains its own auto exposure system in the form of a sensor that measures the light reflected from the subject and controls exposure by adjusting the duration of the flash. To use this type of flash, you put your camera in manual exposure mode, set the shutter speed to the camera's sync speed, and set the ISO and aperture to match the corresponding settings on the flash unit. The flash unit handles the exposure calculations. Because the camera is in manual exposure mode, this kind of flash is sometimes called a manual flash, although that term seems more appropriate for a flash with no exposure automation.

> **Dedicated flash:** These flash units are called dedicated because their design is dedicated to a specific camera brand. In fact, the flash usually carries the same brand name as the camera, although some third-party flash units are available for the most popular camera brands such as Canon and Nikon. Like the non-dedicated flash, it is typically much more powerful than the camera's built-in flash, includes a tilt and swivel head, and may offer additional features such as an auto-focus

assist lamp. The flash connects to the camera's hot shoe or a special sync cable that, like the flash itself, is dedicated to the specific camera brand and model. The dedicated flash, such as the one shown in figure 9-11, integrates with the camera's automatic focus and exposure systems much like the built-in flash. In effect, it becomes a more powerful extension of, or replacement for, the built-in flash. A dedicated flash is sometimes called a TTL flash because it links to the camera's Through The Lens (TTL) exposure system.

What are flash guide numbers?

Flash power for portable flash units is described by a *guide number,* which was originally developed as a tool to help photographers manually calculate and set flash exposure. The guide number is given in feet (or meters) at a given ISO, usually ISO 100. The higher the guide number, the more powerful the flash. You can use the guide number, along with a little math, to determine the correct aperture to use.

You calculate the exposure by dividing the guide number by the flash-to-subject distance to determine the correct *f*-stop. For example, if your subject is 20 feet from the flash and the flash unit's guide number is 120 ft. at ISO 100, then the equation would be:

120 (guide number) / 20 (distance in feet) = *f*-6

Most flash units today have their own built-in automatic exposure systems, or they connect to the camera's Through The Lens (TTL) metering system, so you won't need to use the guide number to calculate exposures manually. However, the guide number remains a useful reference point for comparing the light output of different flash units and for quickly calculating maximum flash distances.

Built-in and dedicated portable flash units in higher-end cameras often offer an impressive range of features. Methods and naming conventions for these features vary by camera manufacturer, but they include:

> **Flash exposure compensation.** As with exposure compensation, flash exposure compensation allows you to reduce or increase the exposure by setting a negative or positive compensation amount. Generally, the compensation is set in increments of 1/3 stops up to plus/minus 2 stops. This feature allows you to compensate for flash exposure errors due the unusually high or low subject reflectance, adjust flash exposure for creative control, and balance flash and ambient light levels for flash fill when you're shooting in bright light and want to reduce shadows on a subject's face.

9-11
© Charlotte K. Lowrie | wordsandphotos.org

PRO TIP

Dedicated flash units should be used only on the specific camera brand(s) and models for which they were designed. The flash unit communicates with the camera through a series of electrical contacts in the hot shoe connector, and different camera manufacturers use different voltages to send signals through the various contacts. A voltage mismatch can cause serious damage to the sensitive electronics in the camera or flash.

> **Flash exposure lock.** This feature allows you to set the flash exposure for a specific object in the frame. Generally, you focus on the area where you want to lock the flash exposure, press and hold a button, which fires a preflash to calculate exposure and retain it in memory. Then you recompose the image and shoot the picture.

> **Red-eye reduction.** One of the most vexing problems with flash photography is the appearance of a red glow in a subject's eyes as the light from the flash reflects off the back of the retina. The problem occurs only when the flash is positioned very close to the lens and the subject's pupils are open wide because of a low ambient light level. The red-eye reduction feature fires a low preflash light that helps to narrow the subject's pupil and thus lessen the occurrence of red pupils in the final image. Although it helps some, the red-eye reduction feature is seldom 100 percent effective. For optimum results, ask the subject to look at the camera during the red-eye reduction flashes. Better yet, increase the separation between the lens and the flash by using an accessory flash instead of the camera's built-in flash.

> **Remote flash triggering.** Some newer portable flash units are designed to work with remote triggering systems that enable you to set up multiple flash units that are fired simultaneously from a central control point at the camera. Some remote triggering systems are simply optical sensors that

fire a slave flash when the sensor detects the pulse of light from the master flash unit. Others are wireless remote devices that use infra-red or radio-frequency transmitter/receivers to trigger and control the flash units. Some of the more advanced dedicated flash units can retain a measure of exposure automation control over the remote units. So with a few light stands, an umbrella or two, and multiple flash units, you can simulate studio lighting on location without schlepping around the studio flash heads and power pack.

AC-Powered flash

One interesting segment of the market for flash lighting equipment is the small, low-power AC-powered flash units. A typical example of this kind of flash unit has a screw-in base, just like a household light bulb or a photoflood, and it's compact enough to fit into most of the same light fixtures and sockets. Each flash unit includes a built-in optical slave sensor to fire the flash when it detects the pulse of light from a master flash unit attached to the camera. You can also get versions that you can connect to the camera with a PC sync cord and some self-contained units that don't have to be screwed into a separate light socket.

These AC-powered flash units are quite inexpensive compared to other photographic lighting equipment, so it's not surprising that they form the basis of some low-cost, entry-level lighting kits. You can also purchase the flash units separately and use them as replacements for photoflood bulbs to convert low-end

PRO TIP

Flash exposure compensation is ideal when you want to add a small pop of light. Just use a negative flash compensation setting to reduce the flash exposure to the point that it just supplements the ambient light by opening up shadows and adds a sparkle to the eyes.

hot light kits to flash. As you might expect of a product of such small size and low cost, AC-powered flash units have a limited feature set, including:

> Many of the units do not include modeling lights, which makes it difficult to anticipate the lighting effect without trial-and-error testing.

> Most of them offer relatively low light output. While they're generally a little more powerful than the typical built-in flash unit in a camera, they don't usually match the light output of a middle-of-the-road accessory flash unit, much less a small studio strobe. Still, they offer adequate power for some limited uses.

> The light output isn't adjustable and the flash units don't offer any exposure automation. All exposure calculations and adjustments are strictly manual.

> Each AC flash is a sealed, self-contained unit. The flash tube and modeling light (if it has one) are not replaceable, so when any component fails, you must replace the entire unit. Given the low cost of each one, that's not too much of a concern.

Despite their low cost, small AC-powered flash units aren't very attractive as a general-purpose primary lighting tool. However, they're handy to have around

for specialty applications (such as copy stand lighting, or an ID photo station) and as supplemental lights that you can hide in tight spaces on a room set or architectural interior.

Power pack and head systems

Full-fledged studio strobe light systems come in two basic configurations. The traditional workhorse of the photographic studio consists of one or more separate flash heads, connected to a power pack that powers and controls all the heads. The other configuration is called a monolight, which I cover in the next section.

The individual flash heads of a power pack and head strobe system each contain a flash tube and modeling light in a lightweight unit that is easy to position on a light stand. The flash head usually accepts interchangeable reflectors and a variety of accessories such as barn doors, snoots, umbrellas, and softboxes. Each flash head is connected to the power pack by a cable, and the power pack is connected to a wall outlet (or battery pack) for electrical power and to the camera for shutter synchronization.

A typical power pack supports one to four flash heads, although some can handle more. The power pack contains the actual flash generator, plus controls for distributing the power from the power pack among the flash heads and for varying output of the flash and modeling lights. Because the controls for all flash heads are located on the pack, you can easily adjust all the flash heads from a single location.

Power pack and head systems range from around 400 watt/second to 4800 watt/second, and a typical studio strobe system is around 1200 - 2000 watt/second. The power rating is the maximum output from the power pack, and that power is divided among the flash heads. Even after distributing the power to four flash heads, the light output from each head of a typical studio strobe system easily exceeds the output of all but the most powerful portable accessory flash units, and studio strobes usually recycle much faster than battery-powered accessory flash units.

PRO TIP

If your flash pictures have a dark spot at the bottom of the frame, the problem may be an oversized lens. Large lens hoods, super telephoto lenses, very large-aperture lenses, and very wide lenses can all partially obstruct the light from built-in flash units.

9-12
© Charlotte K. Lowrie | wordsandphotos.org

The modeling light is another important feature of most studio strobe systems (both power pack and monolight). The modeling light is a relatively low-power continuous light mounted in the flash head along with the flash tube. At 50-150 watts or so, the modeling light isn't bright enough to use as the primary light to make an exposure and it doesn't generate too much heat, but in a dark room, it's enough to allow the photographer to position and aim the flash head and preview the light and shadow it creates on the subject. The better strobe systems control the light output of each modeling light so that it varies in proportion to the light output of the corresponding flash tube. Proportional modeling lights make it much easier to preview and evaluate lighting ratios and other nuances that you can't see with non-proportional modeling lights that show only the light positions.

Monolights

A monolight is a studio strobe system that combines a flash head and power pack in one compact unit. This makes the flash head heavier, but more efficient, since there is no power loss to resistance in a long cable between the flash head and the flash generator, as there is in a power pack and head system. The efficiency of monolights, such as the one shown in figure 9-12, are one of the reasons they are becoming increasingly popular in photographic studios.

NOTE

The power of studio strobe systems is rated by the electrical capacity of the power pack — measured in watts per second. The rating allows for rough comparisons of different systems, but it does not reflect a measurement of the actual light output of the system, which depends on the efficiency of the flash tube, cabling, and reflectors, among other factors. Although you can safely assume that a 1000-watt/second system will produce more light than a 100-watt/second system; there may be substantial differences in the actual light output from two different 1000-watt/second systems.

The flash head portion of a monolight usually accepts interchangeable reflectors and accessories just like its counterpart in a power pack and head system. In fact, many of the accessories are often interchangeable between monolights and separate flash heads from the same manufacturer.

Because each monolight contains its own power pack, it plugs directly into a power source with a power cord. Like power pack and head systems, most monolights feature controls that enable you to vary the light output of the flash tube and modeling light, but since those controls are located on the head, you need to move around to each light to make adjustments instead of making all the adjustments from one central location.

To avoid having sync cords strung from light to light all over the studio, most monolights include a built-in optical sensor to fire the slave strobe automatically when the sensor detects a pulse of light from the main light. That way, only one monolight needs to be connected to the camera for synchronization with the shutter.

Monolights range in power from under 100 watt/second to 1500 watt/second or more. Typical units are usually in the range of 300-600 watt/second, but if your needs are modest, you might get by with 160 watt/second units. The total power rating of a set of four typical monolights is roughly comparable to the power rating of a typical power pack and head system that supports four heads.

What to Look For in a Studio Strobe Lighting System

Regardless which studio system you get, it's important to evaluate the system. Here are some factors to consider.

> **Reliable performance:** Whether you spend a little or a lot on a studio lighting system, the system is only good as long as it works. Murphy's Law says that equipment breaks when you need it most, which can leave you scrambling for alternatives. As a result, it's important to evaluate lighting systems in terms of the availability of repair centers, the cost of repairs, the expected life of the system, and the ability to easily rent replacement heads or packs. You can check the reputation of the manufacturer by talking to other photographers and dealers.

> **Expandability:** Another consideration is how extensive the manufacturer's

selection is when you buy the system and the probability that the company will still be in business and will have compatible gear and replacement parts available months or years later when you want to expand your system. A good quality strobe system can last for a photographer's entire career, but it's frustrating to have a system that's been discontinued and has no upgrades available from the original manufacturer. Also, look around to see if other companies offer accessories for the system you're considering—an indication that the system is recognized and supported by others in the industry. If you need to add another flash head to your inventory, it's generally less expensive to add a head to a pack and head system than it is to buy an

Continued

additional monolight. However, the monolight is usually less expensive than replacing the power pack if you've reached the maximum number of heads that your power pack supports, or you need more total power.

> Power: A key consideration in purchasing a studio lighting system is how much light output you need for the type shooting you plan to do. Shooting head-and-shoulders portraits or table-top product shots don't require as much light output as shooting full-body fashion shots, large product shots, or room sets. Also consider the range of apertures that you want to use. If you typically shoot portraits at f-5.6, you don't need (or want) as much power as you do if you shoot products at f-22. If you do both, then the system should provide the variable output to cover the entire range. Ultimately, you have to evaluate the output of the specific system you're considering and factor in the number of flash heads you'll have in the system. A four-head kit with a total power of 400-640 watt/seconds is probably sufficient for shooting individual and small group portraits. For bigger subjects, you'll need more power.

> Adjustability: The ability to adjust the power of the flash heads determines the range of exposures that you can use, and also how much you have to move the lights around to get the proper exposure. If you can fire the flash head(s) only at full power,

you'll have to move them forward or back to get the exposure you want. But with flash heads that allow you to dial down power in increments, you'll spend less time moving lights. Power increments range from full stop to third-stop settings or continuously variable.

> Recycle Time: Another consideration is how quickly the lights recycle and are ready for another full-power flash. This becomes a critical factor in fast shooting situations such as fashion, but is less of an issue with still-life photography. Typically, you pay more for faster recycle times and the flash tubes and other components may not last as long if you fast recycle the system constantly.

> Modeling lights: Most photographers consider modeling lights to be an essential feature of a studio strobe system. While any modeling light is better than none, you really need true proportional modeling lights if you're going to do any sort of critical lighting judgments. That means that not only must each modeling light vary in brightness in proportion to the light output of its corresponding flash tube, all the lights on the set

need to be proportional to each other to give an accurate preview of the overall lighting scheme. If all the strobe lights on the set are from the same manufacturer and series, you've got a much better chance of achieving this goal than if you attempt to mix lights from various manufacturers.

> Slave features: Almost all current monolights (and many power packs too) include some form of built-in optical slave or other wireless triggering device. If the system features optical slaves, make sure it isn't so sensitive that sunlight triggers it accidentally or causes an overload that prevents slave flash heads from firing in direct sunlight. If you're using infrared or radio-frequency wireless devices with multiple systems in your studio, be sure that the systems don't cross fire.

> Set up and transport: If you do location work and want to take the lighting system, you need to consider the ease or difficulty with which the system can be disassembled, transported, and reassembled on location. You also need to think about the power requirements at the location. The total power requirements for a studio strobe system are usually quite modest, but the availability of outlets may be an issue. Each monolight requires its own wall outlet (or extension). In pack and head systems, only the pack is plugged into an electrical outlet.

> Cost: When calculating the overall cost of the system, it's important to include spare parts, such as flash tubes, cables, and modeling light bulbs, as well as accessories and light modifiers including reflectors, softboxes, diffusion panels, umbrellas, an overhead rail system or light stands, and so on.

TOOLS FOR MODIFYING AND MANIPULATING THE LIGHT

The range of tools for photographic lighting is impressively broad and potentially overwhelming. However, each tool serves a specific purpose for shaping, modifying, containing, blocking, reflecting, or redirecting light. Some lighting kits include basic tools such as reflectors and umbrellas so that you can begin shooting as soon as you unpack the kit. But over time, you'll want to add other tools to the system to get more precise lighting results.

Most lighting instruments start out with a point source light from a relatively small light bulb or flash tube that emits light in all directions. The way that light is constrained, directed, focused, filtered, or diffused as it travels from the bulb to the subject can harness an inefficient scattering of light and give it the efficiency and punch of a focused spot beam or spread and diffuse it into a soft light that seems to wrap around the subject.

PRO TIP

Many dealers also sell used lighting equipment, and this can mean big savings for you, whether you're buying a whole lighting system or shopping for a used flash head and other components to add to an existing system. Be sure to buy spares. Having a spare flash head for the system is as important as having a backup camera body and lens.

Light shaping starts with construction of the lighting instrument itself and the bowl shaped reflector that helps catch light that would be wasted spilling out to the sides and back of the light head and redirecting it toward the subject. A deep bowl reflector with a shiny interior confines the light to a narrower field than a shallow dish reflector with a white interior. Lenses and mechanisms that adjust the bulb position in the

reflector further shape the light in spot lights. There are hundreds of different lighting instruments available, but most photographers work with just a few on a regular basis.

Reflectors and diffusers

The simplest of all lighting tools is the *reflector*. Any surface that reflects light can be used as a reflector, from a polished silver mirror to a simple piece of white foamboard or card stock. Reflectors come in sizes ranging from a few inches to a few feet across and may be composed of rigid panels, semi-rigid foldable panels, or the popular collapsible metal hoops that support stretched fabric reflective surfaces. As if that definition weren't broad enough, many people loosely apply the term reflector to any similarly shaped panel, whether its purpose is to reflect, block, absorb, or diffuse the light. Hence the popular five-in-one "reflector" kit shown in figure 9-13. The collapsible hoop supports transluscent diffuser material, and the reversible zippered cover provides white, silver, and gold reflectors, plus a black absorber panel. Although they all redirect light in some way, their effects and effectiveness are very different from each other.

> **Silver reflectors:** A silver reflector is used to redirect the light from a source in another direction with minimal change in the intensity and quality of the light source itself. A polished mirror surface can maintain essentially the same quality and light intensity as the original light source. The more common silver fabric reflector has a matte surface that scatters the light some, which makes the light a little softer and contributes to a loss of approximately one *f*-stop of light compared to the original light.

PRO TIP

Perhaps the most-used lighting accessory of all is the basic light stand. It's a simple device — just a collapsible three-leg base supporting a telescoping center pole. It allows you to easily position the lighting instrument attached to the top of the stand. When looking for a light stand, be sure to get one that is heavy enough to support the weight of your lighting instruments and attachments, and make sure the clamps on the center pole are strong and easy to use. Check the diameter (3/8" or 5/8") of the stud on the top of the light stand to ensure that it matches the mounting base of your lights.

9-13

X-REF

See Chapter 10 for more information on using reflectors, including examples.

Direct sunlight bounced off a silver reflector tends to be too harsh for portraiture and most other subjects, unless you're going for a relatively hard light effect. On the other hand, the efficiency of a silver reflector is perfect for bouncing light from a more diffuse source such as an overcast sky to fill shadow areas of the subject.

> **Gold reflectors:** A gold reflector is essentially the same as a silver reflector except that its golden color tints the reflected light, which adds warmth to the subject. You can use the gold reflector to counteract the excess blue in the reflection of the light from a north sky, or to simulate the golden glow of sunset lighting. The gold color also reduces the intensity of the reflected light slightly compared to a silver reflector. How much depends on how dark the gold color is and how shiny or matte the surface.

> **White reflectors:** Like silver reflectors, white reflectors redirect the main light source. However, unlike the silver reflector, the white reflector has a white matte surface that diffuses any light that strikes it, transforming even a hard point-source light into a soft diffuse light. The white reflector reflects light over its entire surface, so the reflector becomes a secondary light source. White reflectors are much less efficient than silver reflectors — with a loss of approximately two *f*-stops or more.

White reflectors do a great job of simultaneously softening and subduing a strong harsh light, such as direct sunlight, and making it suitable for a fill light for an outdoor portrait. On the other hand, a white reflector isn't usually efficient enough to function well when reflecting a dull light such as an overcast sky.

> **Black absorbers:** An opaque black panel is the opposite of a reflector. Instead of reflecting light, it absorbs most of the light that strikes its surface. You use it to control unwanted reflections. For example, placing a black panel just outside the frame on the shadow side of a portrait head can significantly reduce the amount of light that's reflected into the shadows — a handy trick when you need to increase the contrast of an image.

Another common use for an opaque black panel is to create portable open shade conditions wherever you want. You can mount the black panel on a light stand, and then position it between the subject and the sun so that it creates a pool of shade for your subject. The effect simulates shooting the subject on a porch or under the overhang of a building. In this case, the black panel functions as a kind of gobo (go-between) commonly called a *shade*.

> **Diffusers:** A diffuser is a white translucent panel, which looks a lot like a standard white reflector but works very differently. A diffuser is a surface that diffuses and reduces the intensity of light when you place it in the path of the light that is falling on the subject. A diffuser can transform a hard, point-source light, such as direct sunlight, into a soft, diffuse light.

X-REF

See Chapter 10 for an example of using a diffuser to soften direct sun.

Other light modifiers

Here is a list and short description of the most common lighting system tools and accessories.

> **Acetate or gel:** A transparent colored sheet that modifies the color of light. Commonly referred to as a gel, which is an abbreviation of gelatin filter. Gels are normally mounted on studio lights using frames that attach to the light and hold the gel a few inches away from the light to reduce problems

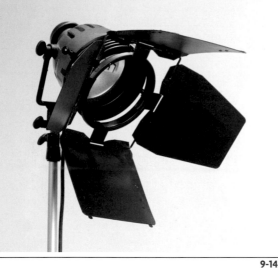

9-14
Image provided by Dreamstime.com

with overheating. Small gels can be affixed directly to the flash head of accessory flash units.

> **Barn doors:** An adjustable attachment for a light consisting of one or two pairs of hinged black panels that attach to the front of the reflector and can be folded at various angles to control spill. See figure 9-14.

> **Boom:** A horizontal extension arm added to the top of a light stand to allow the light affixed to the end of the boom to be cantilevered out and over a subject or set. A boom arm typically includes a counterweight on the opposite end of the arm and a mechanism to adjust and lock the angle of the boom.

> **Cookie:** Cookie is short for cucoloris. It's a device, usually a perforated metal sheet that attaches to a focusing spotlight to produce a light and shadow pattern, such as leaves, across a subject or background. Cookies are sometimes motorized to create a moving shadow pattern to simulate light passing through snow or rain.

> **Effects light:** Any light that is used to create an effect, such as a hair light in a portrait, rather than light the overall scene.

> **Flag:** A device used to block light and create a shadow or control spill. Flags can be any opaque material, such as foam-core, cardstock, or metal, and are usually black. Flags are frequently rectangular objects that are clamped or taped to a light stand, much like a flag on a flagpole, hence the name.

> **Gobo:** Short for "Go Between," gobo can refer to any of a number of lighting tools that are placed between a light source and the subject to block or control the light. In common usage, gobo refers to a large panel that is placed some distance from the light and contains cutout holes that create an interesting light and shadow pattern in the scene. Gobos often create the effect of light shining through doors, windows, and Venetian blinds, such as the example in figure 9-15.

> **Honeycomb:** A lighting accessory that attaches to the front of the reflector on a light and consists of a grid of hexagonal cells that resemble a honeycomb (see figure 9-16). A honeycomb grid restricts the spread of the light and increases its directionality.

> **Projection spot:** A lighting instrument that features projection optics to create a focused light output. Often used to cast the image of a gobo or cookie onto a background or subject.

> **Scrim:** A device, usually made of wire or fiberglass screening, that attaches to a light like a gel filter to reduce the light intensity with minimal diffusion.

> **Seamless paper:** Long rolls of heavy-weight paper that are used to provide a nonreflective background. The rolls of paper are over eight feet wide and available in white, black, and a variety of colors. By mounting the roll on stands or hanging it from the wall and then unrolling the paper down the wall and across the floor so that it transitions from floor to wall in a smooth curve, you can

9-15
© Bryan Moberly | moberlyphotography.com

9-16
Photo by Robert Lerich | Dreamstime.com

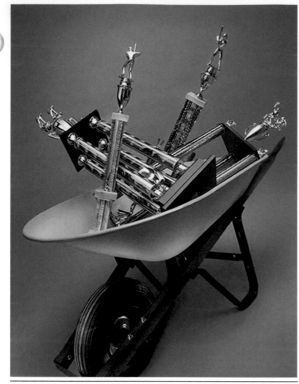

9-17
Photo by Dean Lavenson

9-18

provide a seamless background look like the background in figure 9-17.

> **Snoot:** A lighting accessory shaped like an inverted cone that attaches to a light in place of the normal reflector and constricts the light into a small spot. See figure 9-18.

> **Softbox:** A lighting accessory shaped like a large box that has one or more layers of diffusion material and baffles to create a soft lighting effect. (See figure 9-19.) The softbox attaches to the light source like a big reflector that contains layers of diffusion to soften light. Softboxes come in a variety of sizes and shapes and may have white, silver, or gold baffles. They are usually made of heat resistant fabric supported by metal or fiberglass rods in the corners. Like an umbrella, the goal of the softbox is to transform the raw light of a flash head or other light into a soft light. Because the light shines through a softbox instead of bouncing off it indirectly, the light tends to be more directional than the light from an umbrella.

> **Spill:** Light from any source that falls on anything other than the subject at which it is pointed. Spill light can sometimes be useful in filling shadows or backgrounds, but it can also be a problem, creating unwanted reflections and causing lens flare. It can be controlled with flags, barn doors, or gobos.

> **Spot:** A lighting instrument that is capable of confining its light output to a small spot, usually by

means of a focusing system with reflectors or lenses or both. In some cases, a light that is fitted with a deep reflector and honeycomb attachment or a snoot can successfully function as a spot.

> **Strip light:** A light with a reflector that is much longer than it is wide, and thus puts out a long, narrow strip of light.

> **Tent:** A lighting technique that surrounds and covers a subject with diffusion material and then lights the subject by shining light through the diffusion material to create a soft, shadowless light. The tent includes an opening through which the camera lens fits. Tents also reduce unwanted reflections from shiny subjects. Figure 9-20 shows an unusual subject posed inside a prefab tent called a lite cube. It's a pop-up tent composed of white fabric stretched on metal hoops, like the collapsible reflectors. Another panel (with a shooting slit for the lens) attaches to the open front when you need a fully enclosed tent.

> **Umbrella:** A lighting accessory shaped like an umbrella that mounts on a light so that the light shines into or through the umbrella to spread or diffuse light and create a soft lighting effect.

X-REF

See Chapter 14 for examples of tent lighting.

9-19

9-20

(See figure 9-21.) The umbrella opens and closes with the same mechanism as a rain umbrella. The umbrella shaft attaches to the light so that the light shines into the concave interior of the umbrella. Normally, the light head points away from the subject so that the subject is lit by the light bouncing off the umbrella's inner surface. The umbrella becomes a large, dish-shaped reflector. Umbrellas come in a variety of sizes and may have white, silver, or gold reflective surfaces. Some umbrellas are translucent to allow them to function as diffusers rather than reflectors. Like a softbox, the goal of the umbrella is to transform the raw light of a flash head or other light into a soft light. Because the light bounces off a curved surface in an umbrella instead of shining through a softbox, umbrella light tends to spread out more and be less directional than the light from a softbox.

CONTROLLING LIGHT INTENSITIES

Lighting tools are all about controlling light, and one of the key things you need to control is how much light reaches the subject — in other words, the brightness of the light. Obviously, you need enough light on the subject to achieve a good exposure, but there's more to it than that. You also need to control relative brightness of different portions of scene — highlights and shadows, modeling to define form, and so on.

BRIGHTNESS VERSUS DISTANCE

Light intensity varies with the distance from the light source. The closer you are to the light source, the brighter the light. Conversely, light intensity falls off as distance from the source increases.

You can see the effect of light falloff over distance in figure 9-22. The main light source is just outside the frame on the right, and naturally, the light is brightest on the right side of the bags. The light falls off noticeably across the face of the bags, and the leather gets darker the farther you go to the left.

9-22
Photo by Alicia McGinnis

INVERSE SQUARE LAW

The phenomenon of light fall as distance from the light source increases happens at a consistent and predictable rate, as explained by a principle of physics called the Inverse Square Law, which states that the intensity of light is inversely proportional to the square of the distance from the source.

So, if you double the distance from the light source, the light intensity is reduced to one-forth (the distance times two is two, two squared is four, and the inverse of four is one-fourth). The same formula works in the opposite direction. If you reduce the distance from the light source by half, the light intensity increases by a factor of four (the distance divided by two is one-half, one-half squared is one-fourth, and the inverse of one-fourth is four).

The diagram in figure 9-23 may help you visualize how this works. Light spreads out as it travels farther from the source. The amount of light energy striking a given square at some distance from the source spreads out to cover four squares at double that distance from the source, which means that each square

gets only one fourth of the light energy at the doubled distance.

Have you got all that?

To put it in photographic terms, doubling the distance between the light source and subject reduces the brightness by two stops, and halving the distance between the light source and subject increases the brightness by two stops. In other words, any time you change the light to subject distance by a factor of two, you change the brightness of the light on the subject by two stops.

Of course, if you increase or decrease the distance by some other amount besides double or half, the Inverse Square Law still applies, but the math gets a little more complicated. For example, to make a one-stop change in the light intensity, you change the distance from the source by a factor of 1.4, and so on.

LIGHT RATIOS

The difference in brightness between the highlights and shadows in a scene or subject is called the light ratio. A high ratio creates greater contrast. The ratio

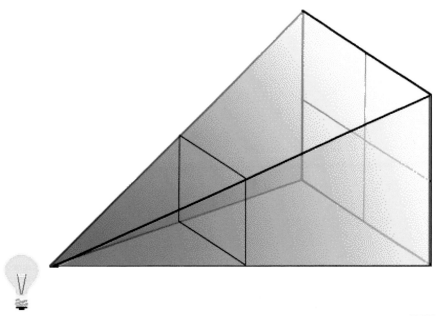

9-23

describes in *f*-stops the difference between highlights and shadows. So doubling the lighting ratio equates to a one-stop change between highlights and shadows. Here are some examples of lighting ratios.

> **1:1 ratio** — A flat lighting where the subject is evenly lit with essentially no dominant shadows. The exposure on both the highlight and shadow sides meter essentially the same. Figure 9-24 shows a test subject with flat lighting. Notice how it lacks much of the modeling that defines the three-dimensional form in the higher light ratio examples that follow.

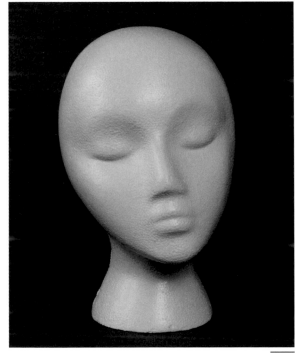

9-24

9-25

> **2:1 ratio** — There is a one f-stop difference between the highlights and shadows. Shadows are visible but very light. Figure 9-25 shows the test subject lit with a 2:1 ratio. This is the minimum light ratio that shows effective modeling to define the form.

> **4:1 ratio** — The highlights are four times or two f-stops lighter than the shadows. With this ratio, the shadows are dark but still show texture and detail. In figure 9-26, you can see the strong three-dimensional modeling that the 4:1 ratio provides.

> **8:1 ratio** — In this ratio, the highlights are eight times or three f-stops lighter than the shadows. This is a contrasty ratio in which either highlight or shadow detail may be lost. The 8:1 light ratio shown in figure 9-27 starts getting into the realm of excessive contrast. The starkness of the shadows begins to hide, rather than enhance, the form.

9-26

9-27

Is it true that tungsten, or hot lights, create color temperature problems?

Color temperature has traditionally been a challenge with hot lights. The problem is that their light output and color balance change slightly as the line voltage fluctuates or the lamps age. Also, there's often a noticeable color variation between different types of lamps, such as photofloods compared to quartz-halogen lamps. However, the slight color shifts aren't as much of a problem with digital cameras as they were with film because you can shoot Raw and/or set a custom white balance. Shooting Raw gives you the opportunity to compensate for any color inconsistency during processing, and setting a custom white balance at the beginning of each shooting session offsets any color shift from the nominal standard for tungsten light and ensures that your colors will be accurate and neutral.

How do I decide how many lights or flash heads I need to get started?

You can begin with just a single light and one or more reflectors of various sizes. You can achieve some good results with a one-light setup, but it's limiting, and using a single light effectively actually takes more skill than using multiple lights. Many lighting kits come with two lights, and that is sufficient for the main light and a fill light. I'd say that two lights is a minimum starter kit, with three being preferable. Most standard portrait lighting schemes use four lights (main, fill, hair, background), so that's probably the recommended base inventory of lights.

What is a specular highlight?

A specular highlight, sometimes called a hot spot, is a pinpoint reflection of the light source reflected from a shiny surface, such as a chrome car bumper, the rim of a glass, or ripples of water. Specular highlights render as pure white and are not factored into the lighting ratio of the scene.

How do you build a lighting scheme in the studio? Where do you start?

Well, you don't just turn on a bunch of lights and start moving them around randomly until you stumble onto something that works. Instead, you need to build the lighting scheme methodically, one light at a time.

It helps to start by visualizing the finished effect you want to achieve, and then you place each light where it needs to be to contribute to that effect. I usually start by emulating some natural lighting situation that I've observed somewhere, and then I adapt and improve upon that basic lighting situation as needed.

When it comes to placing the individual lights, I usually start with the primary light — the one that will define the shape of the main subject — and then add other lights. The process goes something like this:

1. Turn on the main light and position it to create the light and shadow pattern that defines the subject's form or other feature that you want to accentuate. Move the light around some to try different angles and effects. With just one light, you'll be able to see the effect of the main light in stark contrast.

2. Add a fill light to open shadows and reduce overall contrast ratio of the main subject to acceptable levels. More often than not, this means adding a large soft light from near the camera position. Be careful not to overpower the main light.

3. Add another light (or lights) as needed to fill in the background and illuminate the rest of the scene. Sometimes your fill light will provide all the general illumination you need on the background. Other times you may need one or more separate lights dedicated to lighting the background. As you add background lights, pay attention to any unintended effects they may have on the main subject lighting.

4. Add accents and details as needed. This is when you add finishing touches such as a hair light or kicker on a portrait.

5. Refine and adjust the lighting as needed. You may need to adjust one or more of the lights to fine-tune their position slightly, or you may need to bring in some barn doors or flags to knock out a reflection or control some spill.

This is just one approach. Other approaches are equally valid. For example, you might choose to start with the fill light first to establish an overall light level on the set. Then you could add the main light to accent the primary subject and bring it out of the background with a punch of brightness and contrast.

The important thing is to have a plan for developing your lighting scheme and to build the lighting systematically according to that plan.

In a photographic studio, the photographer has absolute control over every nuance of the lighting for each photograph. However, most photographs aren't taken in the controlled environment of the studio. Instead, the photographer must venture out of the studio to find and photograph subjects, such as figure 10-1 in their natural environments. In most cases, photography at remote locations outside the studio means working with whatever existing light is available.

By necessity, a photographer's approach to available light photography is fundamentally different from studio photography. The emphasis is on analyzing and adapting to the light that is available at the subject's location rather than creating your own lighting scheme from scratch as you do in the studio.

This chapter explores some typical available light sources and situations with examples of how different photographers handled those situations. Although I can't possibly provide comprehensive coverage of the many varied light situations that you might encounter, the images on these pages encompass the work of several photographers in a wide range of lighting conditions.

ADAPTING TO EXISTING LIGHT

In many cases, working with available light simply means recognizing the good qualities of whatever light is available and making the best of it. In some cases, you may be able to manipulate or supplement the available light to enhance your photograph. In other cases, you may elect to replace some (or all) of the available light with portable photographic lighting that ranges from a simple on-camera flash unit to a full set of portable studio lights. Even when you decide to replace the ambient light at a location with photographic lighting, you must still deal with the existing light, if only to ensure that you eliminate its influence on your photograph.

10-1
Photo by Dan Dry

There are distinctly different approaches to photography that are particularly evident in how different photographers work with available light.

> **Photojournalistic:** Some photographers take a photojournalistic approach. They see their role as that of an observer and recorder of the world around them and seek to do so with minimal interference. Some of the more extreme practitioners of this approach refuse to use any sort of supplemental lighting whatsoever, but most will use a reflector or flash fill occasionally if it's necessary to get the shot.

> **Artistic:** Other photographers take a much more hands-on approach to location lighting. They see the pre-existing lighting as a starting point and actively look for ways to manipulate and supplement that lighting to create the finished photographs they envision.

Both approaches are valid, and they sometimes overlap significantly. A photographer who normally tends to take the photojournalistic approach may sometimes need to manipulate the lighting heavily to get a shot that tells the story they want to present. In contrast, a photographer who normally adjusts the lighting of each shot may sometimes encounter situations in which no lighting manipulation is needed.

WORKING WITH DAYLIGHT

The most common form of available light for photography is daylight — the direct or reflected light of the sun. From dawn to dusk, daylight is available to contribute at least some illumination for most any subject located outside of a windowless room or a deep cave.

Unless you're in the Arctic or Antarctic in midwinter, you can count on having at least a few hours of daylight each day, but you can't necessarily count on the quality of that light. Sunlight changes direction constantly during the day as the sun makes its arc across the sky, and the brightness and character of the light changes with time of day and atmospheric conditions.

None of those changes are within the photographer's control. You can't reach out and move the sun to a different angle or adjust the position and density of a cloud to create more or less diffusion. Instead, you need to become a keen observer of the quality of the naturally occurring light and how it affects your subject; and then be selective about when and how you take the picture. Sometimes, that means grabbing the shot in the brief moment when you see that the light is right, and other times it means waiting for the light to change (hopefully, for the better). Sometimes, you might change the camera angle or reposition the subject to take better advantage of the naturally occurring light.

TIMES OF DAY

Perhaps the most predictable changes in sunlight come with different times of day. As the sun starts its daily journey low in the eastern sky, the early morning light is warmer in color and not as bright as it will be later in the day, and it's often softened by fog or mist left over from the night before, as in figure 10-2.

Mid-day sun creates a very different effect, as in figures 10-3 through 10-5. The sun is higher in the sky and its bright light creates sharp contrast between the brilliant highlights and the short, dark shadows. The dense shadows create an opportunity to play with shadow patterns (figure 10-3), and the crisp lighting enhances some industrial subjects (figure 10-4), which makes for good abstract studies. On the other hand, mid-day sun is not usually the preferred lighting for people, but can be appropriate when the goal is to accentuate a colorful costume and striking pose (as in figure 10-5) instead of flattering lighting on the subject's face.

10-2
Photo courtesy Brian Grant / Dreamstime

10-3
Photo by Dan Dry

10-4

10-5
Photo by Dan Dry

10-6
Photo by Dan Dry

most photographers consider the warm tones to be highly desirable and stick with the daylight color setting to record them without adjustment.

PRO TIP

If you want to exaggerate the warm tones of evening sunlight, set your camera's white balance to a higher color temperature than normal daylight. The cloudy or shade settings may do the trick.

10-7
Photo by Ramon Rodriguez

As the sun begins to descend to the west in the late afternoon, the shadows get longer and less intense as a result of the lower angle and decreasing brightness of the sun. Compare the length and openness of the shadows in figure 10-6 to the short, dark shadows of figure 10-3. Both images were shot in direct sun, just at different times of day.

Evening sunlight changes color as well as angle. It takes on a warm, yellowish glow, which you can see in the color of the flagstones in figure 10-6 and in the bride's flesh tones and the yellowish greens of the garden setting in figure 10-7. You could adjust your camera's white balance setting to compensate for the color shift and neutralize the colors in the scene, but

As daylight wanes and evening gives way to dusk, the light changes even more. When the sun dips below the horizon, distinct shadows disappear, and so does the warmth of sunlight. Even after careful color correction, pictures such as figure 10-8 take on a distinctly cool tone as a result of being lit by the scattered reflections of the blue sky rather than the direct light of the sun.

10-8
Photo by Dean Lavenson

ATMOSPHERIC CONDITIONS

Before reaching the Earth's surface, sunlight is filtered, reflected, scattered, and blocked by haze, clouds, rain, fog, and more. All these atmospheric conditions can change the character of the light drastically. As a photographer, you need to be attuned to these changes and how they affect the lighting on your subjects.

On a clear day, direct sunlight creates crisp, high contrast lighting with gleaming highlights and dense shadows. In figure 10-9, the photographer used the brightness of the direct sun to emphasize the radiant white of the bride's dress in contrast to the deep shadows behind her.

In figure 10-10, the photographer used the strong contrast of direct sunlight in a different way. Catching this beautiful young Indian woman posed so that most of her face is in shadow allows the sunlit highlight to outline the shape of her face. It's an unusual approach to outdoor portrait lighting, but it works well in this case.

10-9
Photo by Ramon Rodriguez

Indirect sunlight has a very different character. In figures 10-11 and 10-12, the subjects were both photographed outdoors in daylight, but were in the shade instead of in direct sunlight. The light is from an open expanse of blue sky, which furnishes a large, diffuse light source instead of the stark point source of direct sunlight. This is the classic *open shade* lighting, and it's generally considered a more flattering light for portraiture than direct sunlight. Open shade is a soft light that produces open, soft-edged shadows and just enough contrast between the highlights and the shadows to create good modeling to define forms.

10-10
Photo by Dan Dry

X-REF

See Chapter 2 for more information on color temperature and setting white balance.

PRO TIP

Open shade lighting is cooler in color than direct sun, but that's easy to correct by selecting the appropriate white balance setting on your camera or by adjusting the color during post processing in your favorite image editor. Some cameras feature a "shade" setting (7500 kelvin) for this purpose.

Notice how the stark contrast in figure 10-10 hides the detail and focuses your attention on the simple line created by the highlighted side of the face. Compare that to the way the softer lighting in figures 10-11 or 10-12 focuses more on three-dimensional form and brings out details in both highlights and shadows.

The clouds of an overcast sky filter and diffuse the harsh sunlight to create another one of nature's soft light sources. The exact effect of an overcast sky depends on the density of the cloud cover.

10-11
Photo by Dan Dry

10-12
Photo by Dan Dry

A light overcast merely softens the sunlight slightly — you still get a directional light and distinct shadows, but the shadows are lighter and softer edged compared to direct sunlight on a clear day. Notice the soft edges of the shadows under the bench and plant stands in figure 10-13. They're not the hard-edged shadows of direct sunlight, but they are still distinct enough to see individual shadows of the cross braces for the plant stand legs.

A heavier overcast diffuses the light more completely so that the entire sky becomes the light source. Distinct shadow edges disappear, replaced by a very gradual transition from highlight to shadow. The diffuse light tends to fill in all but the deepest shadows. For example, in figures 10-14 and 10-15, the eye sockets of the subjects in both pictures are barely darker than the rest of the faces. The shadows under the jaws are only slightly darker. In figure 10-15, the blue tarp casts a noticeable shadow on the wood, but the edge of the shadow is so soft that it defies exact definition.

10-13
Photo by Fred D. Reaves

10-14
Photo by Dan Dry

10-15
Photo by Dan Dry

PRO TIP

Like open shade, the light from an overcast sky is cooler in color (higher color temperature) than direct sun. As a result, images shot under an overcast sky will have a bluish tint unless you set your camera's white balance to a higher color temperature or adjust the color balance during post processing. Some cameras have a "cloudy" setting (about 6500 kelvin) for this purpose.

When storm clouds cover the sky, they can block most of the sunlight, creating a dusk-like lighting condition. The resulting light is usually dim, flat, and rather uninteresting. But it's a different situation entirely when there's a bit of sunlight peeking through breaks in the clouds as in figure 10-16. The dappled patches of sunlight scattered across the landscape create interesting contrasts, especially when areas of sunlit ground are brighter than the dark underbelly of the clouds above.

You can sometimes see this effect at mid-day when the sun shines through gaps in a general cloud cover. Under the right conditions, the sunbeam effect shown in figure 10-17 appears. However, the most dramatic effects usually occur in the early morning or late afternoon when the sun is at a low angle so that it shines under the thick clouds above the subject. For example, in figure 10-18, the sunlight coming in from behind and to the right of the photographer spotlights the lifeguard stand against the dark sky, made darker by the gathering clouds and approaching night.

Getting a good exposure in this kind of high-contrast lighting situation is a challenge. You might get lucky using your camera's matrix metering mode, but it's more likely that the automatic exposure system will overexpose the white lifeguard stand in order to render the dark sky with more midtones. If you're adept at using the Zone System, you could spot meter the

10-16
Photo by Tony Guffy

sky, sand, and the lifeguard stand and calculate the exposure to place each one in the appropriate zone. Perhaps the simplest solution is to recognize that this is a situation that may fool your automatic exposure system and use your camera's exposure compensation feature to shoot a bracket of alternate exposures around whatever the meter indicates.

X-REF

See Chapter 5 for more information on the Zone System and Chapter 3 for information on bracketing.

Atmospheric conditions aren't confined to various levels of cloud cover far up in the sky. You can also encounter atmospheric phenomenon at ground level in the form of fog, mist, haze, and rain or snow. And of course, all these conditions affect the quality of light.

10-17
Photo by Erin O'Mara

directions. The light scatter toward the camera creates the white glow, and the scatter back toward the trees adds some light and subtle color to the bank and trees that would otherwise be stark silhouettes.

In figure 10-20, the fog bank is larger, completely covering the sky. It rises from the bank of the lake and continues up and overhead above the photographer, enveloping the entire scene in very soft light. Notice the subtle shading on the surfaces of the chairs, especially the backs of the chairs closest to the camera. On a clear day, those surfaces would be in deep shadow.

Figure 10-21 shows the effect fog has on the apparent sharpness of the objects in the scene, which is also a result of the light-scattering properties of the water droplets in the fog. The more fog there is between the camera and the subject, the lighter and less distinct that object appears. The foliage in the foreground at the bottom of the frame is relatively sharp, the front of the barn is blurred, but retains some visible detail, the back edge of the barn roof is much less distinct, and the shape of the tree behind the barn is barely discernable.

Fog isn't the only atmospheric condition to create blurring and lightening of distant objects. In fact, any sort of dust, rain, snow, mist, or humidity in the air can cause a similar effect, and does so in most scenic photographs. The strength of the effect is proportional to the amount of moisture or dust in the air. Dense fog, rain, or snow can obscure object detail in a few feet. The haze of a humid day in the southeast might create a similar effect in a few thousand feet. In the dry air of the southwest, you can see clearly for miles, but even there, the distant mountains turn blue and merge with the sky.

Sometimes, fog makes a good photographic subject, as in figure 10-19. Besides being a nice picture of a tranquil scene, this image demonstrates some of the light altering characteristics of fog. Notice that the fog bank almost seems to glow with a soft white light, even though it isn't a light source itself. The light comes from the sky above, but it's being diffused by the water droplets in the fog. Passing through the fog causes the light to lose directionality and scatter in all

10-19
© Charlotte K. Lowrie | wordsandphotos.org

10-20
Photo by Tony Guffy

10-21
© Charlotte K. Lowrie | wordsandphotos.org

WORKING WITH AVAILABLE LIGHT INDOORS

Outdoors, the quality of available light varies with time of day and atmospheric conditions. When you move indoors, you must contend with even more variability in the lighting. The light comes from a variety of sources, such as daylight entering the room through windows and skylights, artificial light from lamps and ceiling lights, and reflections from walls, ceilings, and other surfaces. Light from the various sources differs in brightness, character, and color — and you must sometimes deal with a mixture of light sources within the same scene.

Another significant difference between indoor and outdoor available lighting is that the light sources tend to be much closer to the subjects indoors. When working in close proximity to the light source, small changes in the relative position of the subject can make significant changes to the light on that subject because of the inverse square law. Light is brightest at the source, and that brightness diminishes rapidly as distance from the source increases. Consequently, indoor light levels can vary drastically as you move into or out of the pools of light from the individual light sources.

X-REF

See Chapter 9 for an explanation of the inverse square law.

WINDOW LIGHT

Daylight entering a room through a window, door, or skylight is often considered one of the nicest forms of indoor lighting. One of the things that makes window light attractive to photographers is that it is usually a bright light with good color. In addition, windows are usually the largest light sources in a room, lighting larger areas with more even light level than other typical indoor light sources.

Of course, the quality of light from a window depends on the size and location of the window and on the outside lighting conditions. You get different kinds of light through windows on the sunny and shady sides of a building, and the light is different on sunny or cloudy days. Drapes, shades, and other window treatments (as well as tinted glass) also affect the quality of the light.

Figure 10-22 is a beautiful study of the quality of window light. Notice how the light from the window plays across the adjacent wall. The light is brightest near the corner close to the window and dims gradually toward the left side of the frame. It's a soft light coming from a large area of open sky rather than direct sunlight. As a result, the shadows from the chair are soft-edged and there's no visible shadow from the window mullions.

Figure 10-23 shows a classroom lit entirely by window light. The window itself isn't visible in the frame, but its location behind the teacher on left is clearly evident from the pattern of light on the walls and the highlight on the teacher's head and shoulders. Notice how the pool of light from the window lights the faces of some of the students.

10-22
Photo by Fred D. Reaves

10-23
Photo by Dan Dry

In figure 10-24, the light from the window creates nice modeling across the man's hat and face, with a highlight along the edge of the hat nearest the window. To create this effect, the light outside the window must be soft and diffuse — probably an overcast day.

In figure 10-26, you can see the effect of soft window light from another direction. This time, the light source is behind the photographer, and it's a large open doorway rather than a typical window. Notice the rich detail in the skin made possible by the modeling from the soft directional light.

10-24
© Charlotte K. Lowrie | wordsandphotos.org

10-26
Photo by Dan Dry

Figure 10-25 is another example of an informal portrait by window light. In this case, the window is outside the frame on the left. The light is soft and broad, creating gradual transitions from highlight to shadow, but the dim interior of the room creates strong contrast with a dark background and deep shadows.

Figure 10-27 shows that direct sunlight through a window creates high contrast lighting, just like direct sun outside. The extreme brightness difference between the sunlight and the interior of the room creates the opportunity for dramatic lighting effects. If you expose for the sunlight, as the photographer did in this case, anything not in the direct beam of sunlight coming through the window goes nearly black. Notice how sharp the shadows are and that even the shadows of the window frame on the surface beside the window are lighter than the rest of the room.

10-25
Photo by Dan Dry

10-27
Photo by Fred D. Reaves

10-28
Photo by Dan Dry

A constrained beam of light coming in through a window can create an interesting spotlight effect on a subject. For example, notice the strong contrast between the dark background in figure 10-28 and the subject sitting in a pool of light from a window. The small pool of light in a dark room usually occurs when direct sun beams through a window, and that often creates harsh, hard-edged shadows. In this case, the slight softness of the shadows indicates that a light overcast outside or something on the window that is diffusing the light slightly.

HOME AND OFFICE LIGHTING

There's more to working with available light indoors than just window light. Sooner or later, you must deal with the man-made artificial lighting and homes, offices, and other buildings. The quality and quantity of that light varies tremendously.

The overall light level in a typical private home is often surprisingly low after the sun goes down and window light is no longer making a significant contribution. The general illumination level is often just high enough to allow the occupants to move around the house without stumbling over things in the dark. Table lamps and other task lights create pools of brighter light for reading and other activities.

This scenario creates a real challenge for available light photography. The low light levels make it difficult to get a good exposure, even with slow shutter speeds, high ISO settings, and the camera mounted on a tripod. Furthermore, table and floor lamps tend to create hotspots within the prevailing darkness, and because they sit low and are scattered around the room, it's hard to avoid having them appear in the frame, as in figure 10-29. You're frequently forced to choose between an exposure that renders the surrounding area properly while overexposing the area around a lamp, and one that favors the brighter area around the lamp while allowing the surroundings to go dark.

Good quality available light photography in a residential setting is challenging, but it's not impossible. For the informal portrait in figure 10-30, the photographer needed to find a spot where the existing lighting was favorable and a cooperative subject who could sit still during the 1/10 second exposure.

10-29
Photo courtesy Violet Star / Dreamstime

10-30
Photo by Charlotte Lowrie

Offices, stores, and other commercial interiors generally offer better available light photography potential than residential settings. The overall light level in most offices is significantly higher than the typical home, and the light is usually more evenly distributed with fewer isolated bright spots. Most of the light usually comes from ceiling fixtures, so it's easier to avoid having the light source appear within the frame.

Offices, such as the one in figure 10-31, pose their own challenges for available light photography. Although the light levels are generally higher than what you find in homes, they still fall short of ideal levels for photography. For example, the exposure for figure 10-31 was 1/80 at *f*-2.8 with ISO 400, which is fairly typical. In this case, there is also some window light in the scene, but it isn't bright enough to overpower the interior lights. (It was probably an overcast day, which produced similar light levels in the room from the windows and the interior lights.)

10-31
Photo courtesy Arjun Kartha / stock.xchng

The color of the light is also an issue in many offices. The predominant form of lighting is usually fluorescent ceiling lights, but there is often a mixture of different kinds of fluorescent tubes installed, as well as incandescent lighting and window light. Selecting the appropriate white balance setting is sometimes pure guesswork, and you still may have some pools of off color light somewhere within the image no matter what you do.

PRO TIP

White balance can be problematic when taking available light shots in an office. Shooting in Camera Raw format (if your camera offers that option) gives you the flexibility to adjust the white balance later, when you process the Raw file, instead of having to commit to a white balance setting when you take the picture.

Inconsistencies in the color and brightness of the light sources in a scene can be a problem, but it can also create an opportunity to do something a little out of the ordinary. In figure 10-32, the photographer accentuated the spotlight effect on the hanging meat and the trays on the counter by slightly underexposing the overall scene, which reduced the overexposure of the bright areas and added contrast by making the rest of the scene a little darker.

One of the challenges to shooting people in an office environment is that almost all the light shines down from overhead, which tends to create deep shadows in the eye sockets, under the chin, and so forth. If the subject looks down, the entire face can be in shadow. In figure 10-33, the photographer partially overcame this problem by posing the subject with his head tilted back slightly, which exposed his face to more of the overhead light, but the eye sockets are still shadowed.

10-32
Photo by Dan Dry

10-33
Photo courtesy Daniel Vineyard / Dreamstime

In contrast to the big league facilities, local school gyms often have relatively poor lighting. The light levels are typically much lower than you find at larger facilities. For example, figure 10-35 was shot at the same *f*-2.8 aperture as figure 10-34, but the photographer had to wait for a natural pause in the action in order to catch the young player with the slow 1/40 second at ISO 400 that the lower light levels of the small gym required.

PRO TIP

You might be tempted to use flash to overcome the low light level found in small gyms, but I don't recommend it. A normal on-camera flash unit isn't powerful enough to effectively light a space as large as a gymnasium, but it may be bright enough to distract the players, which could be dangerous. A distracted player might fall or run into other players, benches, or photographers on the sidelines. People could get hurt!

GYM AND STADIUM LIGHTING

Lighting in gymnasiums, arenas, stadiums, and other sports venues runs the gamut from awful to reasonably good.

As a general rule, the facilities designed for professional and major college teams have the best lighting. They're usually engineered to meet the needs of broadcast television with reasonable levels of good-quality light. As a result, there's enough light to support action-stopping shutter speeds, such as the 1/500 second used to shoot the images in the composite shown in figure 10-34, and the light usually has good color too. The light is almost all from overhead, but there's enough of it to provide decent illumination, if not flattering light angles.

Another problem that you may encounter in smaller gyms is poor color quality of the light. To reduce cost, small gyms often use the same kind of mercury or sodium vapor lights typically used in factories and warehouses. These lights emit a discontinuous spectrum that makes it impossible to get good color rendering, no mater how you set your camera's color balance.

X-REF

See Chapter 2 for more information on color balance and color temperature.

10-34
Photo by Tony Guffy

CHURCHES AND OTHER LOCATIONS

Churches and school auditoriums are more examples of challenging locations for available light photography. They are rarely designed with photography in mind. Light levels are relatively low, and mixed-color light sources are common.

For example, the lighting in the church in figure 10-36 includes daylight coming in through the skylights at the peak of the roof, incandescent lamps in the hanging light fixtures, and fluorescent lights along the left wall. Sunlight filtered through a large stained glass window behind the camera adds a red glow to the ceiling beams on the left. Despite all the different light

sources, there's only enough overall light to support an exposure of 1/4 at f-3.5 with ISO 200. Because the camera was mounted on a tripod, the static parts of the image are sharp, although some of the people are slightly blurred due to the slow shutter speed.

Figure 10-37 shows another church with a different lighting challenge. The lights are all the same color, but the location of the lights embedded in and around the alter area creates numerous hot spots that are overexposed when the exposure is set at an appropriate level for the rest of the scene (1/40 at f-2.8 with ISO 200). The shutter speed was pushing the limits of a hand-held exposure with an 80mm lens, so it isn't quite as sharp overall as 10-36.

10-35

10-36

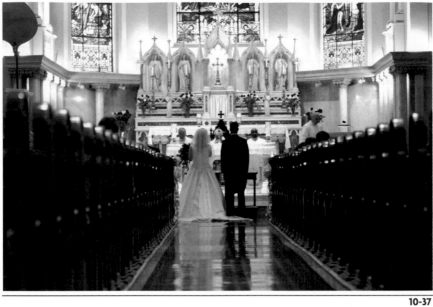

Stage lighting for a concert, play, or other stage production is yet another peculiar lighting situation that you may want to photograph. It's an unusual situation where you have a subject lit by very bright lights, but the rest of the room (and sometimes, the rest of the stage) is in near total darkness. Stage lighting is often characterized by very harsh light from odd directions, which can create hard-edged shadows in awkward locations, but there's nothing you can do about that.

Spot metering is essential for getting good exposures of a subject in a spotlight at a concert, such as the one in figure 10-38. It's the only way to be sure that your camera is basing its exposure calculations on the light reflected from the subject you want to photograph and not the black background or other parts of the stage, which may be lit very differently.

Plays and similar stage productions are usually a little easier to deal with because the entire stage is lit instead of a spotlight isolating an individual performer. The more uniform lighting means that you can probably use your camera's normal metering mode to set the exposure, provided that you can fill most of the frame with the image of the stage. Including too much of the dark auditorium could bias the exposure and cause the stage to be overexposed.

10-38
Photo courtesy Robert Kohlhuber / Dreamstime

AUGMENTING AVAILABLE LIGHT

Sometimes the pre-existing light at a location just isn't quite good enough to produce quality images. Perhaps there's enough light for a decent overall exposure, but it's all from one direction, which creates some unwanted dark shadow areas. You have a choice of shooting a high-contrast image with no shadow detail, or augmenting the available light with some sort of supplemental lighting to make up for the shortcomings of the existing light.

On such an occasion, available light photography means making more light available. When done well, someone viewing the finished image never knows you added any light.

For example, figure 10-39 appears to be an architectural interior lit by the light from the wall of windows plus a few scattered ceiling lights and table lamps. However, although most of the light for this image did come from the windows, the photographer actually added significant supplemental lighting to open up shadows and balance out the difference in light levels between the areas close to the windows and areas

farther into the room. There are photographic lights (strobes, to match the color temperature of the window light) positioned to the right of the camera and hidden at various locations throughout the scene, including behind the central column. The brightness of the supplemental lighting was carefully controlled so that it served as fill light instead of overpowering the window light. In addition, the photographer manipulated the image in Photoshop to bring back detail in the windows that was lost to overexposure in the main shot.

10-39
Photo by Dean Lavenson

SOFTENING THE SUN WITH SHADES AND DIFFUSERS

The direct light of the mid-day sun is just too harsh for many photographic subjects. The softer light of an overcast sky or open shade creates a more pleasing effect for portraits, fashion shots (such as figure 10-40), flowers, and many other subjects. However, nature doesn't always cooperate by providing shade from the direct sun or a strategically positioned cloud to filter the harsh sunlight.

It's fairly easy to change the light on a small subject. All you need is an opaque panel to create some shade or some translucent material stretched on a frame to diffuse the light. With these tools, you can convert the direct sunlight on the test subject shown in figure 10-41 to a more pleasing light.

10-41

10-40
Photo by Alicia McGinnis

> To create an open shade effect, position an opaque panel between the sun and the subject so that the subject is in its shadow. Figure 10-42 shows the effect of placing a black panel just outside the left side of the frame so that it blocks the direct sun. The test head is now lit by the open sky above and on the right side of the frame. As a result, the right side of the test head is now the highlight side instead of the sunlit left side in figure 10-41. Notice how much softer the shadows are in 10-42.

10-42

10-43

> To simulate the diffuse light of an overcast sky, position a diffuser between the sun and the subject. Figure 10-43 shows the result of placing a diffusion panel vertically, just outside the left side of the frame. Notice that the subject is now lit by a soft light coming from the left. The highlights are on the left side of the head, just as they are in 10-41, but the shadows are much softer and the light wraps around the subject now because the diffuser acts as a large light source. The right side of the test head is getting a strong fill light from the general skylight — the same light that creates the open shade effect in 10-42. That light is present in 10-41, too but it appears much darker compared to the overpowering brightness of the direct sunlight and the reduced exposure that the sunlit subject requires.

FILLING SHADOWS WITH REFLECTORS

Another way to soften and subdue shadows is to use reflectors to bounce light into the shadow areas. The reflector serves as a fill light, adding light to shadows to reduce excess contrast and improve detail in the shadow areas.

A reflector can be as simple as a piece of white cardboard or foamboard. You can also purchase specially made photographic reflectors in a variety of colors and reflective surfaces. The most common reflectors are matte white, matte metallic silver, and matte metallic gold.

> Use a white reflector to bounce direct sunlight back into the shadows of a subject. For example, figure 10-44 shows the effect of a white reflector positioned adjacent to the lens on the left so that it bounces light up under the chin and nose. This

199

is an exaggerated effect for demonstration purposes. Moving the reflector around to a more vertical orientation on the right side of the camera would produce a more subtle effect that would probably look more natural.

reflector, just compare figures 10-45 and 10-46. Figure 10-45 is an example of normal open shade lighting with the light coming from the top and right sides of the frame, and 10-46 shows the effect of adding a silver reflector positioned low and to the left of the camera to reflect light up into the shadows. Again, this is an exaggerated effect. You can easily reduce the intensity of the reflection by moving the reflector further back from the subject or positioning it at a less efficient angle.

10-44

10-45

> Use a silver reflector to open up shadows in open shade or overcast sky lighting conditions. A plain white reflector often isn't very effective under an overcast sky or open shade, but a silver reflector surface is much more efficient at bouncing the less intense light. To see the effect of a silver

10-46

10-47

> Use a gold reflector to open up shadows in open shade or overcast sky lighting conditions while adding a warm color tint to the reflections. Figure 10-47 shows the effect of positioning a gold reflector surface similar to the silver reflector in figure 10-46. Notice the warm tone in the shadows under the chin, along the left cheek, and in the left eye socket.

LIGHTING WITH ON-CAMERA FLASH

When the existing light just isn't adequate, you may need to add some light of your own, and the simplest way to do that is with an on-camera flash unit.

Most digital cameras include a built-in flash, and it often pops up and fires automatically when the camera senses that the ambient light level is too dim to enable you to shoot at a reasonable hand-held shutter speed. Typically, the camera's built-in flash is fully integrated with the exposure system so that the flash output and exposure are all handled automatically. The result is the typical snapshot lighting as in figure 10-48. The lighting is a little harsh, but you get a good, sharp image, even in near darkness.

10-48

Having a built-in flash unit that pops up when needed is certainly convenient, but the design constraints imposed by the need to incorporate the flash into the camera body can limit the usefulness of the built-in flash. The main problem is its limited range. The typical built-in flash just doesn't have enough light output available to effectively illuminate a subject that is more than about 10-12 feet from the camera. That's enough range to cover the usual snapshot subjects, but it falls short from the power you need to reach out and cover larger groups from greater distances. The built-in flash is also limited to firing straight ahead, which doesn't allow you to bounce the flash off the ceiling to create a more natural light as is the case in figure 10-49.

10-49

Making Light Available on Location

Some professional camera models don't include a built-in pop-up flash. Instead, they are designed to deliver a similar level of exposure automation when used in conjunction with an external flash unit attached to the camera's hot shoe connector. An external flash unit is usually significantly more powerful than the typical built-in flash, which gives it much more range, and since the external flash is powered by a separate battery pack, using it doesn't drain the camera's battery. Many external flash units allow you to angle the flash head up or to the side for bounce effects.

To get the full benefit of all the automatic features, you must use a *dedicated* flash unit designed specifically for your camera brand and model. The flash unit normally must come from the same manufacturer as the camera. In addition to exposure automation, some of the high-end flash units offer advanced features such as dual flash heads for simultaneous direct and bounce flash. The result is noticeably better lighting than you can get from a smaller built-in flash unit, as you can see in figure 10-50.

The same flash units that are designed for use with the professional camera models will also work on some of the more advanced consumer digital SLRs — provided you're willing to pay the rather hefty price. Most cameras will also work with a range of dedicated and non-dedicated external flash units from a variety of third-party manufacturers, albeit without some of the advanced features and exposure automation that are available from the brand-name units.

PRO TIP

Some third-party external flash units offer plenty of power at a very attractive price, but they don't integrate with the camera's automatic exposure system, which can make them cumbersome to use. Typically, you must set the camera for manual exposure, and then select matching aperture settings on the camera and flash. A light sensor on the flash controls the exposure by adjusting the flash output. The system works reasonably well most of the time, but it's neither as convenient nor as accurate as a dedicated flash linked to the camera's auto exposure system.

PRO TIP

Be careful about using a shoe-mount flash unit that isn't designed specifically for your camera model. The trigger voltages on the contacts between the flash and the camera body aren't the same on all cameras, and using mismatched units can fry sensitive electronics. There's usually no problem with the simple manual or non-dedicated flash units that have only one contact point on the bottom of the hot shoe. It's the dedicated flash units that attempt to integrate the flash with the camera's exposure system that can cause problems. Don't swap flash units between different brand cameras or use third-party flash units that aren't guaranteed compatible with your camera.

10-50
Photo by Alicia McGinnis

DIRECT FLASH

The most common way to use an on-camera flash to light a scene is to point the flash head directly toward the subject — it's called *direct flash*. That's the basic default setup for external flash units, and if you're using the camera's built-in flash, you have no other option.

The flash head is a very small, bright, point-source light, which creates a hard light with strong highlights and dark, hard-edged shadows. The hard light is what gives flash snapshots such as figures 10-48 and 10-51 their typical crispness. It's an effective way to get light on the subject, even if it isn't the most flattering kind of light.

The hard light of direct flash casts a dark, hard-edged shadow behind the subject. Depending on the position of the subject and the surfaces behind it, the shadow might be more or less of a distracting element of the picture. For example, in figure 10-51, the grooms-man's shadow is mostly hidden — you can see only thin shadow outline on either side of his upper legs. On the other hand, in figure 10-52, more of the shadow is visible along the left side of the subject.

10-52
Photo by Ramon Rodriguez

10-51

Shadows tend to be more pronounced when the camera is rotated for a vertical shot. The reason is that the flash is normally centered above the lens when the camera is in its normal horizontal orientation. This causes the shadow to be centered directly behind the subject, thus hiding most of it from view. Rotating the camera for a vertical composition moves the flash to the side of the lens instead of above it, which offsets the shadow to the opposite side of the subject where more of the shadow is visible. To avoid this problem, consider using a flash bracket that allows the camera to rotate from horizontal to vertical while keeping the flash centered above the lens.

The shadow that the flash casts from your subject is only visible if it is cast upon a surface that appears in the picture. For example, notice the groom's shadow on the wall behind the couple in figure 10-53. It's clearly visible because the wall is just a few feet away and directly in line from the flash to the subject.

10-53

You can sometimes avoid having the shadow appear in the finished picture by selecting camera angles and subject positions that hide the shadow. One of the simplest ways to do that is to avoid having a wall behind your subject. For example, in figure 10-54, the shadows of the groom and the cake both disappear through the doorway behind the cake and are broken up by the various objects instead of creating silhouettes on a flat wall.

10-54

Another characteristic of direct flash is its propensity for creating a spotlight effect when you photograph a subject outdoors or in a large open space such as a party room. You can thank the inverse square law for this effect, which is clearly evident in figure 10-55. The camera and flash work together to properly expose the couple on the dance floor, but the light from the flash falls off sharply as distance increases, so the people, tables, and other objects in the distance are dark from underexposure.

Photo by Ramon Rodriguez

BOUNCE FLASH

You can transform the hard, point-source light from an on-camera flash unit into a much softer light by bouncing the light off of a ceiling or wall instead of pointing it directly at the subject. The indirect light bounced off a large surface creates a much softer light that is more flattering for most subjects. For example, compare figure 10-56, which was shot with bounce flash, to the direct flash shot in figure 10-48. Notice the softer highlights and smoother modeling in 10-56.

PRO TIP

Bounce flash also scatters light around the room to increase the general illumination level and reduce the isolating effect of a brightly lit subject against a dark background.

In order to use the bounce flash technique, you need an external flash unit with a tilt head that allows you to aim the flash head toward the ceiling. The technique won't work with the camera's built-in flash unit or an external flash that is locked into a straight-ahead direct-flash position. With the proper equipment, the bounce flash technique is simple to do. Just keep the following points in mind:

> You need to be in a room with a low, white ceiling. Eight-foot high ceilings work best. Bouncing the flash off a very high ceiling isn't practical due to excessive light falloff reducing the brightness level. A colored ceiling will absorb too much light and/or create a color cast in your photograph.

> Simply point the flash head up toward the ceiling as demonstrated in figure 10-57 and then frame and focus your shot normally. Ideally, you direct the flash at a point on the ceiling roughly half way between the camera and the subject, but the position isn't critical. Most anywhere above and in

front of the subject will do. Just don't aim the flash at a point that is behind the subject.

10-57
Photo courtesy Piotr Przesol / Dreamstime

> If you're using a dedicated flash that integrates with your camera's automatic exposure system, there's usually no need for any exposure compensation or other adjustments. The automatic exposure system should work normally to ensure proper exposure. If you're using a manual or semi-automatic flash, be sure to select the widest available aperture setting to maximize the working range of the flash.

> Remember that the maximum working range of the flash is reduced because of the inherent inefficiencies of bouncing light off the ceiling. Check your exposures frequently and switch back to the direct flash technique if the subject gets too far away from the camera for good bounce flash exposures.

PRO TIP

If a low white ceiling isn't available, you can try softening your flash with one of the many bounce accessories on the market. The bounce accessory is usually an angled reflector card that attaches to your flash. You point the flash up so that the light bounces off the reflector and then to the subject. None of the products I've tried work as well as a ceiling bounce, but most of them create a slightly softer light than direct flash.

USING FLASH FILL

In addition to using your flash as a replacement light source when the available light is totally inadequate, you can also use it as a supplemental light to augment the existing light. For example, in figure 10-58, the photographer posed the model in a scene with heavy backlighting, and then used an on-camera flash to add enough light from the front to bring out full detail in the model's face and clothes.

10-58
Photo by Alicia McGinnis

Dealing with the Dreaded Red-Eye Effect

We've all seen flash photographs in which a bright red glow appears in the subjects' eyes. It's rarely (if ever) a desirable effect, but it happens all too often. In order to avoid the red-eye effect, you need to understand what causes it.

Red-eye occurs when the direct light from the flash bounces off the retina at back of the subject's eye and back into the camera lens. That can happen only when the subject is looking straight at the camera, the pupil is open wide due to low ambient light levels, and the flash is positioned very close to the lens axis, as is the case with any flash that is built-into the camera body.

To help alleviate the problem, many built-in flash units (and some external accessory flash) have a red-eye reduction mode that blinks the flash before opening the shutter and triggering the main flash to take the picture. The series of pre-flashes is supposed to cause the subject's pupils to contract, thus reducing the red-eye effect.

The trouble is that this kind of red-eye reduction often doesn't work very well. The pre-flashes aren't bright enough to be effective unless the camera is very close to the subject, and they may increase the likelihood that your subject will blink and their eyes will be closed in the final shot. Furthermore, the red-eye reduction pre-flashes cause a significant delay between pressing the shutter release button and the actual exposure. The delay makes it difficult to catch good expressions in posed shots, and it's likely to cause you to completely miss un-posed shots of children and pets.

A more reliable way to eliminate red-eye is to move the flash away from the lens. If light from the flash strikes the subject's eye at an angle, it can't bounce straight back into the camera lens, so there's no red-eye effect. Of course, moving the flash isn't an option if it's built into the camera body. On the other hand, the red-eye problem is a powerful argument for switching off the camera's built-in flash and using an external flash unit instead.

Making Light Available on Location

For a typical snapshot subject, it takes only a few inches of separation between the flash and the lens to create enough angle to eliminate red-eye. That's why most shoe-mount accessory flash units are designed to raise the flash tube and reflector above the top of the camera by three to five inches. It makes the flash unit more bulky, but it gets rid of a lot of red-eye problems.

As you move farther back from your subject, you need more physical separation between the flash and the lens to maintain enough angle to avoid red-eye. Consequently, many press and wedding photographers use flash brackets that position the flash head about eight to twelve inches above the lens, which is usually enough to shoot small groups without worrying about red-eye problems. For larger groups, which you must photograph from greater distances, there are adjustable-height flash brackets available that can raise the flash a foot or more above the lens.

The flash has to be pointed directly at the subject to cause red-eye, so bouncing the flash off of the ceiling or wall is another sure-fire way to avoid red-eye. The problems with this approach to red-eye management are that it doesn't work outdoors or with the camera's built-in flash, and indoors you need a powerful flash unit to compensate for the light loss from bouncing.

If, despite your best efforts, you end up with a picture of a subject with red-eye, all is not lost. Most image editor programs include features that enable you to quickly retouch red-eyes by selectively replacing the red with black. Most of these programs are easy to use and fairly effective, but none of them are perfect. It's far better to avoid the red-eye problem in the first place.

The technique is called *flash fill* because the sun or other available light source acts as the main light source and the flash functions as a fill light — opening up the shadows cast by the main light, reducing contrast, and lowering excessively high light ratios, just like the fill light in a studio lighting scheme. In the studio, the fill light is often positioned close to the camera, so it makes sense that an on-camera flash unit can play that role out in the field.

The key to the success of the flash fill technique is being able to control the light ratio between the existing light and the flash. That can be a tricky thing to accomplish with a manual flash, but it's easy to do if your camera has a flash exposure compensation feature. Just follow these steps:

1. Set the exposure for the existing light component of the picture using whatever meter reading and auto exposure modes are appropriate for the lighting conditions. You can use aperture- or shutter-priority auto exposure, or any other exposure mode *except* a preprogrammed scene that includes flash settings that would conflict with the settings in step 2. (Refer to your camera's manual to learn what scenes and program modes might have such conflicts.)

2. Set the flash component of the exposure for one to two stops underexposure. Simply find the button, dial, or menu that controls flash exposure compensation on your camera and adjust the setting to somewhere between -1 EV and -2 EV. The job of the flash is to partially fill in the shadows, without brightening those shadows up to match the highlights. This exposure compensation controls just how dark or light the shadows become.

3. Frame and shoot the picture and then check your results. If you don't like the light ratio between the highlights and shadows, adjust the flash exposure compensation setting in step 2 and try again.

The color temperature of an on-camera flash is approximately the same as normal sunlight, so the flash fill technique mixes well with daylight. It's especially useful for lightening the harsh shadows created by direct sunlight. In figure 10-59, the photographer deliberately overexposed the lower part of the dress to create a glowing effect. The bride's upper body is lit by a combination of open shade coming through the archway and flash fill from the camera. Without the flash fill, the bride's side closest to the building would be much too dark.

10-59
Photo by Ramon Rodriguez

You can also use flash fill indoors. It's the perfect counterpoint to strong window light. In figure 10-60, the main light is a large bright window at the left side of the frame. Flash fill from the camera controlled the light

10-60
Photo by Ramon Rodriguez

ratios to keep the shadows from being too dark. In this case, the flash fill was also bounced to soften the effect and subdue the shadows on the wall behind the couple.

USING PORTABLE STUDIO LIGHTS

When the existing light at a location is inadequate and an on-camera flash doesn't provide enough additional light, you need to bring out the big lights — portable versions of the lights you'd use in the studio. Sometimes there's no other way to get the shot except to convert a remote location into a temporary photographic studio, complete with whatever lighting equipment you need to get the job done.

Sometimes there's just not enough existing light to get a decent exposure, and sometimes there's something wrong with the existing light that makes it unsuitable for photography, such as bad color, awkward placement, and so on. When you encounter

such a situation, it's usually best to just turn out all the existing lights and start from scratch lighting the scene with your own lights.

That's exactly what photographer Dean Lavenson did in figure 10-61. He started with a dark room and added lights as necessary to achieve the desired effect, just as he normally does in the studio. He built up an intricate lighting scheme using separate lights for the wall, the sign, the cabinet, and every other major object. He did incorporate a few lights from the original scene as accents, including the examination light and the computer screens.

The interesting highlights that play across the chair cushions and several other surfaces are the result of a technique Dean calls *painting with light*. He works with an assistant to take multiple exposures as he moves around the scene highlighting details with a fiber optic light wand. Then he selects the details he likes from the various exposures and composites them into the base image using Photoshop. It's a laborious process that produces some stunning results.

A typical location photo shoot doesn't usually require such an elaborate lighting setup — a simple shot with two or three lights is more the norm. The point I'm trying to make with this admittedly extreme example is that once you make the decision to convert a location into a temporary photography studio, anything goes.

PRO TIP

Don't skimp on the quality of your extension cords. The wire gauge must be more than enough to handle the load without getting hot, and plugs and insulation must be built to withstand heavy use. Standard household extension cords just don't cut it! Heavy duty outdoor extension cords are a better choice, and extra-heavy commercial-grade cables are better still.

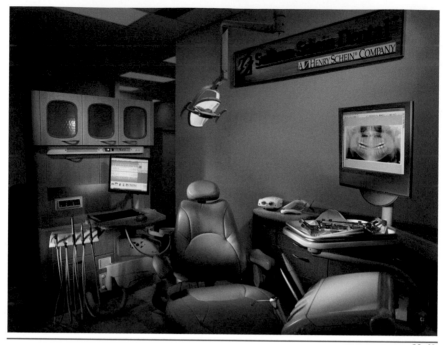

10-61
Photo by Dean Lavenson

Be Cautious of Overloading Electrical Circuits

Photographic lighting equipment can require a lot of electrical power, especially if you're using quartz and tungsten hot lights. When using the lights in a temporary studio setting, there's a real risk of your lights overloading the electrical circuits at your location. That's something you want to avoid if possible. At the very least, it's an inconvenience to have to locate and reset a tripped circuit breaker, and interrupting power to room lighting, office equipment, and other devices on the same circuit could be more than a minor inconvenience.

Q&A

What are the differences of available light, ambient light, existing light, and natural light?

All these terms refer to the light that the photographer finds lighting subjects at locations outside the studio, and generally speaking, they are used interchangeably. However, the terms do have slightly different connotations that some photographic purists use to draw distinctions between different kinds of light.

> **Natural light:** The most restrictive of the terms. It implies that the light is of natural origin (from the sun) and not man-made or altered.

> **Existing light:** Implies the pre-existing light that the photographer finds at the scene. It includes natural light from the sun and also man-made light from electric lights in homes and offices, but excludes any supplemental light supplied by the photographer.

> **Ambient light:** Light from the surroundings. In most cases, the term is functionally equivalent to existing light, but some photographers use it in mixed lighting situations to designate the background light level and differentiate it from whatever supplemental lighting the photographer adds.

> **Available light:** A broader term that includes all the natural and man-made light available at the scene, and also whatever supplemental light the photographer has readily available. The general connotation of supplemental light includes reflectors and diffusers, and sometimes even a flash fill. However, the old joke is that available light can include "all the light you can make available," and that you sometimes need a whole truck load of lighting equipment to get a good available light shot.

When using photographic lighting equipment, how can I avoid overloading the electrical circuits?

You need to be aware of the demands your lighting equipment will place on the electrical circuits and take steps to ensure that you don't overload any one circuit with your lights. For example, an individual flash unit may draw only a few amps, but a 1000 watt quartz light demands nearly two-thirds of the entire capacity of a typical 15-amp household electrical circuit. You typically need several lights to adequately light your subject, and the total electrical load can be significant, so you need to spread that load out over several circuits.

The secret to avoiding overloaded electrical circuits is lots of long extension cords. Instead of trying to plug all your lights into the nearest electrical outlet, use the extension cords to distribute the load to multiple outlets. Since several outlets may be on the same circuit, it's best to avoid using adjacent outlets along a common wall. Using outlets from opposite sides of a building or a large room increases the odds that the outlets are actually on separate circuits.

Chapter 11

MAKING PICTURES OF PEOPLE

Few types of photography are more gratifying than creating a portrait that not only captures the subject's personality, but that also becomes a portrait the subject will treasure for years. But portraiture is challenging because, unlike inanimate objects, people tend to sit still for only so long before they become bored and ultimately irritated. Many people are often nervous about having their picture made, and, unless you, the photographer, can calm and reassure them, the subject's nervousness inevitably shows up in the portrait. It's essential that you get all the artistic and technical aspects of the photograph right, but you don't have the luxury of taking as much time as you want to fiddle with composition, focus, lighting, and exposure. When you're shooting a portrait such as the one in figure 11-1, you must shoot fast, while you have the cooperation of the subject.

This chapter covers some of the basic exposure considerations and lighting patterns for portraits and other pictures of people. It's enough to get you off to a good start with photographing people. When you're ready to explore the topic in more depth, you can refer to some of the many books that are available on exposure and lighting for portraits, and still more books on poses and other aspects of portraiture, wedding photography, and related specialties. Although the lighting and exposure may seem complex at first, if you capture the person with a great, natural expression that reveals their personality and vitality, you've already mastered the most important aspect of portraiture.

Photo by Ramon Rodriguez

THE GOALS OF PORTRAITURE

There are several goals in portraiture, all of which are important in making a successful portrait.

> **Capture the subject's essence:** Whether you are making a portrait of a man, woman, or child, the primary goal is to reveal the person's personality. This goal has nothing to do with lighting or

exposure; instead, it has everything to do with your ability to interact with the subject and to put them at ease. Developing a rapport by chatting with the subject before the portrait session often makes the difference between a "camera smile" and a smile where the subject is genuinely engaged with the conversation. As you chat with the subject, study the person's face looking for characteristics and features that you want to play up and downplay in the images, whether it's an exuberant grin or the intent gaze of the child's eyes in figure 11-2.

> **Create three-dimensional lighting:** Another goal of lighting in portraits is to create a three-dimensional appearance in a two-dimensional medium. With portraits, the goal is to wrap the light around the subject, revealing texture and shadows that define and emphasize the subject's strongest features and characteristics. And, of course, the eyes must look alive and sparkling. Most portrait lighting is characterized by the following:

> **Soft light:** Soft light minimizes lines and wrinkles, and it's generally a more flattering light. Hard light tends to be too harsh for portraits except in the rare instances where the goal is a very dramatic special effect.

> **Directional light:** You need enough visible highlight and shadow to define the form of the subject's face. For a natural effect, that usually requires a light angled slightly down and across the face. You don't get enough

shadow definition if the lighting is too low in contrast and/or a frontal light coming from the camera position.

> **Close light:** Having the light source positioned close to the subject creates a noticeable falloff

11-2
Photo by Dan Dry

11-3
Photo by Alicia McGinnis

in light intensity across the face, which enhances the modeling effect of the directional light.

> **Catch light:** You need at least one light source positioned so that the subject's eye catches a reflection of the light and bounces it back to the camera, as shown in figure 11-3. This catchlight creates a lively sparkle in the eye, and without it, the eyes look dull and lifeless. Normally, the main light and/or fill create the catchlight, but if they don't, you may need to add a light for this purpose.

> **Determine the exposure:** The proof of any image, especially the case with portraits, is in the print. Getting a good print starts by getting a good exposure in the camera. Regardless of how adept you are at using image-editing programs, if you don't get the exposure right in the camera, your images won't have optimal detail throughout highlights and shadows, good tonal range throughout the image, and a high-quality final file that isn't degraded through over editing. The other advantage is that getting it right in the camera takes far less time than fixing it in Photoshop.

X-REF

Refer to Chapter 4 for more information on metering modes and techniques.

By and large, the onboard reflective light meters featured in most digital SLR cameras are accurate and dependable. However, if the background of a portrait is very dark (as in figure 11-4) or very light, the meter reading may be unduly influenced by the background. One way to avoid having the background influence the meter reading is by using an incident meter that reads the amount of light falling on the subject rather than the amount of light that is reflected by the subject. Another approach is to use your camera's spot metering mode to read the subject's flesh tone and base your exposure on that. Don't forget to adjust the indicated exposure for the difference between the subject's skin tone and the average reflectance for which the meter is calibrated.

Another exposure consideration is how you want to render the background and the subject in relation to the background. If the light in the scene is too bright to use a wide aperture to blur the background, you may want to use a diffuser, scrim, or even a neutral-density filter to get the wide aperture you need for a shallow depth of field.

PRO TIP

Normally, bracketing your shots by shooting alternate exposures a stop or so over and under the metered exposure helps ensure that you get an optimum exposure. However, the technique doesn't always work when shooting pictures of people, because the optimum exposure and the optimum expression seldom occur in the same frame. Bracketing may be necessary in difficult lighting conditions. However, a better exposure strategy for a portrait session where you control the lighting is to start with a quick test shot, then analyze the histogram, and retest. When you get the exposure right, shoot everything at that setting (unless and until you change the lighting). That way, the only variable is the subject's expression.

11-4
Photo by Dan Dry

NATURAL-LIGHT PORTRAITS

Environmental portraits, such as figures 11-5 and 11-6, are a popular alternative to traditional studio portraits for high school seniors, engaged couples, family groups, and others. There are obvious advantages to photographing the subject in a location where they feel natural and at ease, instead of the alien environment of a photographic studio. And the selection of location and background for the photo can create a context for the portrait and make a statement about the subject.

Environmental portraits can be in most any environment, indoors or out, but the natural light of an outdoor location has a special appeal for the subject and the photographer alike. Natural light can be beautiful,

but it can also be harsh, unflattering, and difficult to work with. The trick is to find an attractive location with light that is flattering to the subject. The following list describes some natural-light situations and how to deal with them:

> **Direct sun:** Although the brilliant light of the direct mid-day sun is often highly desirable for scenic photography, it's the most challenging and least flattering light for portraits. Most photographers avoid shooting portraits in mid-day sun because the light produces strong, sharp-edge shadows, overly bright highlights, and the light is generally too harsh to make pleasing portraits.

Mid-day sunlight can, however, be modified to achieve acceptable portraits. One approach is to

11-5
Photo by Ramon Rodriguez

11-6
Photo by Ramon Rodriguez

place the subject's back to the sun, and then illuminate the subject with fill flash (as shown in figure 11-7) or by bouncing sunlight from a reflector and toward the subject. With two reflectors, you can use a silver reflector as the primary light source, and then use a white reflector as a secondary source to fill shadow areas. Alternately, you can block the harsh overhead sunlight by moving the subject under an awning, onto a porch, or into the shade of some trees or a building. You can also use a large sheet of diffusion material, placed between the sun and the subject, to reduce the intensity of sunlight and soften it enough to create a more flattering light.

> **Sunset and sunrise:** The time just before and during sunset is when the warmest and most intense color of natural light occurs creating vibrant golden color and soft contrasts that define and enhance textures and shapes. It's a great time for fashion shots such as figure 11-8. Likewise in the early dawn, the gold and red hues emerge. For fashion and commercial photographers, the prized golden hour begins just as the sun emerges over the horizon, and again in the last hour before sunset. This light is especially good for fashion work because the light is direct and at a low angle without being excessively harsh. Light during these times may require diffusion and reflectors to fill shadow areas.

11-7
Photo by Alicia McGinnis

11-8
Photo by Alicia McGinnis

> **Open shade:** When the subject is positioned under a tree, awning, or overhang, as is the case in figure 11-9, the harsh overhead light is blocked, and the subject is illuminated by a diffuse light from the open sky that is directional enough to provide modeling on the subject's face. The light in such a shaded area is soft, and has medium to low contrast, which is usually a naturally flattering light that requires little or no supplemental fill from reflectors.

> **Overcast sky:** The classic example of diffuse light is the light of an overcast day. A layer of clouds covers the sky and diffuses the sunlight, which creates gradual shadows with soft edges and low subject contrast. This type of even lighting can make flattering portraits, as shown in figure 11-10.

↳ How to warm up a photo in Photoshop.

11-9
Photo by Alicia McGinnis

However, because an overcast sky is overhead lighting, it sometimes produces unattractive shadows in the eye sockets and under the nose and chin, and doesn't usually create good catchlights in the subject's eyes. Although the light is generally even, there is also typically some directionality to it that you can use to your advantage. You can use flash fill or a silver reflector to fill in shadows or to add catchlights to the subject's eyes. As figure 11-11 demonstrates, flash fill is also a good way to add some much needed pop to the dull, flat light of a heavy overcast.

X-REF

See Chapter 10 for some more examples of open shade and window lighting.

> **Window light:** Not all natural light is outdoors. The natural daylight coming in through a window can be among the most beautiful light you can find. This directional light can range from relatively hard to soft depending on the size of the window and the outside light conditions. Obviously, beams of direct sunlight streaming through a window create a hard light, but a large window that opens onto a clear north sky creates a nearly ideal soft light with enough directionality to provide excellent modeling. A reflector is useful for redirecting some of the light into the shadow side of the subject's face when the subject is positioned at an angle to the window.

11-10
© Charlotte K. Lowrie | wordsandphotos.org

11-11
Photo by Dan Dry

For example, figures 11-12 and 11-13 were both lit with just window light and a reflector. In figure 11-12, the window is just outside the frame on the right. The subject is posed against an off-white wall, so some bounce light is coming from that wall and the adjacent walls outside the frame. A large silver reflector beside the camera provides a stronger fill light and catchlights in the eyes. In figure 11-13, the subject is posed against the glass of a large window. Most of the window is open and serves as the main light, but a black card on the other side of the glass behind the subject turns that portion of the window into a mirror to create an interesting reflection. Again, a silver reflector to the left of the camera provides a fill light and creates catchlights in the eyes.

11-12
Photo by Ramon Rodriguez

PRO TIP

North-facing windows provide even, indirect light for portraits. By contrast, south-facing windows catch more of the direct sun rays. Windows on the shady side of a building can provide light that is comparable to a north window. Also, large windows produce a softer light with more "wrap around" quality than small windows.

11-13
Photo by Ramon Rodriguez

Rendering Backgrounds

For an environmental portrait, the background is part of the story because it puts the subject in the context of their work or leisure-time environment. But the background should always complement the subject without stealing the spotlight. You can control how the background is rendered by varying camera-to-subject distance as well as the aperture to render the background as sharp or blurred as you want. You can also affect the background rendering with your choice of lens; a telephoto lens will provide less background sharpness than a wide-angle lens provides.

For studio portraits, the choice of backgrounds ranges from seamless papers and hand-painted muslins, to specially built sets. Traditional papers and muslins are held in place with affordable background stands. Walls or sets are typically mounted on rollers so that they can be easily moved and interchanged. Improvisation also provides creative opportunities to create unusual backgrounds from found materials and locations around the studio, such as an interesting brick wall or fireplace.

ARTIFICIAL-LIGHT PORTRAITS

In the studio, the photographer has complete control over the lighting. It doesn't matter whether the lights are studio strobes or accessory flash units, hot tungsten lights or cool fluorescents; the important thing is the control you have over positioning and modifying the light to suit your vision and goals. You can use that control to create images, such as figure 11-14.

Although you can shoot a successful portrait with one light and some reflectors, most portrait lighting schemes usually employ four lights that each serve a specific purpose, contributing to the overall effect. Here's an overview of the four lights in the typical portrait lighting scheme and what they do:

> **Main light:** The main light defines the form by casting shadows from the subject's nose and other facial features. It's usually the brightest light, and as such, it establishes the overall exposure by lighting the all-important dominant highlights on the face. In most cases, the main light needs to be a soft light, such as an umbrella or softbox. Figure 11-15 shows my test head lit by the main light alone. In this case, the light is positioned about 45-degrees to the left of the subject's nose and about 45-degrees above the subject's eyes. As you experiment with the main light placement, study the shadows that are created on the facial plane, particularly under and to the side of the subject's nose. These shadows create the modeling on the face to give the face dimension.

11-14
Photo by Alicia McGinnis

11-15

> **Fill light:** The fill light opens up the shadows cast by the main light and reduces overall contrast ratio. The fill light is typically a large, soft light that is positioned on the opposite side of the camera from the main light. It's usually a stop or so less bright than the main light. Figure 11-16 shows my test head lit by the fill light alone. In this case, the light is positioned just above and to the right of the camera. The fill light doesn't necessarily have to be a separate light — a well-placed reflector can often do the same job.

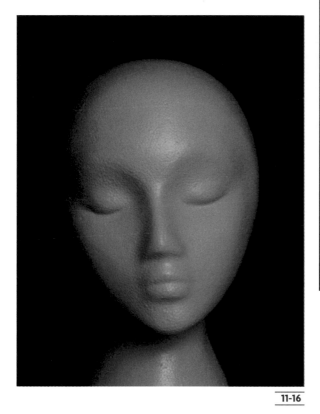

11-16

> **Hair light:** The purpose of the hair light is to add a highlight to the hair and create a rim of light along the back of the head and shoulders to help separate the subject from the background. The hair light is usually a small spotlight or a regular flash head or light with a snoot or grid attachment to help confine its light to the desired area and control unwanted spill. To do its job, the hair light needs to be aimed down onto the back of the subject's head from a position well above and behind the subject. Mounting the hair light on a boom facilitates proper positioning. Figure 11-17 shows the test head lit with the hair light alone.

11-17

> **Background light:** As the name implies, the background light lights the background. Sometimes enough spill from the main and fill lights provides an adequate light level on the background. If so, you don't need a separate background light. However, there's a distinct advantage to lighting the background separately. It allows you to control the brightness of the background independently of the lighting on the subject, and you can create interesting light falloff patterns across the background. The background light may be one or two lights depending on the effect desired. They

are usually positioned behind the subject and pointed toward the background, so they don't spill any light onto the foreground subject. Figure 11-18 shows the test setup with only the background light on. In this case, the background light is behind and below the subject, pointed up at the muslin background material.

> **Putting it all together:** All four lights, working together, create the effect shown in Figure 11-19.

11-18

11-19

PRO TIP

When choosing a lens, the goal should be to avoid distortion to the subject's face. This can usually be accomplished with a short telephoto lens, for example, an 80-105mm lens (35mm format equivalent) at a distance of 4 to 6 feet from the subject render the face in a pleasing and realistic manner. A wide angle lens exaggerates perspective, making features closest to the lens look larger and further features look smaller. Conversely, a longer telephoto lens tends to flatten perspective.

Over the years, photographers have developed and refined several standard lighting schemes for portraiture. These traditional lighting schemes have proven useful to emphasize the subject's strongest features or to minimize features such as a long, narrow face. Here are some of the most commonly used lighting setups and ideas on when to use them.

BROAD LIGHTING

Broad lighting is when the main light illuminates the side of the subject's face that is closest to the camera in a three-quarter view as shown in figure 11-20. This lighting pattern works well for subjects with thin or narrow faces because it makes the face appear wider. To create a broad lighting effect, follow these steps:

11-20

1. Start with the subject's head position angled away from the camera slightly in a two-thirds or three-quarters view.

2. Place the main light above and to one side of the subject. The exact position can vary significantly — you can combine broad lighting with one of the other lighting schemes, such as Rembrandt, loop, or split lighting (described later in this chapter). The important thing is that the main light be on the same side of the subject's nose as the camera.

3. Place the fill light as needed to fill in the shadows from the main light. Because the position of the main light varies, so does the position of the fill light. However, the most common position for the fill light is probably straight in front of the subject's nose.

NOTE

For this lighting demonstration series, I deliberately chose a hard main light and fairly high lighting ratios in order to accentuate the distinctive nose shadows of each lighting scheme.

SHORT LIGHTING

Short lighting is the exact opposite of broad lighting — the main light illuminates the side of the subject's face that is farthest away from the camera, as shown in figure 11-21. This lighting pattern works well for thinning full faces. To create a short lighting effect, follow these steps:

1. Start with the subject's head position angled away from the camera slightly in a two-thirds or three-quarters view.

11-21

light. However, the most common position for the fill light is next to the camera on the opposite side from the main light.

SPLIT LIGHTING

Split lighting lights only one side of the face, leaving the opposite side in shadow. This lighting scheme, shown in figure 11-22, is often combined with high lighting ratios to produce a very dramatic effect. However, it can also be a very subtle effect if you keep the light ratios low with a generous amount of fill light. Like short lighting, split lighting tends to elongate the face, so it works well for subjects with full faces. However, the strong cross lighting exaggerates laugh lines and other wrinkles, so it tends to be more useful for young subjects who haven't yet developed

2. Place the main light above and to one side of the subject. As with broad lighting, the exact position can vary significantly in order to combine short lighting with one of the other lighting schemes, such as Rembrandt, loop, or split lighting (described later). The main light must be positioned on the opposite side of the subject's nose from the camera. Because the subject's face is angled away from the camera, this puts the main light well off to one side — sometimes more than 90 degrees from the camera position.

3. Place the fill light as needed to fill in the shadows from the main light. Because the position of the main light varies, so does the position of the fill

11-22

deep wrinkles or for men who consider their wrinkles to be character lines. To create the split lighting effect, follow these steps:

1. Start with the subject's head in any position from looking straight into the lens to angled away from the camera in a two-thirds or three-quarters view.

2. Place the main light almost level with the subject's eyes and about 60 degrees off to one side of the subject. Move the light further off to the side (more toward 90 degrees from the subject's nose axis) until the highlight on the subject's opposite cheek just disappears. The highlight/shadow demarcation line should run straight down the nose and split the chin and forehead fairly evenly.

3. Place the fill light about 90 degrees from the main light. Doing this usually puts the fill light close to the camera, just to the opposite side of the camera from the main light. For a dramatic effect, use a very weak fill light or reflector. For a more subtle effect, use a stronger fill to create a 2:1 or 3:1 ratio with the main light.

REMBRANDT LIGHTING

Rembrandt lighting, shown in figure 11-23, takes its name from the famous Dutch painter, Rembrandt van Rijn. It's characterized by the distinctive inverted triangle-shaped highlight on the cheek on the shadowed side of the face, which is reminiscent of the lighting seen in many Rembrandt portrait paintings. It's also called 45 degree lighting because of the position of the main light. Rembrandt lighting is often combined with short lighting to flatter oval or round faces by making the face appear narrower. To create Rembrandt lighting, follow these steps:

1. The subject's head can be in most any position from looking straight into the lens to angled

11-23

away from the camera in a two-thirds or three-quarters view.

2. Place the main light approximately 45 degrees above the subject's eye level and 45 degrees to one side of the nose axis. Adjust the angle and height of the light as needed to create the distinctive inverted triangle highlight on the opposite cheek bordered by the eye socket, nose shadow, and the outer edge of the cheek itself. The nose shadow needs to extend far enough off to the side to merge with the cheek shadow in order to create the bottom point to the triangular cheek highlight. The shadow from the bridge of the nose should connect with the eye socket, but it should not obscure the eye.

3. Place the fill light just off the nose axis on the opposite side from the main light. This usually puts the fill light close to the camera, just to the opposite side of the camera from the main light, but if the subject's head is angled strongly away from the camera, the fill light may be on the same side of the camera as the main light.

LOOP LIGHTING

This lighting setup creates a "loop" shadow under the nose, as shown in figure 11-24. This lighting style brings out the brilliance of the subject's eyes. To create loop lighting, follow these steps:

11-24

1. The subject's head can be in most any position from looking straight into the lens to angled away from the camera in a two-thirds or three-quarters view.

2. Start with the main light approximately 45 degrees above the subject's eye level and 45 degrees to one side of the nose axis as in Rembrandt lighting. Bring the light in toward the nose axis until the nose shadow forms a loop-shape just below and to one side of the nose. The nose shadow should not extend out far enough to connect with the cheek shadow or down far enough to reach the edge of the lip, nor should it disappear into the side of the nose. That leaves you considerable leeway to adapt this basic lighting scheme to work with a variety of different facial structures.

3. Place the fill light at about eye level on the opposite side of the nose axis from the main light, separated about 60 to 90 degrees from the main light.

BUTTERFLY LIGHTING

Butterfly lighting, shown in figure 11-25, gets its name from the butterfly-shaped shadow under the subject's nose. It's also known as Paramount lighting because it was used extensively by Paramount Studios in the heyday of their starlet promotions in the 1930s. This classic glamour lighting setup enhances high cheekbones and a beautiful face. The main light is placed in a high position but not so high that it creates deep shadows under the nose and eye sockets. To create butterfly lighting, follow these steps:

1. The subject's head position needs to be angled to one side of the camera and not looking down. If the subject looks straight into the lens, you'll have trouble positioning the lights and camera along the same axis. A downward tilt of the head can make it very difficult to position the main light so that the nose shadow doesn't extend over the lips.

11-25

2. Start with the main light approximately 45 degrees above the subject's eye level and straight ahead of the subject's nose. To help maintain the proper head and light positions, ask the subject to point her nose at the light stand for the main light. Adjust the height of the main light so that the eye sockets are well lit and the nose shadow creates the butterfly wing shape, without extending down to the edge of the lip.

3. Place the fill light at about eye level, just below and beside the main light. The original plan for this lighting scheme called for the main and fill lights to be stacked with the main directly above the fill, and both of them on the subject's nose axis. However, I've found that it works just as well for the fill light to be positioned between the main light and the camera, and it's a little easier to position the lights that way.

OTHER PORTRAIT LIGHTING SCHEMES

The traditional portrait lighting schemes can be invaluable as a reference and starting point for your own experimentation and exploration, but you shouldn't feel constrained by them. You don't have to stick with the traditional lighting schemes or the traditional studio settings — you can use your imagination and try a wide range of different effects. Don't be afraid to move the lights or the subject. The "right" light is achieved when the angle of the person's face and the angle of the light create a three-dimensional shape of the subject.

For example, consider figure 11-26, for which the photographer transported his studio lights to a court room to create a virtual studio for this portrait of a lawyer. The main lighting on the face is very close to the standard loop lighting scheme. Instead of the usual hair light across the top of the head and shoulders, this portrait features a light along the left side of the subject that ties into what appears to be window light on the door and flag in the background.

Figure 11-27 is another example of an imaginative use of lighting for an executive portrait. In this case, the subject is outdoors, but posed in such deep shade that the shadowed surroundings, such as the horse sculptures on the right are just silhouettes against the sunlit background. The subject would be a silhouette too if it weren't for a strong light coming in from the left — probably a powerful studio strobe. The strong cross light is just a little shy of being split lighting.

Figure 11-28 is another example of how the fundamental principles of lighting and exposure can serve you well whether you're shooting individual portraits or for editorial or stock assignments. This image was taken for stock to show merging of cultures. The exposure was ISO 100, f/19, 1/250 sec. using a Hasselblad H1 camera with a Kodak Pro 645 Digital back and an 80mm lens.

11-26
Photo by Dean Lavenson

11-27
Photo by Dan Dry

11-28
© Charlotte K. Lowrie | wordsandphotos.org

11-29
Photo by Alicia McGinnis

TIPS FOR OTHER PEOPLE PICTURES

Not all pictures of people are individual portraits, but many of the same fundamentals of lighting and exposure apply. Here is a compendium of tips for some of the other people pictures besides portraiture:

> **Fashion photography:** Fashion has a lot in common with portraiture — especially the environmental portraiture that's so popular today. Many of the settings and lighting techniques are the same. The big difference is that the emphasis of photos such as figures 11-29 and 11-30 is on the image the model is projecting with the clothes, hair, makeup, pose, setting, and attitude instead of the real person inside those clothes. The purpose of the picture is to sell a product, not create a cherished memory for the subject or their family.

11-30
Photo by Alicia McGinnis

11-31
Photo by Ramon Rodriguez

> **Group portraits:** Small groups, such as the family in figure 11-31, are really portraits with multiple subjects. The lighting is same as for an individual portrait, but you can't be as fussy about the exact positions of each person's head in relation to the lights — you can't get the perfect nose shadow for all members of the group simultaneously. One trick that helps is to use softer light overall for more leeway in positioning.

Larger groups, such as the wedding party in figure 11-32, are more of a challenge. It's best to shoot large groups outdoors if possible, because the sun and sky create a large, uniform light that is difficult to replicate indoors. If you're forced to shoot inside, move your lights as far back as possible to minimize the light falloff that causes those members of the group that are closer to the light to be in brighter light than those who are farther away. Use at least two lights, one as a main and the other a fill. A single light is sure to cause bad shadows on someone.

11-32

When positioning couples or groups, look for the interplay of their combined forms. With groups, begin by placing one person, and then arrange others around that person for a pleasing composition of shapes and sizes. To ensure sufficient depth of field, shoot at a narrow aperture so that all faces are equally sharp. If the light is low and requires a wide aperture, position the subjects on the same plane perpendicular to the lens axis.

> **Weddings and special occasions:** Weddings and other special occasions are especially challenging to photograph. They include everything from romantic portraits, to large groups, to candid shots. Time limitations generally preclude elaborate lighting setups, so everything must be done quickly and smoothly. And it's a once-in-a-lifetime event, so every shot has to count — there will be no opportunity for reshoots.

If the weather cooperates, shoot outside as much as possible to take advantage of the natural light for shots such as figure 11-33. Natural light is faster, easier, and more dependable than any photographic lights you can carry to the location.

When you must move inside, use an accessory flash unit that is capable of bounce lighting in order to avoid the harshness of direct flash wherever possible. Consider using a bounce diffuser accessory to further soften the light from the on-camera flash. Figure 11-34 was shot with bounce flash with an additional diffuser accessory on the flash.

11-33
Photo by Ramon Rodriguez

11-34
Photo by Ramon Rodriguez

Q&A

The lighting, exposure, and composition for my portraits look good, but there still seems to be something missing. What's wrong?

Lighting, exposure, and composition are all important factors in making good photographs, and getting those factors right is your primary concern when taking a picture of an inanimate object. But a portrait is a photograph of a living, breathing human being, and the emotional content of the picture, as evidenced by the subject's facial expression and body language, is at least as important as the technical considerations.

Portrait photographers sometimes use the acronym *ESP* as a reminder that *Expression Sells Pictures*. It's apropos because it often seems like you need some of the other kind of ESP (extra-sensory perception) to get portrait subjects to relax and give you the kind of expression you're both looking for. You need to make a connection with your portrait subject on a personal level in order to bring out that expression.

Some photographers have a natural talent for quickly developing a rapport with a subject, others just don't. If you don't instinctively "connect" to people, try assuming the role of a director coaching an actor. Ask your subject to imagine a situation, such as a pleasant experience or meeting a dear friend, and then capture the resulting expression that appears on the subject's face.

If I'm mixing ambient light with fill flash, how do I determine the exposure for the flash?

Start by determining the proper exposure for the ambient light. If you're in a situation that calls for flash fill, there's probably a stark contrast between the highlights and some dark shadows, so you'll probably need to use your camera's spot metering mode to read the highlights and apply exposure compensation to adjust for any differences in reflectivity between the highlight and the middle gray for which the meter is calibrated. Next, decide how much difference you want between those highlights and the shadows that will be filled in by the flash. Set the exposure compensation for the flash to achieve the desired difference. Generally, 1 to 2 stops of negative flash-exposure compensation is usually a good starting point.

What should be the point of sharpest focus in a portrait?

The eyes, and in particular, the eye closest to the camera should be the sharpest point in the image. In a group portrait, there will usually be a central person around whom others are arranged, and the central person's eyes should be in sharpest focus.

How can I minimize wrinkles in an older subject?

Two factors tend to accentuate wrinkles: hard light and light that rakes across the wrinkled surface at an angle. Therefore, to minimize facial wrinkles, you need to use softer lights and/or reduce the angle at which the light strikes the face by moving your main light to a more frontal light placement. To create a clean jaw and neckline, ask the subject to stand with one foot on a stool, and then to turn and face the camera while leaning slightly toward you. This action helps stretch the neck to minimize the appearance of loose skin and jowls in mature subjects.

Chapter 12

GETTING INTO THE ACTION

12-1
Photo by Dan Dry

Photographing action presents the photographer with challenges unlike those found in any other photographic specialty. Whether the subject is a major sports event, such as the Kentucky Derby (see figure 12-1), or the more subdued action of a family outing staged for an advertising illustration (see figure 12-2), the photographer is confronted with the need to distill the essence of a dynamic situation into a single image.

Meeting that artistic challenge requires the ability to anticipate the action, the vision to recognize the defining image, the timing to capture just the right moment, and the technical skill to record it. And a healthy dose of good luck, too.

I can't pass along an Irish good luck charm on these pages, but perhaps the discussions of exposure considerations for shooting action can help you successfully capture the moment when your own intuition or good fortune put you in the right place at the right time for that great action image.

12-2
Photo by Dean Lavenson

SHOOTING THINGS THAT MOVE

Shooting stationary photographic subjects is easier than shooting things that move. When the subject is static, it doesn't create many exposure constraints. For static subjects, you can use any combination of shutter speed, aperture, and ISO that delivers the correct amount of light to the image sensor in your camera. You can use a low ISO setting for minimal noise, and then select your aperture depending on the depth of field you need. The shutter speed can vary significantly without affecting the shot.

For static subjects, you can use a small aperture and a slow shutter speed, or a larger aperture and faster shutter speed. If the subject isn't moving during the exposure, then the shutter speed doesn't make any difference as long as the camera is relatively stable.

The only constraint on shutter speed selection is that it needs to be fast enough to control the camera shake of a hand-held shot — and you can easily eliminate that concern by using a tripod.

Moving subjects, on the other hand, present the photographer with a completely different set of issues. Any movement of the subject while the shutter is open creates a blur in the finished image, so selecting a shutter speed that controls that blur is a critical factor in the exposure. All of a sudden, shutter speed becomes the top priority as you seek the ideal balance between shutter speed, aperture, and ISO. So naturally, this is the time to use your camera's shutter-priority exposure mode, which allows you to set the shutter speed while the auto-exposure system determines the aperture.

12-3
Photo by Dan Dry

When you're shooting action, the movement of the subject isn't the only movement you need to consider. In many cases, you must also contend with significant amounts of extra camera movement as you pan, tilt, zoom, and generally move around to follow the action in the viewfinder. Then, when the decisive moment (such as the falling jockey in figure 12-3) arrives, you punch the shutter release in a frenzied attempt to grab the shot. All this jostling around exaggerates the relative motion between the camera and the subject and requires even higher shutter speeds if your goal is to generate a sharp image.

For most action shots, the photographer's vantage point is some distance from where the action takes place. (Believe me, you don't want to be in the middle of the track as the thundering hooves of a dozen horses gallop toward you. It's scary enough to be on the other side of the rail.) That means that telephoto lenses (in this case, 450mm) are necessary to get frame-filling shots such as figure 12-4. Telephoto lenses magnify camera shake as they magnify the image, which is yet another reason why most action shots require high shutter speeds to control all the camera and subject movement.

12-4
Photo by Dan Dry

EXPOSURE CONSIDERATIONS

Because of their location, most action shots must be done with available light. After all, you can't usually invade a sports field such as the one shown in figure 12-5 with a bunch of photographic lights. You must rely on the existing light, whether it's daylight or the artificial lights of a stadium, arena, or other venue.

Furthermore, the subject is usually too far away for an on-camera flash to be effective. (The typical built-in flash has a maximum range of about 15 feet, and you're rarely that close to any action taking place outside of the home.) Even if you're close enough to use a flash, it's often not advisable to do so because a flash that is close enough and bright enough to produce a good exposure would be distracting (and potentially dangerous) for the participants in most sports. You can sometimes get away with using flash if you're shooting casual activities of kids and pets, but even then, you should be mindful of the disruption the blinding light of the flash can cause.

We've already established that most action photos require high shutter speeds to control both subject and camera motions. Shooting at high shutter speeds is no problem if you have lots of light. According to the sunny-16 rule, the base exposure for a sunlit subject with the default ISO of 100 is f-16 at 1/100. Bumping the shutter speed up to 1/500 puts the aperture at f-7, which is near the middle of the aperture range of a typical lens. At 1/1000, the aperture is still f-5, and at 1/2000, the aperture is f-3.5. The 1/2000 at f-2.8 exposure that the photographer used for figure 12-6 shows that real-world exposures in daylight conditions may vary slightly, but usually stay remarkably close to the sunny-16 rule.

All these aperture/shutter speed combinations are very usable — but that's in full sun on a sunny day.

12-5
Photo by Tony Guffy

12-6
Photo by Dan Dry

You won't have as much light to work with on a cloudy day, at an indoor arena, under stadium lights (see figure 12-7), or in many other situations. To maintain the fast shutter speeds you need to control subject and camera movement, you may need to open up two to four stops or more, which is beyond the aperture range of most lenses (especially telephoto zooms that tend to top out at around f-4). Fast lenses with larger maximum apertures are available, but they're expensive. So, the only other solution is to boost the ISO setting as much as necessary to allow you to shoot at a reasonable aperture/shutter speed combination.

12-7
Photo by Tony Guffy

Of course, cranking up the sensitivity of your camera's image sensor by increasing the ISO setting also increases the amount of digital noise in your finished images. Digital noise is a problem in product shots, where crisp detail and smooth tones are critically important, but action photos are all about capturing that dynamic moment, and a little noise is a small price to pay for the ability to get the shot in the conditions that exist. Still, you need to be aware of the tradeoffs involved in increasing the ISO setting and push it only as far as necessary.

So, to summarize the exposure considerations for action photography, here's a hypothetical mental checklist for balancing the exposure elements:

1. Set your camera for shutter-priority automatic exposure or manual exposure mode, so you can directly control the shutter speed selection. If you must use a preprogrammed shooting mode or scene, choose the sports/action mode, but I don't recommend that option because you don't have as much direct control.

2. Select the lens focal length you want to use (either the focal length of a prime lens or the focal length setting of a zoom lens), and calculate the slowest safe shutter speed for hand-held shots. To do so, first convert the lens focal length to its 35mm equivalent by applying the conversion factor for your camera. For example, if you're using a 120mm lens (or zoom setting) and the conversion factor is 1.5, then the 35mm equivalent is 180mm. The slowest hand-holding speed is the inverse of the effective focal length, which is 1/180 in this example. You can skip this step if you use a tripod or other camera support to eliminate camera shake as a constraint on shutter speed.

3. Evaluate the subject motion and select a shutter speed fast enough to freeze that motion (assuming that freezing the motion is your goal, which is normally the case). The shutter speed you select depends on the speed and direction of the subject motion. For fast-paced sports action, you probably want to use 1/500 or faster. For kids playing, a shutter speed between 1/125 and 1/250 may be fast enough.

4. Compare the results of steps 2 and 3, and set the shutter speed to the faster of the two.

5. Set the camera's metering mode as appropriate for the subject and take a light level reading to determine whether the light is bright enough to support an exposure at an aperture that is within the range that's available on your lens. For most sports and action subjects, matrix or multi-area metering works best, but you may want to use average or spot metering in some circumstances.

Most cameras take a meter reading and display the exposure settings, complete with over/under exposure warnings, in the viewfinder when you half-press the shutter release button.

6. If step 5 indicates that the shot would be under exposed, even if you use the maximum aperture available on your lens, then increase the ISO setting as needed to achieve a good exposure. If this requires such a high ISO setting that digital noise becomes objectionable, you need to return to steps 2 and 3 and reevaluate the shot. You may need to use a shorter focal length lens that you can hand-hold at a slower speed, and accept that you won't be able to stop all the motion, so you need to look for pauses and peaks in the action that you can shoot at a slower speed without excessive blur.

This list may seem long when you read it here, but with a little practice and experience, you can use this checklist to determine an exposure in a matter of a few seconds.

SHOOTING SPORTS

Great sports shots take planning — things happen much too fast to react to them after the fact. By the time you see something happening and reach for the camera, the moment is gone. To get great shots like figures 12-8 and 12-9, you have to be in the right place at the right time, watching the action unfold in the viewfinder.

You need to know the sport well enough to anticipate where the action will take place, and position yourself to capture that action. Figure 12-10 shows sports photographers lined up along the sidelines of a major sporting event. In some cases, the competition for prime spots can be fierce. For example, on the first Saturday in May, there are dozens of photographers and video crews vying for a spot on the first turn at Churchill Downs, in position to take the classic Kentucky Derby shot shown in figure 12-11 with the horses rounding the turn and the famous twin spires of the clubhouse in the background.

12-8
Photo by Dan Dry

12-9
Photo courtesy of Ron Hilton/Dreamstime

12-10
Image provided by Dreamstime

12-11
Photo by Tony Guffy

Just as you need to anticipate where the action will occur and position yourself accordingly, you also need to anticipate your exposure in advance and pre-set your camera with the ISO, aperture, and shutter speed you expect to use. You don't have time to be fumbling with exposure settings when you're busy trying to follow fast-moving action. One of the great advantages of digital photography over film is the ability to see results immediately, which allows you to test your exposure settings and make adjustments just moments before an important shot.

PRO TIP

When fast reactions are essential to catching just the right action, consider setting your camera for manual operation. Even the fastest auto-exposure and auto-focus systems take time to perform their calculations, which contributes to the slight delay between pressing the shutter release button and the image being recorded on the camera's sensor. Presetting exposure and focus in manual mode minimizes shutter lag and allows your camera to respond a split second faster; thus improving your chances of getting just the right shot.

STOPPING THE ACTION

For most action shots, you want to freeze all subject motion to keep the subject sharp. For that, you need a fast shutter speed. The only question is, how fast is fast enough.

As a general rule, 1/500 second is fast enough to stop most human actions, although you may need an even faster shutter speed to freeze details such as the head of a golf club in mid swing. You can use slower shutter speeds with slower-moving subjects, but it's unusual to be able to get much below 1/125. Also remember that the direction of movement makes a difference. Big actions moving across the frame require a faster shutter speed than smaller actions that occur along the lens axis.

The 1/2000 shutter speed that the photographer used for figure 12-12 was fast enough to freeze not only the major motion of the horse, but also it's mane and saddle number flapping in the breeze.

In contrast, a much slower shutter speed was sufficient to stop most of the action of the bowler in figure 12-13. The bowler is moving much slower to begin with, the motion is more aligned with the lens axis, and the photographer used a normal focal length instead of a telephoto. All these factors combined to enable the slow 1/45 shutter speed to control all the motion except a little blur of the bowler's right arm. It's amazing just how slow you can go in just the right conditions.

Another way to capture a sharp image of an active subject is to shoot the natural pause that often occurs at the peak of a motion. Peak actions, such as a basketball player at the apex of a jump shot, or the golfer in figure 12-14, are often dramatic poses that give the illusion of movement, even though the subject is actually relatively still for a fraction of a second. Because you're actually capturing a momentary pause in the subject movement, you can often do so with a slower shutter speed than would be required to freeze the full action.

ACCENTUATING THE ACTION

Freezing all subject motion isn't the only way to shoot action photos. Sometimes, allowing the moving subject to blur the image creates more of a feeling of motion than a perfectly sharp image.

One way to accomplish this is to keep the camera steady and shoot at a shutter speed that is slow enough to allow some, or all, the subject motion to blur. Figure 12-13 shows this kind of deliberate blur in the bowler's right arm. Notice that the lack of camera movement produces a relatively sharp background in contrast to the moving subject.

Figure 12-15 shows another form of deliberate blur, called *panning*. In this technique, you move the camera to track your subject's motion during an exposure with a slow shutter speed. The camera motion blurs the background, but since the camera is moving *with* the subject, that subject is less blurred than the background.

The technique works best with action going across the frame, not coming toward or away from the camera, and the strength of the effect depends on how much motion occurs while the shutter is open. For example, figure 12-15 was shot at 1/8 second, using a telephoto lens, which exaggerated the panning motion. Figure 12-16, on the other hand, was shot at 1/30 using a wide angle lens, thus producing a more subtle effect.

12-15

© Charlotte K. Lowrie | wordsandphotos.org

12-16

Photo by Dan Dry

X-REF

Panning is a great technique, but it takes practice (and some luck) to pull it off successfully. I describe the technique in more detail in Chapter 6.

SHOOTING KIDS, PETS, AND PEOPLE IN MOTION

Photographing kids and pets may not seem like a sport, but like sports photography, it's a situation that requires you to capture images of a moving subject. It doesn't really matter whether the movement is part of an organized sport or the general activities of the people around us, you still need to use shutter speeds that are fast enough to freeze action, and the critical importance of the shutter speed selection means that you'll probably be working in shutter-priority mode.

PRO TIP

Giving shutter speed priority in exposure selection doesn't always mean using your camera's shutter-priority mode. If you use your camera's aperture-priority mode and select the largest aperture available for your lens, the auto-exposure system will automatically select the fastest shutter speed available for the current light level.

Any time you're trying to capture motion, it's easier to do so outdoors in daylight, where you have plenty of light to support the fast shutter speeds you need to use to freeze subject motion. In figure 12-17, the photographer chose 1/1000 to catch a close-up of a flying bicyclist in mid air.

As you move into shaded areas or indoors, the lower light levels naturally restrict your shutter speed selection, but you can get some nice shots at moderate shutter speeds if the action isn't too raucous. For example, 1/125 was fast enough to catch the youngsters playing in the shade in figure 12-18.

Indoor light levels are often so low that you're forced to use slow shutter speeds, even after increasing the ISO setting to its maximum. Slow shutter speeds can't stop any significant subject motion, but as Figure 12-19 demonstrates, you can still get good photographs by capturing your subject during natural pauses and peaks in the action. In this case, a 1/15 second exposure caught this young pool player lining up a shot. At that shutter speed, you must be concerned about camera movement as well as subject movement, so a tripod or other camera support is necessary.

12-17
© Charlotte K. Lowrie | wordsandphotos.org

12-18
Photo courtesy Rayna Canedy/Dreamstime

12-19
© Charlotte K. Lowrie | wordsandphotos.org

Fortunately, kids and pets aren't always in motion. They have their quieter moments in which they present almost stationary targets. If you can catch your subject at one of these brief interludes, you can forget about subject motion and use any shutter speed that you need for the correct exposure. In figure 12-20, the dog remained motionless during a full one-second exposure. Although this example is extreme, it shows that it is possible to shoot normally active subjects with very slow shutter speeds.

Actions of children and pets are far less predictable than a more structured activity on a sports field, so getting into position to capture them is much more difficult.

12-20
© Charlotte K. Lowrie | wordsandphotos.org

Fortunately, there's at least one offsetting advantage that can make things a little easier, and that's the ability to get close enough to the action to use flash. The camera's built-in flash typically has a very limited range, but range isn't an issue when the action takes place barely more than an arm's reach away (see figure 12-21), and it's usually sufficient to light a subject anywhere within the same residential room with the photographer.

12-22
Image provided by Dreamstime

12-21
Photo courtesy Scott Rothstein/Dreamstime

One problem with the camera's built-in flash is that the direct flash creates a very harsh light with hot highlights and hard, dark shadows. Using a more powerful flash unit with a tilting head gives you the option of bouncing the flash off the ceiling, which produces a much more pleasing and natural lighting effect as shown in figure 12-22.

PRO TIP

Sometimes, simply pointing a camera at children causes them to change their behavior — they stop the activity that you want to photograph and begin posing for the camera. To minimize the chances of that happening, turn away from the children and pretend to focus your camera on something else that's the same distance away and in same light. Use this decoy target to preset the exposure and focus, and lock in the settings. Lower the camera and watch for the right moment. When the moment comes, you can quickly raise the camera and shoot before the children have time to change what they are doing.

Is shooting sequences a good way to capture sports action?

Most digital SLRs, and many other digital cameras, have the ability to shoot short multiframe sequences at the rate of several frames per second. Many photographers seem to think that firing off a burst of shots is the best way to capture any action. But that's not necessarily so.

For a lot of sports action, shooting a multiframe sequence isn't the best way to capture the exact instant of peak action. A single well-timed shot is often better than a multiframe sequence, just as a well-aimed rifle shot has a better chance of scoring a direct hit on the bulls-eye than a shotgun blast. On the other hand, the shotgun is more appropriate than a rifle for very fast-moving game and when it's more important to get several close hits than it is to score a precise bull's-eye. Similarly, shooting sequences can be an effective way to get off more shots in quick succession than you could do manually, and it does give you more chances at getting a usable image of some very fast-moving subjects.

If you do decide to use sequences to capture sports action, it's important to remember a couple of common limitations on the feature. First, the multiframe bursts are usually limited to a few frames, so you must resist the temptation to begin a sequence too early or else you may run through all the frames before reaching the peak action you want to capture. Second, after shooting a sequence, swriting those images to the memory card may take several seconds, and you may miss other shots while you wait for the camera to catch up.

How high can I push the ISO setting before digital noise becomes objectionable?

All camera sensors exhibit increased digital noise as the sensor's sensitivity increases with changes in the ISO setting. However, the sensors in different cameras exhibit varying amounts and kinds of noise. Some cameras deliver excellent results at the default ISO setting but show marked increase in noise with modest increases in the ISO setting. Other cameras show a more gradual increase in noise at higher ISO settings. The only way to know for sure how your camera reacts is to test it, and then you can judge for yourself how much digital noise is too much for the kinds of images you plan to create.

Chapter 13

PHOTOGRAPHING NATURE

Since the early days of photography, photographers have been drawn to the abundant subject matter available in nature. It remains as true today as it was when Ansel Adams was conducting classes in Yosemite Valley. Like the film photographers before them, digital photographers are often inspired to create images that record and interpret the natural beauty they find around them, whether it's a scenic landscape in a spectacular location such as in figure 13-1, a colorful sunset at a favorite vacation spot, or a flower in a backyard garden.

Photographing nature means shooting with available light. Obviously, it's impossible for a photographer to light a sweeping landscape, and it's seldom practical to light other nature subjects. Fortunately, it's also unnecessary because nature subjects are located outdoors where the ultimate light source, the sun, provides plenty of illumination — at least during daylight hours. As a result, nature photographers seldom need to supply any lighting. At most, you might use a small reflector or portable flash as a supplemental fill for some smaller close-up subjects.

Okay, I realize that I'm generalizing about nature photography being available light only. Granted, there are situations in which photographers carry lighting equipment out into the field, usually to photograph nocturnal animals. Also, photographers sometimes bring small specimens back to the studio and photograph them under controlled conditions. But both of these circumstances are relatively rare.

However, just because you can't create the lighting for a nature photograph from scratch the way you can light a product or portrait in the studio, doesn't mean that the quality, direction, and color of the light is any less critical to your photograph. Photography is still all about recording the light reflected from your subject. The difference is that, in nature photography, the strategy is to observe and select the light instead of attempting to actively manipulate the light.

13-1
Photo courtesy of PDphoto.org

Selecting the Light and Exposure for a Landscape

Scenic landscapes like figure 13-2 can make breathtakingly beautiful photographs when the light is right. The same scene can be dull and uninteresting in different light.

You can't reach out and move the sun and clouds to change the angle and character of the light, so landscape lighting is all about selecting the season and time of day when the sun is in the best position to light the scene naturally. You may get lucky and arrive upon a scene just as that special lighting situation occurs. Sometimes, you can see the light beginning to take shape and only need to wait a while for it to develop.

Other times, you may find a scene that you want to photograph, but the light is just not right, and you have no choice but to return at another time or day when the light is better. For example, if you're looking to the west, at an east-facing side of a mountain, the morning sun will light the trees on that mountainside in their full color, but by mid-afternoon, the eastern side of the mountain is in shadow, bathed in a softer light that's shifted toward the blue. Later in the evening, the same mountainside will be silhouetted against the setting sun.

Generally, you want to shoot the sunlit side of a hill or mountain as shown in figure 13-3. You want the sun to be behind the camera, shining onto the scene you want to photograph. You can also get some nice effects with the sun shining across the scene from one side, but you rarely want to shoot into the sun unless you are trying to capture a sunrise or sunset. Of course, there are always exceptions to these general rules depending on the effect you're going for.

13-2
© Charlotte K. Lowrie | wordsandphotos.org

13-3
Photo courtesy PDphoto.org

Early morning and late afternoon sun produce more dramatic effects with longer shadows and warmer light as seen in figures 13-4 and 13-5. Mid-day sun minimizes shadows for more uniform lighting. In open terrain, mid-day light tends to be a little less interesting, but it may be the only time of day when the sun reaches down into a deep valley or gorge as in figure 13-6, or into a clearing or stream in a deep forest.

PRO TIP

A good topographic map and GPS receiver can be handy tools to help analyze the lay of the land and plan a return trip to a promising landscape when the light might be better. The GPS receiver makes it easy to pinpoint your exact position and angle of view, and a detailed map of the terrain lets you identify the features you want to photograph and then make some good guesses as to what portions will be in sunlight or shade at different times of the day. If you don't have a GPS, a small pocket compass is enough to get yourself oriented to the basic sun positions, even on an overcast day.

13-4
Photo by Tony Guffy

13-5
Photo by Dan Dry

SETTING THE EXPOSURE FOR LANDSCAPES

A classic scenic landscape often comes very close to being the theoretical "average" photographic subject for which light meters and automatic exposure systems were designed. As a result, you can usually get good results from your camera's automatic exposure system in most of the light metering modes. As you select the most appropriate metering mode, keep the following points in mind:

> If your scene includes lots of high contrast areas, use average metering mode to keep any of the contrast extremes from biasing the exposure too much. For most scenic photos, average or multi-segment metering mode should work equally well.

> If your scene includes a large area of clear sky like figure 13-7 and you want to concentrate on the terrain, point the camera down slightly to reduce the amount of sky in the frame while you meter the scene and lock the exposure. Then reframe the shot and take the picture.

13-6
Photo courtesy PDphoto.org

13-7
Photo courtesy PDphoto.org

> If you're going for a dramatic effect, such as the last rays of the setting sun on a mountain top as shown in figure 13-8, use your camera's spot metering mode to isolate the key interest area and expose for that.

> Scenery doesn't usually move, so you can use aperture-priority exposure mode and select the aperture based on the depth of field you need. Many digital cameras also include a Scenery program mode as well, but I prefer and recommend aperture-priority for the additional control it gives the photographer.

> If you frame a distant scene with some much closer rocks or trees as in figure 13-9, you may need to use a very small aperture for adequate depth of field. That, in turn, means using a slow shutter speed to get the equivalent exposure. Set your lens to its hyperfocal distance to maximize depth of field, and use a tripod to keep everything sharp despite the slow shutter speed.

X-REF

For more information on depth of field and hyperfocal distance see Chapter 7.

PHOTOGRAPHING MOVING WATER

Waterfalls are popular photographic subjects, as are rivers, streams, and waves at the seashore. Moving water presents a particular challenge for nature photographers.

Normally, you want to keep the central subject of a photo sharp. Shooting moving water such as in figure 13-10 means using a fast enough shutter speed to stop the motion of the water so that glimmering highlights are crisply frozen in position in the final image. This approach produces an accurate rendition of the scene, but it can be a little static. Allowing the glittering highlights on the water to create a motion blur in the image, as in figure 13-11, often evokes the feeling of a softly flowing stream better than the sharp image.

13-8
Photo courtesy PDphoto.org

13-9
Photo courtesy PDphoto.org

13-10
Photo by Alicia McGinnis

13-11
Photo by Alicia McGinnis

You can easily achieve this effect by simply using a slower shutter speed. How slow depends on the speed of the water. Here's the general procedure for shooting the moving water effect:

1. Start by mounting your camera on a sturdy tripod to eliminate camera movement so that everything but the water stays sharp. Frame and focus your shot.

2. Select shutter-priority (or manual) exposure mode so you can directly control the shutter speed selection.

3. Set the initial shutter speed selection according to the speed of the water and shoot a test shot.

   > For a waterfall or fast-moving stream, start with a shutter speed of about 1/8 second.

   > For a slow-moving stream or lazy waves lapping at the shore, you will need a slower shutter speed, so start at about 1/2 second.

4. Evaluate your results and then adjust the shutter speed and reshoot as needed to get the desired effect. To get more detail in the water, use a faster shutter speed. To increase the motion blur effect, use a slower shutter speed. As you adjust the shutter speed to find the best setting, do it in full stop increments. Smaller changes in shutter speed don't usually produce a significantly different effect.

CAPTURING WILDLIFE

Wildlife, such as in figure 13-12, are particularly challenging to photograph. They are, by definition, wild animals that are unpredictable and usually wary of humans. Sometimes you can observe and photograph insects and some small animals up close, but it's very difficult (and potentially dangerous) to get close to most wildlife outside of a zoo.

13-12
Photo courtesy PDphoto.org

So, photographing most wildlife is a matter of stalking a quarry that is elusive, uncooperative, and located a long distance from the photographer's vantage point. Doing that successfully takes knowledge of the animal's habits, plus skill, patience, and a long telephoto lens.

You're on your own when it comes to developing the knowledge and patience parts. The best I can do is offer general tips on getting good exposures with telephoto lenses:

> Long telephoto lenses such as the one used for figure 13-13 magnify camera shake, so fast shutter speeds are required if you expect to get sharp images with a hand-held camera. As a rule of thumb, use a shutter speed that is faster than the reciprocal of the lens focal length. So, with a 400mm telephoto lens, you need to use 1/400 shutter speed or faster.

> A lens with an image stabilization feature can help reduce, but not eliminate, the camera shake problem. Image stabilization typically enables you to get sharp results from hand-held shots at shutter speeds that are about a stop slower than you can with a regular lens. (Unfortunately, image stabilized lenses are quite expensive.)

> In low light situations (most anything less than full mid-day sun), boost the sensitivity rating (ISO setting) so you can use a faster shutter speed at the same light level.

> If you use automatic exposure, use shutter priority mode so that you can select a shutter speed that adequately controls camera shake with the tele-photo lens. Alternatively, you can use aperture priority mode and set the aperture to the maximum available on the lens, thus ensuring that you will be shooting at the fastest possible shutter speed. You'll usually want to avoid the camera's pro-grammed exposure modes because they don't give you enough control over shutter speed selection.

> Watch out for backlighting and other situations that might fool your camera's meter and auto-exposure system, such as the sky being reflected off the water in figure 13-14. As you pan to follow a moving animal, lighting can change very quickly. Be ready to switch to spot metering mode and/or override the auto-exposure with exposure com-pensation or manual exposure settings.

> Use a tripod or other camera support to stabilize the camera and minimize camera shake. Using a monopod or sandbag can enable you to shoot at shutter speeds that are a stop or so slower than you can hold freehand. A good solid tripod can add even more to the range of shutter speeds that will produce sharp results.

> Put your camera in silent mode. If your camera gives you the option to disable its beeps, clicks, and other confirmation sounds, be sure to turn them off. Animals usually have very keen hearing and are easily startled by unusual sounds, and you don't really need to hear your digital camera imitating the sound of a film camera's film advance motor as you fire off each frame.

Domestic animals, such as the dog in figure 13-15, are much less wary of humans, which makes getting close enough for a good shot somewhat easier. As a result, you can sometimes photograph them up close with normal lenses, although a short telephoto or zoom helps maintain a reasonable working distance, which allows you to photograph the animal without interfering with its activity. (Besides, you may be more comfortable with a fence between you and a skittish thoroughbred horse or a prize bull.)

PRO TIP

Photographing animals using your camera's built-in flash can produce a red-eye effect, just as does in humans. The eyes are often glow green instead of red, but the basic effect is the same. The camera's red-eye reduction feature is totally useless with animals because the pre-flash that's supposed to reduce pupil size interrupts what they were doing and scares them away. It's best to avoid using flash when photographing animals. If you must use flash, use an external flash unit instead of the camera's built-in flash, and bounce the light from the flash off the ceiling to further reduce the chances of getting the glowing eye effect in your photograph. If all else fails, fix it in Photoshop.

SHOOTING BEACH AND SNOW SCENES

Beach scenes, such as figure 13-16, and snow scenes can make great photographs when they are properly exposed. But getting a good exposure with most cameras is a challenge because such scenes tend to fool light meters.

13-15
Photo courtesy of PDphoto.org

13-16

The camera's built-in meter and exposure system is set up to calculate the correct exposure for an average scene, adjusting the exposure as needed to adapt to differing light levels. The problem is that a scene that contains large expanses of highly reflective water, white sand, or whiter snow reflects far more light than the average scene.

There's no way for the camera to tell the difference between a highly reflective scene (such as a beach or snowscape) and a normal scene in brighter light. The camera detects more light entering the lens and reacts as though the light is brighter, instead of light colored objects in the scene reflecting more than the normal amount of light. The result is an underexposed image, such as figure 13-17, with sand or snow that is gray instead of white. It can sometimes be an interesting effect, but it's not an accurate rendering of the scene.

The only way to address the problem of getting a good exposure of a scene that contains a lot of unusually light tones and reflective surfaces is to use some sort of manual exposure compensation. You can use the camera's exposure compensation (EV bias) feature to tell the auto-exposure system to give the image more exposure, or you can meter off of a gray card instead of the bright scene and lock in that exposure. Of course, you can also switch to manual exposure mode and set the aperture and shutter speed yourself. Measuring the light falling on the subject with an incident light meter is probably the best way to determine the proper exposure for a scene with unusual reflectance, but if you don't have an incident meter handy, you can use the following guidelines to adjust your exposures:

> Exposure compensation for a typical beach scene (see figure 13-16) is about plus one stop.

> Exposure compensation for a typical snow scene (see figure 13-18) is about plus two stops.

13-17
Photo courtesy Pavel Gribkov/Dreamstime

13-18
Photo courtesy Peter Weber/Dreamstime

13-19
Photo by Dan Dry

> Test your exposure and read the histogram. Because the subject is composed of mostly light tones, the hump in the histogram should be to the right of center, but the peak shouldn't be jammed against the right side of the histogram. If your camera display shows highlight clipping, you can expect to see scattered clipped highlights, but there shouldn't be large areas that are blown out.

Remember that the best shots aren't always the most accurate rendition of the original scene. Try adjusting the exposure for effect. You can deliberately underexpose the scene even more than normal by using spot metering mode and basing your exposure on one of the lighter tones in the scene. Doing so produces an image that's much darker than normal overall, but with some richly detailed highlights. If you use the same technique in reverse (spot meter on a darker tone), you create a forced high-key effect, such as figure 13-19, with all the lighter tones washed out to white and unusually open and luminous shadows.

CAPTURING THE SKY AND CLOUDS

Nature photographers seem to like photographing sky and cloud formations, either by themselves or in combination with scenic landscapes. And no wonder — sunrise, sunsets, big fluffy clouds at mid-day, and storm clouds all make for interesting pictures, such as figure 13-20.

Getting the proper exposure for a dramatic skyscape can be tricky. Sometimes your camera's meter and auto-exposure system produces an excellent exposure on its own. Other times, you can override the auto-exposure settings to get the effect you want. The following tips may help:

> For a deep blue sky with a few cirrus (wispy) or cumulus (fluffy) clouds, such as figure 13-21, you can probably use the indicated automatic exposure.

13-20
Photo by Dan Dry

13-21
Photo courtesy PDphoto.org

> For a light blue sky, or one with more coverage of white clouds, meter the sky and then apply plus one stop exposure compensation.

> For a sunrise or sunset where you want to emphasize rich color, meter the sky and then apply minus one stop exposure compensation. Bracket around that exposure. Check your results and make additional adjustments if needed.

> Storm clouds such as those in figure 13-22 often average out to be reasonably close to middle gray, so you can use the metered exposure without adjustment. If the clouds are especially dark, meter the sky and then apply minus one stop exposure compensation to keep the auto-exposure system from lightening up the clouds.

> If the sun is in the frame, as it is in figure 13-23, don't use the average or multi-segment metering modes. Switch to spot metering mode and select a middle tone, such as the gray underside of a cloud, on which to base your exposure. You can often find a good middle gray tone in a sunrise or sunset. If the darkest clouds are lighter than middle gray, meter the darkest area, and apply plus one stop exposure compensation.

13-22
Photo by Tony Guffy

13-23
Photo by Tony Guffy

Capturing Rain, Fog, and Atmospheric Effects

There's a natural inclination to think of rain, snow, and foggy conditions as a bad time to take pictures, but the unusual lighting effects can be beautiful as you can see in figure 13-24. As you can see in figure 13-25, the soft diffused light is very flattering to many subjects and the brightness range of the scene is usually well within the camera's dynamic range, which means that you don't need to sacrifice detail in highlights or shadows because of excessive brightness range, as often happens on a sunny day.

The soft light also makes metering and exposure easy. Light is usually distributed fairly evenly across the frame, so average and multi-segment metering modes both work equally well and seldom need any exposure compensation unless the subject matter is unusually dark or light. It's a good thing that metering is easy and reliable, because light levels are usually relatively low and highly variable, which makes manual exposure guidelines almost useless for shots such as Figure 13-25.

PRO TIP

When shooting in inclement weather, you must take care to protect your camera gear from getting wet. One good technique is to pull a plastic garbage bag down over your camera mounted on its tripod. Make small slits in opposite sides of the bag for the lens hood and eyepiece, and tape them into place. You can reach up into the bag from below to operate the camera controls while keeping the camera completely covered. It helps to wear a broad brimmed hat to further shield the camera while you frame and focus.

13-24
© Charlotte K. Lowrie | wordsandphotos.org

13-25
Photo by Tony Guffy

LIGHTING FLOWERS AND NATURE CLOSE-UPS

Nature photography runs the gamut from the broad expanses of scenic landscapes to the close-up views of flowers and other small natural objects. Besides the difference in scale, close-ups such as figure 13-26 differ from landscapes and wildlife photographs in that flowers and other close-ups are one kind of nature photo where you can realistically expect to be able to exercise some control over the light.

Like other nature photography subjects, flowers, insects, and other small subjects are usually located outdoors where there is plenty of natural light available. Often, all you need to do is look around to find a nice specimen in good light. One very effective technique is to find a flower head in full sunlight and a background that's in the shade. Figure 13-27 shows

an example of this natural spotlight effect that causes the flower to stand out in sharp contrast to the dark background. If the situation doesn't occur naturally, you can place a black card behind the subject to create a similar effect.

13-26
© Charlotte K. Lowrie | wordsandphotos.org

273

13-27
© Charlotte K. Lowrie | wordsandphotos.org

13-28
© Charlotte K. Lowrie | wordsandphotos.org

When shooting flowers and other small subjects, keep these points in mind:

> Shooting small subjects positioned close to the camera means working with shallow focus, and that means that you need good depth of field control, whether your goal is to stretch the depth of field enough to cover a couple of flower blooms, or whether you want shallow depth of field to throw a background out of focus.

> Use aperture-priority auto-exposure so you can control depth of field with the aperture selection.

> Multi-segment metering mode will work well most of the time, but you may need to switch to spot metering to isolate the main subject if the background is especially dark (see figure 13-27) or light (see figure 13-28).

The big difference between photographing a landscape and a flower such as figure 13-29 is that when the light isn't right on the landscape, all you can do is wait for it to change, but if the light isn't right on the flower, you may be able to change it. For example, if a flower is in full sun, but you want a softer light, you could use a diffuser to soften the harsh sunlight, or simply have a friend stand so that they cast a shadow on the flower, thus creating open shade lighting for the flower.

13-29
Photo by Alicia McGinnis

Q&A

How can I get a good exposure of both the sky and the ground in a landscape?

The sky is usually much lighter and brighter than the ground, which means that when the ground is properly exposed, the sky is overexposed and washed out. One way to work around the problem is to set your camera up on a tripod and shoot a series of frames at different exposures, each properly exposed for a portion of the image, and then combine the images in Photoshop or another image editor. Better yet, shoot a multistep bracket and merge them into a 32-bit high dynamic range image. Shoot the exposure bracket in 2-EV increments by changing the shutter speed, not aperture.

How can I avoid awkward shadows and overexposure in flash close-ups?

When it comes to using flash to light flowers and other small subjects that may be very close to the camera, some extra care (and equipment) may be required. At normal working distances (more than about four feet), the camera's built-in flash or an external shoe-mount flash will usually work normally. However, as the distance between the camera and subject decreases, the problems tend to increase. Even at minimum power, the flash may be too bright, causing the subject to be overexposed. Also, the lens and/or lens hood may create a shadow on the subject.

To address these problems, special flash units are available that are designed just for close-up photography. To eliminate the possibility of a lens shadow, the flash unit typically mounts to the front of the lens like a filter or lens hood. There may be a pair of flash heads sitting on either side of the lens or the flash head may be a ring that encircles the lens. Positioning the light as close as possible to the lens axis nearly eliminates any visible shadow from the flash by placing the shadow directly behind the subject. To control the overexposure problem, the close-up flash units are usually relatively low power and connected to sensitive exposure control module mounted on the camera's hot shoe that links to the dedicated TTL flash exposure controls. Using these specialized close-up flash units enables photographers to shoot close-ups in low light that wouldn't be practical otherwise.

Chapter 14

TAKING PICTURES OF OBJECTS

Object photography is one of the biggest categories of photographic subjects. Images of objects surround us every day in catalogs, magazine advertisements, and Web pages that show pictures of products. Images such as figures 14-1 through 14-3 are designed to capture our attention, sell a product, evoke a mood, or illustrate a concept.

14-2
Photo by Dean Lavenson

14-1
Photo by Dean Lavenson

Photographing inanimate objects is fundamentally different from photographing people, pets, or even nature subjects. It's almost always done in a photographic studio (or on a location set that the photographer turns into a temporary studio) and the photographer has complete control over subject placement, camera position, lighting, and everything else. An inanimate object doesn't get tired or moody like a person does, and there's no need to be concerned about capturing facial expressions. As a result, the shooting pace can be more deliberate, allowing more time for precise lighting adjustments and special techniques that aren't practical with living subjects.

For example, the basic design and the lighting in figure 14-1 are both starkly simple, but the concept relies on absolute precision and attention to detail. It took hours to set up the shot, clamping the forks in position and making tiny adjustments to get them aligned perfectly with each other, with the camera, and with the lights.

The setup for figure 14-2 was even more elaborate. It required building a rig to drop the pepper into the glass in such a way that it passed through the beam of a light sensor that triggered the flash after a delay that had to be adjusted precisely to the millisecond. The photographer had to conceive of the shot, figure out how to pull it off, build and test the rig and light sensor circuit, and then shoot it — with excellent lighting and perfect exposure, I might add.

Personally, I've always considered object photography to be the purest expression of photography as an illustrative art form. The photographer has a measure of control from concept through to completion that isn't possible when photographing people or nature. There's more opportunity to actively create an image instead of observing and recording naturally occurring scenes. What's more, it's often a solo effort or the result of close collaboration with an art director, and relies less on contributions from models or the cooperation of nature.

LIGHTING STILL LIFES AND SMALL PRODUCTS

There's a long tradition of the still life as a subject in the visual arts. In painting and drawing, the subject is often a flower arrangement or a bowl of fruit. In photography, it's more likely to be a product, such as the shoes in figure 14-3, and the flowers are relegated to the role of set dressing. Because the subject itself is usually static, and often mundane, it's frequently not enough to simply record an accurate representation of the subject, it's up to the photographer to create an appealing image with a good composition and interesting lighting.

14-3
Photo by Alicia McGinnis

Unlike portrait photography, with its named lighting schemes that have evolved over the years, the lighting for small product photography tends to vary tremendously. That's part of the fun for the photographer. You can analyze the product and create an individualized lighting scheme to bring out the subject's unique characteristics. You can choose a direct frontal light to emphasize color, a softly directional light to show three-dimensional form, or a hard light raking across the subject to accentuate an interesting texture. You can emulate natural light, go for the high drama of theatrical-style lighting, create an otherworldly effect, or anything else that strikes your fancy.

14-4
Photo by Dean Lavenson

Rarely do you find natural light that provides the kind of lighting you need for a really good small product shot. Sometimes an outdoor setting or window light at an indoor location will give you a good starting point, but even then, you usually need to manipulate the naturally occurring light with diffusers and reflectors, or supplement it with flash fill.

In the location shot of an artisan's hands trimming a piece of pottery in figure 14-4, the main light source is a large window outside the left side of the frame. The single dominant light source raking across the scene gives the image dramatic impact while looking totally natural. However, that naturalness is an illusion. The photographer supplemented the window light with a reflector just outside the frame on the right, and another beside the camera. Without those reflectors, the shadow areas would lack detail.

Usually, what looks like a natural-light setting for a small product shot is actually a set constructed in the photography studio. Figure 14-5 is one such example. It appears to be a quaint potting shed, lit by the light coming through the window, which is balanced and offset by another light source outside the right side of the frame — perhaps a large open door. But it's all a little too perfect. It's highly unlikely that you'd find this ideal balance of light in real life, and if you did, it would last for only a minute or so. You'd have to be incredibly lucky to be in the right place at the right time to catch that fleeting moment. Constructing a set in the studio gives the photographer control over the lighting and the time to get it right. Carefully imitating a hypothetical natural-light scenario makes the image more believable.

14-5
© Bryan Moberly | moberlyphotography.com

This particular set was lit with studio flash, but it could have been done just as easily with continuous lights such as tungsten, quartz, or HMI lights. For most small product photography, the choice of studio light source is determined by availability and the photographer's preference, not dictated by the subject. After all, flower pots won't sweat from the heat of hot lights, squint at the brightness of continuous lights, or flinch at the sudden burst of light from flash.

Studio sets for small product photography don't have to be as elaborate as constructing a potting shed, complete with a window. In figure 14-6, the set is nothing more than a few planks of weathered wood, with a handful of sand and a piece of rope as set dressing. The lighting is also relatively simple. The main light is a large softbox, positioned about 60-degrees to the left of the camera and pointing down at a similar angle. The fill light is positioned just over the photographer's left shoulder. Another softbox, positioned low on the right, opens up the right side of the bottles and creates a nice vertical highlight on the bottle caps.

14-6
Photo by Alicia McGinnis

The studio is a place where the photographer has complete control, so there's no reason to be limited to emulating natural environments. Sometimes the best way to create the desired effect is with an imaginary setting and unconventional lighting, such as in figure 14-7. The subject is several very large and unusually colored freshwater pearls. (In fact, these are museum-quality specimens and there was an armed guard in the studio.) They're posed on a sheet of black plexiglass that gets its gradation from the deliberate glare created by placing the main light — a large softbox — above and behind the subject, pointed back toward the camera. Two more softboxes on either side of the camera provide frontal lighting as a counterpoint to the main light. A white reflector sitting on top of all three lights creates a white roof for the setup and fills in what would otherwise be a black reflection in the top of the glass orb and the pearls. A single bare-bulb lamp is positioned to peek into the set where the right-front softbox meets the top reflector. It creates a small, bright highlight on the glass orb and on each pearl, which gives them a touch of sparkle, much like the catchlight in the eye of a portrait subject.

In figure 14-8, the photographer took a different approach to imaginative lighting for a small product. The main light for the overall scene is above and behind the saw, positioned so that it lights the board and the top edges of the saw, but not the side toward the camera. The saw blade is lit by a separate accent light that is carefully aimed and shuttered with barn-doors to restrict its light to just the blade. A colored light hidden behind the saw creates a pool of red light on the background, and the photographer added a couple of touches of red to the front of the saw to create some continuity between the subject and the background. This kind of specialty lighting can take hours of experimentation, and the finished image is often a composite of several exposures. In this case, the blade, the saw, and the background were shot separately and then combined to create the finished image.

14-7
Photo courtesy of American Pearl Company and the Latendresse Family

14-8
© Bryan Moberly | moberlyphotography.com

LIGHTING FOOD

In some respects, photographing food is just like photographing any other small product in the studio. The main difference is that the subject itself is generally more appealing than most ordinary commercial subjects, so there's less need for lighting gimmicks to add artificial interest. Instead, the goal of food photography is usually an accurate rendering of the subject (which is challenging enough), combined with an interesting background treatment to complement the food without overpowering it.

Consider, for example, figure 14-9. The main light is a softbox, positioned above the peppers on the right side. It provides both the highlights on the upper surfaces of the peppers, and the modeling that defines their forms. A reflector near the camera is all that is needed to open up the fronts of the peppers. A background light coming in from the lower-left creates a nice gradation that is bright enough to provide contrast with the shadowed lower sides of the red peppers and then gets dark enough to make the highlighted top and stem of the green pepper to really pop.

14-9
Photo by Dean Lavenson

In figure 14-10, the photographer used a different lighting technique. The main light is positioned high, on the left, almost behind the grill, so that it rakes across the cut surface of the grilled chicken, bringing out its texture. It also creates the sparkling highlights on the slices and defines their back edges. Another light, positioned to the right of the camera, lights the fronts and tops of the slices and serves as a general fill light. The spotlight effect on the background is created by a third light shining down on a piece of rust-brown background paper positioned well behind the grill.

14-10
Photo by Dean Lavenson

Photographing food does require some special considerations. You must remember that you're attempting to photograph a perishable product that can melt, wilt, dry out, shrivel up, or otherwise change with time — and sometimes does so very quickly. That's not too much of a concern with a subject such as the peppers in figure 14-9, but it's a major issue with a subject such as the salad in figure 14-11. Within just a few minutes of being placed under hot tungsten or quartz lights, the water droplets evaporate and the salad greens begin to wilt.

and just as quickly wilts or dries out other foods, making them unattractive. Flash is now the king in the food studio because it minimizes the heat problem, therefore maximizing the time the food can be on the set under the lights and still look good. The extra working time afforded by using flash is absolutely essential when you need to prepare and position multiple dishes in one shot, such as in figure 14-12.

14-11
Photo by Dean Lavenson

14-12
Photo by Dean Lavenson

In the old days, when slow photographic films and hot lights were the only tools available to photographers, it was common practice to create meticulously hand-painted models of food and to photograph the models instead of the real thing. The substitute food models could stay under the lights as long as necessary to get the shot, but creating the models was time consuming and expensive, and the fake food raised the ire of truth-in-advertising advocates.

Nowadays, almost all food photography is done with real food, carefully selected and prepared for the studio session.

Furthermore, most photographers today avoid using hot lights for food photography because the heat from the lights quickly melts ice cream and other cold products,

PRO TIP

Freshly prepared foods don't remain at their best for very long. Even without the excessive heat of hot lights, it's hard to work fast enough to get the background, lighting, and camera angle all just right before the food starts to wilt. Consequently, it's common for the food stylist to prepare at least two batches of food. The first batch serves as a stand-in while the photographer takes as much time as necessary to light the set and shoot a series of tests. Then, when everything else is ready, the stylist substitutes a fresh batch of food for the final shot.

LIGHTING SILVER AND REFLECTIVE PRODUCTS

Silver and other similar reflective products have little or no color of their own. Instead, they reflect their environment, particularly the studio lights. You can see that phenomenon at work in figure 14-13. The right side of the polished metal tool reflects the bright white of the main light and also a strip of blue gel placed there to add some color to the subject. The left side of the tool reflects the fill light on the left and also picks up a streak of red from the cloth. The top edge of the tool is black because the darkness of the studio ceiling overhead doesn't give it anything to reflect.

When lighting jewelry, silverware, and other polished metal objects, you need to remember that each reflective surface is a mirror that is defined more by the environment that it reflects than by the light that strikes it directly. Consequently, lighting a reflective object is as much an exercise in lighting the environment for the object as it is lighting the object itself. To get clean bright highlights and light areas in a reflective subject, you need to surround it with a lot of clean white lights and reflectors. You may also want some dark areas in the environment for contrast.

14-13
Photo by Dean Lavenson

The photographer used two rectangular diffusers angled over the jewelry in figure 14-14 to create a mostly white environment for the gold petals to reflect. The camera is pointed straight down, through the gap between the diffusers. The light behind the diffuser at the upper left is closer, and therefore brighter, than the one behind the diffuser at the lower-right, so the torn paper background and rose cast soft shadows down and to the right. If you look very close, you can see the difference in brightness of the reflections in the jewelry, too.

14-14
Photo by Alicia McGinnis

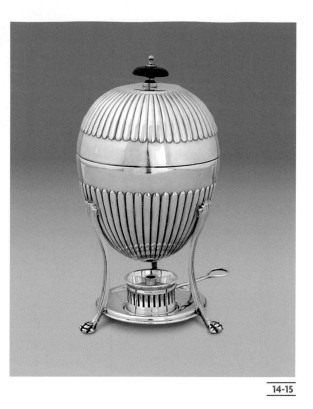

14-15

Convex objects, such as the domed lid of the silver tureen in figure 14-15, can reflect the entire studio. That could create undesirable results if you don't control those reflections. The solution is a technique called *tent lighting,* in which you place the subject inside a tent made of diffusion material and then light the subject by directing lights through the diffusers. The subject is surrounded by soft light because every surface of the tent either diffuses or reflects light. In this case, the tent is made of three rectangular diffusers that are clamped together to create a sort of box over the subject. The back of the box is open to allow for the sweep of the background. The camera-side of the tent is closed with more diffusion material,

and the lens pokes through a vertical slit, which you can see appearing as the dark line in the middle of the lid.

PRO TIP

A pop-up shooting tent is a convenient alternative to building your own tent lighting rig. The cube of white nylon fabric is held open by spring-loaded hoops, much like those in collapsible reflector panels or the sun shades for automobile windshields. One side of the cube opens to allow access to the interior. Velcro tabs allow you to attach interchangeable backgrounds to the floor and back of the cube. When you don't need the tent, it folds flat and collapses with a twist. Pop-up shooting tents come in several sizes, ranging from small cubes that are suitable for shooting individual pieces of jewelry, to larger cubes that can accommodate a silver tea service.

Tents Aren't Just for Reflective Subjects

Tent lighting was developed to control the reflections in silver and gold jewelry and other highly reflective subjects. However, there's another characteristic of tent lighting that makes it useful for some non-reflective subjects as well.

Because tent lighting bathes the subject in diffuse light that is reflected from all sides, it is (or can be) almost totally free of shadows. The absence of shadows is sometimes desirable for certain kinds of catalog illustrations and for product shots that will have their backgrounds dropped out or blended into a large solid-color background for text.

Tent lighting is perhaps the easiest way to achieve the shadow-free effect — provided the soft, uniform light of the tent supplies enough shape definition to keep the subject from looking like a flat paper cutout. The trick is to create some modeling by making the light brighter on the top or on one side of the tent, but to keep the off side bright enough to subdue the shadows. The only shadows that remain are directly beneath the subject.

The alternative to tent lighting for shadow-free small product photography is to place the subject on a clear glass shooting table and position background paper under the table. This setup provides enough physical separation between the subject and the background to allow you to light them independently, which enables you to eliminate shadows completely.

PRO TIP

Sometimes, tent lighting can be too uniform. The absence of any color or dark contrast can make your subject look unreal, especially when you're shooting chrome or silver. You can easily address the problem by hanging strips of colored material (paper, fabric, or gel) inside the tent where it will be reflected in the subject. Placing colored gels on the lights or the outside surface of tent diffuses the color for a more subtle effect.

Lighting Glass and Transparent Subjects

Like silver, clear glass is another substance that doesn't have much color of its own. Because almost all the light that strikes a piece of clear glass passes straight through, the glass object can be almost invisible to the human eye — and to the camera. Unlike opaque objects, which we see by the light reflected by the object, we perceive clear glass by observing distortions of objects behind or inside the glass, specular highlights (intense reflections of a light source) on the edges of the glass object, and some glare or weak reflections from the shiny surface of the glass.

NOTE

Completely clear, transparent glass (or acrylic plastic) creates the greatest lighting challenges. Colored or frosted glass is much easier to work with because it usually has enough color or surface texture to be visible on its own, so there's less need to resort to special lighting techniques. Opaque glass objects reflect light normally and you can use the same lighting techniques you'd use for ordinary substances such as wood or painted metal.

14-16

Figure 14-16 shows examples of all these effects at work to make the clear glass decanter clearly visible against the dark wood background. The distortion of the background is clearly visible in the lower half of the decanter, accentuated by the bottle's fluted sides. The facets of the stopper and curved lip of the decanter's mouth create lots of specular highlights — sharp reflections of the light source. The larger surface reflections across the shoulder of the bottle come from the rectangular diffuser panels positioned on either side of the subject.

Figure 14-17, on the other hand, relies almost entirely on well-placed surface reflections to define the shapes of the glassware in this striking image. The reflections come from a single softbox light on the left side of the subject, almost perpendicular to the camera angle. The light creates a primary reflection on the left side of the glass objects, and also shines through the glass to create a secondary reflection on the opposite side. The resulting highlights stand out in stark contrast to the black background. The photographer wrapped the supports for the upper pieces of glassware in black velvet to make them disappear into the background. The glow in the brandy is the photographer's secret special effect, but I suspect that it might have something to do with the fiber optic light that I saw sitting in the corner of his studio.

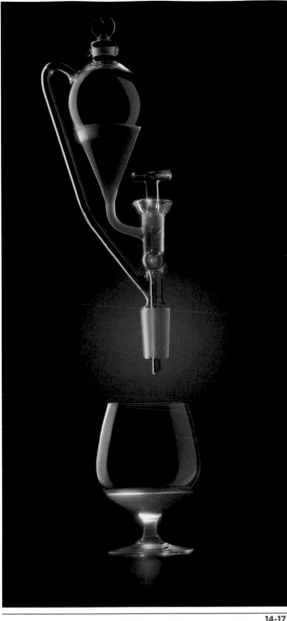

14-17
Photo by Dean Lavenson

through the bottle and the liquid again on its way to the camera lens. As a result, the liquid inside the bottle tends to look darker than you would expect, and you may see distorted shapes and colors from the background. This is a problem if your client cares about the apparent color of the whiskey, perfume, or whatever liquid is in the bottle.

Over the years, photographers have developed some tricks to overcome these problems when photographing transparent liquids. For example, notice the light-colored cologne in a clear bottle in figure 14-18. The bottle is lying on some rope and sand, and normally, you'd be able to see the rope through the bottle. However, in this image, the photographer attached a piece of white paper to the back of the bottle to block the view of the rope and create a clean reflection back through the cologne. Because the bottle is clear and the liquid is very light-colored, a plain white reflector is all that's needed to create a bright, clean look inside the bottle.

14-18
Photo by Alicia McGinnis

Often, the contents of a glass bottle are as important to the photograph as the bottle itself. And when the bottle contains a transparent liquid, it creates some challenges for the photographer. Light striking the front of the bottle normally goes through the bottle and the liquid inside before being reflected from whatever is behind the bottle, and then it passes back

The photographer also used a reflector behind the bottle in figure 14-19 to block the view of the background and improve the lighting through the bottle and a liquid inside. However, in this case the reflector isn't a simple piece of paper attached to the back of the bottle. Instead, the reflector is a freestanding piece of card stock positioned behind the bottle, which sits at about a 45-degree angle so it can catch the light from the large softbox on the right and reflect that light through the bottle and into the lens. The bottle is made of colored glass, so the reflector has to be bright silver in order to pump enough light through the bottle. Getting a reflector perfectly positioned and trimmed to size to fit behind the bottle like this can be a bit tricky, but it's the only way to get the desired results.

14-19
Photo by Alicia McGinnis

LIGHTING LARGER OBJECTS

The only real difference between photographing a small product and a larger object is the matter of scale. Instead of a small product sitting on a tabletop with a three-foot square fabric remnant as a background, the large object probably sits on the studio floor and needs the full eight-foot width of a roll of background paper or a painted muslin backdrop. Larger objects may need to be moved into position on a painted cyc-wall with a dolly or forklift.

NOTE

Some photography studios have a *cyc-wall* (sometimes called a *cyclorama* or *infinity wall*) where the wall blends into the floor in a gentle curve. The cyc-walls in some larger studios extend around two adjacent walls and the corner. The cyc-wall and floor can be painted a solid color to create a seamless background for large product photography.

Despite the difference in the size of the subject, the basics of camera angle, exposure, and lighting remain the same — you just need to do things on a larger scale. For example, adjusting the camera to a higher angle for a small product shot might mean moving the camera up a few inches, which you can accomplish with a few turns on the crank that raises the center post of your tripod. To make the same camera angle adjustment when photographing a larger object, such as the table saw in figure 14-20, you may need to move the camera several feet higher, which is likely to require climbing a stepladder.

14-20
© Bryan Moberly | moberlyphotography.com

14-21
Photo by Randy J. McCaffery

You need to scale your lighting up in much the same way. When photographing large objects, the lights are usually farther away from the subject, so they need to be brighter in order to achieve a similar light level on the subject. (Remember the inverse square law: doubling the distance from the light to the subject reduces the light intensity to one fourth the brightness.) You may need to use more powerful lights to get sufficient illumination levels for good exposures, and you may need more lights just to cover the larger working areas that large products require.

X-REF

For a complete description of the inverse square law see Chapter 10.

Figure 14-21 is an example of needing more lights for a larger product. The lighting scheme is simple, with the main light coming in from the right side. If the whiskey barrels were only about a foot tall, the photographer might have been able to position one light to illuminate the main subject and also spill onto the background. However, the size of the subject requires two lights to cover all the barrels, plus a third light for the background.

As you adapt your small product lighting to larger objects, keep the following points in mind:

> Hard, point-source lights scale up fairly easily. As distance from the subject increases, you need higher light output, but the essential character of a point source light doesn't change. Going from a tabletop setup to a larger product can be as simple as selecting a hot light with a higher wattage lamp, or increasing the power setting on your flash power pack.

> Broad lights are designed to spread their light over a wide area, and they quickly lose their effectiveness as their distance from the subject increases. To scale up for larger products, you need to either go to a larger, more powerful broad light, or replace a single broad light with a bank of two, four, or more lights. You generally want to keep broad lights as close to the subject as possible.

> Soft lights, such as softboxes and umbrellas, achieve their soft effect due to the large size of the light source relative to the size of the subject. Therefore, they need to get bigger in proportion to the size of the product and their distance from the subject in order to maintain that soft light quality. For moderate-sized products, you can compensate by using some of the larger umbrellas (five feet or more in diameter) and softboxes (four by six feet) that are available. For larger products, you need to go to lightbanks, which combine multiple light heads in a single large diffuser that works like a super-sized softbox. Another way to create a large diffuse light source for a large product, is to put one or more lights behind a suitably large piece of diffusion material. The diffusion material might be translucent plastic stretched on a large (4'x8') wooden frame, or white fabric hung from the ceiling of the studio.

> Reflectors also need to get bigger as the subject size increases. Instead of a ten-inch reflector card positioned a few inches from a small product, you may need a large reflector panel eight-feet square positioned a few feet from the subject. (I often use two 4'x8' sheets of white foam board, hinged together along the long sides with white gaffer tape.)

> Overhead lighting for a small product is simple to arrange with a light mounted on a boom stand. To achieve a similar effect on a larger product often requires suspending one or more lights from the studio ceiling. Studios that specialize in large product photography often have a grid of pipes suspended from the ceiling to provide attachment points for overhead lights.

LIGHTING ROOM SETS

Photographers often build room sets in a studio when a product needs to be photographed in its environment and a suitable location isn't readily available. The subject might be kitchen or bathroom cabinets, appliances, flooring, furniture, bedding, or any of hundreds of other products that look best when placed in context of an appropriate surrounding.

Building a room set may sound like a lot of work (and sometimes it is), but it's sometimes the only viable alternative to shooting in cramped quarters such as a bathroom or closet. Even when space isn't such a severe problem, building a studio set is often easier than finding a remote location, getting permission to use it, moving existing furniture out and replacing it with the product, setting up all the lights and camera equipment, shooting the photograph, and then packing up and restoring the location to its original condition.

Besides, the set doesn't have to be as big and elaborate as you might think. Studio sets have more in common with stage backdrops than they do the rooms they try to emulate. Sometimes a set is as simple as one section of wall propped up in the studio and some carpet or a rug on the floor. Figure 14-22 shows a set consisting of two walls joined to create a corner, and there's a window in the wall on the right. Most photographers seldom need a more elaborate set.

14-22
Photo by Alicia McGinnis

At first glance, you might expect that lighting a room set would be very similar to lighting an architectural interior, but you normally have much more control and flexibility in positioning the camera and lights in the studio than you would on location. The set usually consists of only the walls in front of the camera, so the opposite walls aren't there to restrict where you place your camera and lights the way they are in a room at a remote location. Most sets don't have ceilings either, so you can hang lights from the studio ceiling to light your set. As a result, lighting a room set is often more like lighting a large product than it is like lighting an architectural interior.

One thing that you need to think about as you light a room set is that the set will be more believable if the lighting emulates a real room. For example, in figure 14-22, the main light comes from overhead and from the right side. The chair and plant cast shadows to the left onto the wall. That looks right because the window in the wall on the right leads you to expect a light from that side. You can easily imagine another window, just outside the frame on the right, as the source of the light that creates those shadows.

Another lighting technique that helps add interest and makes the set look more believable is the light and shadow pattern across the chair and the picture on the left wall. It mimics the effect of a beam of light coming through a window and the shadows that would be created by the window frame and mullions. The photographer created the effect by cutting window pane sized holes in a piece of foam board placed in front of the light that creates the accent light on the chair and picture. A device for creating this kind of shadow effect is called a *gobo*.

Figure 14-23 is a more extreme example of this same technique. The contrast between light and shadow from the key light and gobo is much greater because the overall light level from the other lights on the set is lower. However, it still looks believable because the effect is that of a room that is being lit by a beam of light from a distant window and there are several obstacles breaking up the light and creating shadows before it reaches the bed. This lighting scheme effectively accentuates the bedding while subduing the details of the set, which happens to be a wall of the warehouse area adjoining the photography studio.

14-23
Photo by Alicia McGinnis

There are two approaches to photographing artwork. One is to shoot the artwork in its normal environment, as in figure 14-24, and the other is a straight-on copy of the artwork itself, such as in figure 14-25. Surprisingly, the environmental shot is usually the easier of the two to pull off because you have some leeway to adjust camera angle and lighting, and the success of the shot is based as much on the overall appearance of the entire scene as it is on the detail of the artwork itself. The straight-on copy requires strict adherence to an established formula that dictates the specific camera and lighting setup. It has the advantage of being a standardized arrangement, but the standard is an unforgiving one.

14-24

LIGHTING ARTWORK AND FLAT OBJECTS

Photographing paintings, mirrors, and other two-dimensional artwork presents some very special challenges. Normally, the goal is to create as faithful a reproduction of the original artwork as possible, so the task is one that demands technical precision rather than creativity.

14-25

Surface reflections and glare are the biggest problems you face when photographing two-dimensional artwork. The problem is worse when there is glass in the frame that covers the artwork, but the glossy surface of the varnish coating an oil painting can create considerable reflection problems too — especially if the piece includes a lot of heavily textured brush strokes. The peaks and valleys of the brush texture are sure to catch and reflect some specular highlights, no matter how carefully you position the lights to avoid it.

Avoiding large-scale glare problems across a piece of artwork in an environmental setting is fairly easy if you remember the rule about angle of incidence equaling angle of reflectance. You're probably shooting the artwork from a slight angle, and you can eliminate most glare problems by simply avoiding putting a light source — either direct or reflected — in a position to shine onto the subject from the mirror image of your camera angle. In figure 14-24, the main light is coming down from the upper-left. Since the

camera is also positioned to the left of the artwork, there's almost no chance of getting any reflection or glare from the main light on the surface of the painting. The fill light is more likely to create a reflection problem since it's positioned to the right of the camera, but it's still to the left of a line extending out from the wall, perpendicular to the painting, so it's in the clear too. On the other hand, moving the fill light a foot or so farther to the right would create a major glare across the entire surface of the painting.

The camera position and lighting for a straight-on copy follows a fixed formula, as outlined in the following steps:

1. Start with the artwork hanging on a wall so that it is straight, square, and plumb. The surface of the painting should be vertical — parallel with the wall. Don't just eyeball the alignment — use a bubble level to get it right. You may need to add spacers behind the bottom corners of a framed painting to get it to hang so that it's plumb instead of tilting out slightly at the top.

2. Drop a plumb line down from the center of the artwork and mark that spot on the floor. Then mark a line on the floor that starts at that point and goes out into the room, perpendicular to the wall. You can use a chalk line or masking tape to mark the line on the floor. To ensure that it's perpendicular to the wall, measure out along the base of the wall and mark points three feet on either side of the centerline; then measure out four feet along the centerline. The diagonal measurements from there to the three-foot marks should be exactly five feet. Add two more lines on the floor, each one starting at the point where the perpendicular line intersects the wall and radiating out at 45-degree angles on either side of the centerline.

3. Position the camera (on a tripod, of course) so that the lens is exactly perpendicular to the center of the artwork and the camera back is parallel to the surface of the painting. To do so, first position

the camera so that it's a comfortable working distance from the artwork and the lens is exactly over the centerline mark on the floor. Then measure the distance from the floor up to the exact center of the artwork and adjust the height of the camera lens to match that measurement. Use a bubble level to ensure that the camera back isn't tilted vertically. Finally, pan the camera to center the artwork in the frame. The camera should be squared up with the artwork.

4. Position two identical lights on the 45-degree lines on either side of the camera to light the artwork equally from both sides. Make sure the lights are far enough away so that their light spreads evenly across the entire surface of the artwork. Use a tape measure to ensure that both lights are equal distance from the artwork, and also measure from the floor up to the center of the light to make sure the height of the light matches the height of the camera lens and the center of the artwork. Carefully aim each light at the center of the painting.

5. Hold a gray card up in front of the artwork and use it to set your camera's white balance and exposure, then photograph the artwork using those settings. Don't use the camera's automatic white balance or exposure features, because artwork often includes nonstandard distribution of colors or grayscale tones that can skew the camera's exposure and color automation.

PRO TIP

Be careful of reflections from glass over the artwork. The glass can act like a mirror, reflecting the camera and photographer, which are both directly in front of the glass. To eliminate reflections, keep the camera (and the rest of the studio) in the dark. If you can't darken the studio, hang black velvet in front of the camera to control the reflections. Shoot through a peephole in the black drape.

Taking Pictures of Objects

Q&A

How can I photograph a television or computer screen?

Attempting to photograph the on-screen image from a television or computer screen can be a little tricky, especially if you also want the television and its surroundings properly exposed. First, it's important to understand that the image on a television or computer screen doesn't pop onto the screen all at once. Instead, it's scanned a line at a time, from top to bottom, and the process occurs about 60 times per second. Therefore, you need to use a shutter speed of 1/60 second or slower to capture the full scan. If you use a faster shutter speed, you'll get only part of the screen image, and the rest of the screen will be black or show only a dim ghost image left over from the previous scan. Furthermore, television broadcasts (and some computer displays) are interlaced, which means that each scan hits every other line and it takes two scans to produce the complete image. To photograph an interlaced screen image, you need to use a shutter speed of 1/30 or slower. You can usually use your camera's automatic exposure system to get a decent exposure for the screen, as long as you make sure the shutter speed is slow enough to capture the full image scan.

Color balance is another area that can be a little tricky. Televisions and computer screens are normally found indoors and you might expect them to have a color temperature that is similar to typical tungsten lights, but that's not the case. The color temperature of most televisions and computer displays is around 6000 kelvin, which is just a tad bluer than standard daylight. As a result, the screen image will look way too blue compared to its surroundings if you use tungsten lights for the rest of the scene. On the other hand, if you use flash to light the surroundings, the screen colors should match up reasonably well.

So, to photograph a television or computer screen with good color and exposure on both the on-screen image and its surroundings, you need to use flash (or another daylight balanced light source) to light the scene, you must use a slow shutter speed (usually 1/30 or slower), and you need to carefully balance the light level of the rest of the scene to match the brightness of the screen image. If you use flash, you need to be concerned only with matching the aperture for the flash exposure with the aperture for the screen exposure. The slow shutter speed doesn't increase the flash exposure.

What is the foam board you mentioned using for reflectors?

Foam board is a versatile product that is very handy to have around a photography studio. It comes in sheets, like cardboard, and consists of a Styrofoam or polystyrene core laminated between smooth paper surfaces. Foam board is light weight, rigid, and easy to cut with a sharp knife. It's available in thicknesses ranging from 1/8" to 1" and sheet sizes ranging from 8"x10" up to 4'x10'. It's primarily used in picture framing, sign making, presentations, and other graphic arts applications, and you can often find smaller sheets (30"x40") available in art supply stores under brand names such as FOME-COR and Gatorboard. For larger sizes, try www.foamboardsource.com.

Architectural photography is one of those photographic specialties that look fairly simple. How hard can it be to point a camera at a building and click the shutter?

But getting great architectural shots like figure 15-1 takes much more effort than most people realize. You need to have a good eye to find interesting and attractive angles that show off the unique features of each building. And dealing with perspective issues can test a photographer's skill. But most of all, architectural subjects can present some exposure and lighting challenges with demanding outdoor locations and confined spaces and mixed light sources indoors.

15-1
© Bryan Moberly | moberlyphotography.com

PHOTOGRAPHING ARCHITECTURAL EXTERIORS

Photographing an architectural exterior has a lot in common with shooting a landscape. You can't move the subject to put it into better light, and you can't light the whole structure yourself with normal photographic lighting instruments. Instead, you must wait for the available light to be right, which usually means waiting for the right time of day for the sun to be in position to light the building in an attractive way.

Architectural exteriors can be more demanding than landscapes because the photographer usually has much less leeway in subject selection. When you set out to photograph a landscape, you pick one that looks good and bypass dozens of others that aren't as attractive. You may be able to do the same with buildings if you're an artist looking for interesting architectural details, but most architectural photography is the result of a commercial assignment to photograph a specific building from an angle that includes a sign or other feature, like the one in figure 15-2. Whether the building is a beautiful piece of architectural sculpture or an ugly utilitarian box, your job is to make it look good, and that requires good light. The trick is to predict when the light will be right, so you can be in position to take the picture when it occurs.

PICK THE TIME OF DAY

Traditionally, most architectural exteriors such as figure 15-3 are photographed in full sun, because the brilliant light and crisp shadows help accentuate the overall form of the structure, bring out the architectural details, and make the building look clean and bright. Of course, you can sometimes get some nice effects under other lighting conditions (even rain, snow, and fog), but full sun has evolved into the standard for a reason — it works.

15-2
Image provided by Dreamstime

Normally, you select the best time of day to photograph an architectural exterior based on the orientation of the building. Pick the time when the sun directly lights the primary façade, main entrance, or other architectural feature that you want to highlight. Keep these tips in mind:

> East-facing buildings need morning sun. The east side of the building is usually shadowed and dull in the afternoon.

> West-facing buildings need afternoon sun.

> The south side of buildings in the northern hemisphere usually gets some sun during most of the day. Select the best time based on which of the adjacent sides you want to include or whether the building is skewed slightly towards the east or west.

> The north side of a building (in the northern hemisphere) often gets little or no direct sun, so the best you can get is open shade lighting. You'll probably want to shoot at mid-day and during the summer months. Avoid low sun angles (early morning, late afternoon, winter days in northern latitudes) that might create a backlighting situation.

15-3

> Mid-day sun generally provides more uniform lighting by minimizing shadows cast to the side and furnishing slightly more illumination on the off side of the building.

> Early morning and late afternoon sun create more dramatic effects with long shadows such as those in figure 15-4. A little later in the day, the light takes on a warmer tone. On the east or west building façades, the low sun angle can actually reduce shadows by reaching farther back under deep overhangs.

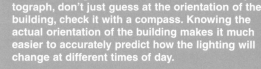

PRO TIP

When scouting a location for an architectural photograph, don't just guess at the orientation of the building, check it with a compass. Knowing the actual orientation of the building makes it much easier to accurately predict how the lighting will change at different times of day.

GET A GOOD SKY

Most architectural photos include a significant amount of sky, and the appearance of that sky can enhance or detract from the finished image. A dull, featureless sky tends to make the whole picture look a little dull, so you usually want to avoid shooting on overcast days. You want either a clear blue sky or an attractive cloudscape like the one in figure 15-5.

15-4
© Bryan Moberly | moberlyphotography.com

15-5

To determine the orientation of a building and predict the optimum time to photograph it, scout the location ahead of time. If it's not practical to visit the site, you can often get a good general idea of the building's orientation by checking its address on an ordinary street map.

PRO TIP

To increase your chances of getting a nice rich blue sky, shoot toward the north on a day with low humidity. In the northern hemisphere, the north sky is noticeably darker, with a richer blue color. Humidity creates haze and light scatter that lightens and washes out the sky color, so the lower the humidity the better.

15-6
Photo by Randy J. McCaffery

Ideally, you can photograph your subject when the light on the building is just right, and the clouds create a pleasant pattern in the sky. However, if you're not lucky enough to have both of those conditions occur simultaneously, concentrate on the building, and worry about the sky later. You can use the magic of digital image manipulation to drop in a blue sky and fluffy clouds from another image later. Just be careful to match the color and direction of the light on the clouds to the light on the building, otherwise the finished image will look subtly "wrong."

GET A GOOD EXPOSURE

In contrast to the challenges of getting the right lighting for an architectural exterior, getting the right exposure is usually relatively straightforward. Because photos like figure 15-6 are usually shot in full sun, the sunny-16 rule normally prevails, and you could just set your exposure manually to 1/100 at f-16 with ISO 100. Most architectural subjects comprise a normal brightness scale, so your camera's automatic exposure system should produce good results, too. You're unlikely to need any exposure compensation unless the subject is unusually dark or light and fills the frame with those extreme tones. When selecting exposure settings for architectural exteriors, keep these tips in mind:

> Black glass and steel construction usually creates a building that is about one stop darker than middle gray. Meter those areas and then apply exposure compensation of *minus* one EV.

> Most medium red and gray bricks are close to middle gray in value. You can use your camera's spot metering mode and base your exposure on those tones without further adjustment.

> Dry concrete, stone, painted siding, and similar building materials are usually about one stop lighter than middle gray. Meter those areas and then apply exposure compensation of *plus* one EV.

> White painted siding, white marble, and highly reflective glass are often two stops brighter than middle gray. Meter those areas and then apply exposure compensation of *plus two* EV.

> As always, shoot a test and then check the histogram to confirm that you've got a good distribution of tones with no clipping at either end of the value scale.

PRO TIP

To keep vertical lines straight and parallel in your photograph, the camera back must be vertical when you take the shot. The swings and tilts of a view camera are designed to allow you to point the camera at an angle to compose the shot and still keep the back straight and plumb. If you don't have access to a view camera, you can shoot with a digital SLR camera that is carefully leveled on a tripod to keep the back vertical. Since you can't tilt the camera to compose the shot, you'll need to compose by cropping the image afterwards. Photoshop and other image editors often include a perspective correction filter that can compensate for some camera tilt, but it's better to avoid the perspective distortion to begin with and not rely on the filter to correct it.

UNUSUAL LIGHTING

The traditional standard of shooting architectural subjects in full sun works well most of the time, but sometimes you may want something different. You can get some dramatic effects from unusual lighting situations such as the prelude to an approaching storm. You can also get great looks like figure 15-7 at sunset or dusk.

Dusk (a few minutes *after* sunset) is an especially effective and challenging time to shoot architectural subjects. In figure 15-8, there's still enough daylight to see the outside of the building clearly, and yet it's dark enough for the sign and interior lights to have equal impact. The mix of colors from a variety of light sources can add some color to what would be a drab building during the day. The fading light of day shifts blue with the absence of any direct sunlight. That makes tungsten lights look even more yellow than usual in comparison. Most fluorescent lights tend to go green, and light from signs and other light sources kick in their own colors.

Images such as figure 15-9 can have a stunning effect, but getting the right exposure is not easy. Your camera's automatic exposure system isn't designed for this situation, and achieving good results on the first shot is unlikely. You can try shooting a test and then adjusting your exposure based on the preview image and histogram. However, given how fast the light changes in those fleeting minutes between daylight and dark, it may be difficult to test, evaluate, and adjust fast enough to get the shot. You might be better off just bracketing like crazy.

15-7
Photo by Dean Lavenson

15-8
Photo by Dean Lavenson

X-REF

If you're not familiar with bracketing, see Chapter 3 for an explanation.

As figure 15-10 shows, architectural photographs are possible later at night if the building is lit by exterior lights or interior light is coming out through lots of glass. However, night exposures can be very tricky. If you decide to attempt a night architectural shot, the following checklist may help:

1. Light levels are usually low, so long exposure times are the norm. Use a sturdy tripod and remote shutter release or self-timer to avoid camera shake. If your camera has mirror lock feature or an anti-shock feature that delays exposure until a few seconds after the mirror flips up, use that too.

2. Set your camera for manual exposure mode. Automatic exposure may not work well because of the long exposures and uneven lighting. Manual exposure mode is more reliable and more controllable.

15-9
Photo by Dean Lavenson

3. Set your camera for spot metering mode and take a meter reading from the lighted area of the building façade. (Aim the camera so that the central spot metering zone of the viewfinder is on the lighted area, and then half-press the shutter release button to engage the exposure system without taking a picture.) Set your exposure based on that area. Light levels are often uneven across the building face, but the lights are typically positioned to highlight interesting architectural details, so you can usually concentrate on the best-lit highlight areas and let the rest go dark.

15-10

© Bryan Moberly | moberlyphotography.com

If the uneven light levels create extreme hot spots surrounded by more dimly lit areas, and important detail is located in both areas, consider shooting a very wide bracket that includes frames with proper exposures for both brightness extremes. Then you can use Photoshop or another image editor to combine those exposures into a single image that retains detail in both highlights and shadows using one of the high dynamic range image techniques.

4. Reframe the shot and shoot a test exposure. Evaluate the preview image and histogram, then adjust the exposure settings, and try again as needed.

5. Mixed light sources are common and they'll create different colors in the image as figure 15-11 clearly shows. You can't match all the colors, but you don't usually need to. Start with the white balance set for tungsten light and then experiment with white balance bracketing to see what setting produces the best effect. Better yet, shoot Camera Raw and deal with color correction when you process the Raw file.

15-11

PHOTOGRAPHING ARCHITECTURAL INTERIORS

Photographing architectural interiors like what is shown in figure 15-12 is at least as challenging as architectural exteriors. You must deal with the same kind of restricted subject assignment and perspective control issues. Plus, you're working indoors, in a confined space, with lower light levels. The ambient light is often inadequate, and supplementing it with photographic lighting can be problematic.

WORKING WITH AVAILABLE LIGHT

The ideal scenario is one in which the ambient lighting from windows and/or indoor lights is sufficient to allow you to get a decent photograph without adding supplemental lighting. Scenes such as figure 15-13 are much too big to light effectively, so you must shoot them by available light.

15-12

When evaluating a scene to determine whether it will make a good available light photograph, pay more attention to whether there is an even distribution of the light rather than its brightness. Perspective control issues dictate that you must work carefully and deliberately with the camera mounted on a tripod, and not attempt to hand-hold the camera. Because your camera will be on a tripod anyway, it's no problem to compensate for low overall light levels by using slow shutter speeds or even short time exposures.

> If there are no windows or if the windows are small and don't admit significant light, you can base your exposure on the artificial light.

> Daylight entering the room through large or numerous windows is usually much brighter than the artificial light inside. Consequently, it will be the dominant light source during daylight hours. Daylight often completely overpowers the interior lighting so that the artificial lights make only a minimal contribution to the overall exposure as seen in figure 15-14.

15-13
© Bryan Moberly | moberlyphotography.com

15-14
Photo by Randy J. McCaffery

> Avoid including in the frame any window that allows direct sun into the room. The extreme brightness difference between the sunlight and the rest of the interior is too great to manage effectively. Unlike architectural exteriors, which almost require a sunny day, interiors are often better on an overcast day because the window light is softer and more uniform on all sides of the building.

> If you want to use the artificial interior lights as the dominant light source in a room with windows, shoot after dark.

DEALING WITH MIXED LIGHT SOURCES

Daylight and artificial lighting are very different colors. To make matters worse, the various artificial lights (tungsten, daylight fluorescent, warm white fluorescent and so on) each has a different color temperature and it's common to have a mixture of different lights in the same scene.

You can color correct your digital images for one light source, but you can't color correct for two or more different light sources simultaneously. Consequently, any room that includes a mixture of light sources is going to show evidence of a color cast around at least some of those lights. In figure 15-15, the photographer deliberately exaggerated this effect to add color and interest to a mostly monochromatic subject.

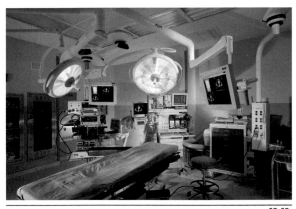

15-15

The only way to prevent the situation is to color correct for the dominant light source and turn off any light source that doesn't match the dominant light's color temperature. When that's not practical or desirable, try some of the following strategies to work with the mixed light sources:

> When the dominant light source is daylight, you can often have some tungsten lights on without creating any unwanted color cast. In situations such as figure 15-16, daylight is so much brighter that it overpowers the tungsten light, leaving just a warm glow around the light itself.

15-16
Photo by Randy J. McCaffery

> When the dominant light is tungsten and there is a window in the scene, daylight coming through the window will have a distinct blue cast. The blue isn't usually objectionable if it's confined to the window itself and doesn't extend into the room. One very effective way to confine the daylight to the window is to hang sheer drapes over the window. If necessary, you can use screens or diffusers to reduce the light intensity at the window.

> Different types of fluorescent lights have different color temperatures and require different color corrections. Ideally, all the fluorescent lamps in a room will be the same type and you can white balance to that color. If the lamp types are mixed, try correcting for the dominant type, or if they are evenly mixed, try an average between the colors. You may need to resort to white balance bracketing to find what setting works best.

> The so called "daylight fluorescent" lamps don't actually match the color of real daylight, but they are sometimes close enough to allow some light mixing with daylight. If color rendition in the scene isn't critical, you may be able to split the difference between the color correction for daylight and for the daylight fluorescents.

> The compact fluorescent lamps that are marketed as replacements for standard screw-base tungsten light bulbs are fairly close to the color temperature of the tungsten lamps they replace. You can mix them freely and use the same color correction for both.

> One of the most common mixed light situations is a mixture of fluorescent and tungsten lights. If one of the light types is clearly dominant, it usually works best to white balance for that light and live with a color cast from the other light. If a prominent foreground object is in the scene, white balance for the light on that object. A color cast in the background is usually much less objectionable.

SUPPLEMENTING AVAILABLE LIGHT

Sometimes the ambient light level in a room is so low that you can't get a good exposure without using such high ISO settings and long exposure times that digital noise begins to degrade the image quality. Sometimes light sources in the frame create hot spots close to the lights and dark corners elsewhere. When you encounter either of these situations, you have no choice but to supplement (or replace) the ambient light as the photographer did in Figure 15-17.

15-17
© Bryan Moberly | moberlyphotography.com

To provide that supplemental lighting, you can use most any lighting instrument you would use for other photographic location lighting, including on-camera flash, portable studio strobes, and tungsten hot lights. However, there are some special considerations when selecting and using the lights for an architectural interior instead of a more common task such as a location portrait — not the least of which is that you probably need more of them.

In most cases, your goal is to light the scene in such a way that it looks natural. In images such as figure 15-18, it isn't immediately obvious that the photographer added light to the scene at all. However, that can be tough to do for two reasons. First, you may be trying to light a fairly large area with a significant distance between the foreground and the far wall. Because light intensity falls off with distance according to the inverse square law, a light placed near the camera may be too bright on the foreground and still not illuminate the far wall adequately. Secondly, because you're usually shooting with a very wide-angle lens in order to encompass as much of the room as possible, there's often not many places to position lights where they won't be in the photograph.

15-18
© Bryan Moberly | moberlyphotography.com

Every scene presents a unique set of challenges for positioning supplemental lighting, and the solutions to those challenges are equally diverse. There is no lighting formula that works all (or even most) of the time. However, you may find the following tips helpful from time to time:

> Position lights as far away from the subject as possible. Increasing the distance between the light and the subject reduces the difference in light intensity on the foreground and background.

> Bounce lights off walls and ceilings instead of pointing them directly at the scene. This softens the light for a more natural effect, spreads the light out over a wider area, and reduces hot spots and shadows.

> If you do need to point a light directly at the scene, try adding a diffuser to the lower half of the light to reduce the light intensity on the foreground.

> Try hiding lights behind furniture and around corners in the scene. Sometimes, this is the only way to get light to distant areas.

> Match the supplemental lighting to the color of the dominant ambient lighting. Use flash to supplement daylight. Use tungsten hot lights to supplement tungsten lighting.

> If you use flash as the supplemental lighting, you can control the ratio of flash to ambient light with your shutter speed selection. The contribution of the flash is the same at all shutter speeds slower than the fastest sync speed. Slower shutter speeds increase the ambient light contribution and faster shutter speeds decrease it.

> If the ambient lighting is fluorescent, neither flash nor tungsten supplemental lights will match. Flash is usually closer. Try lighting the foreground with flash and let the ambient fluorescents fill in the background. A slight color cast in the background isn't usually objectionable, especially if it's a stop or so darker than the foreground.

Determining the best exposure is a balancing act between the ambient light and the supplemental lights. If you use tungsten lights for both, you may be able to start with your camera's built-in meter or auto-exposure system. For flash exposures, a flash meter can give you a starting point. When shooting scenes like the one in figure 15-19, the final exposure is likely to be based on trial and error. Shoot a test, evaluate the preview image and histogram, then adjust the exposure settings and try again.

15-19
© Bryan Moberly | moberlyphotography.com

SHOOTING OFFICE INTERIORS

Offices and commercial spaces typically have lots of overhead fluorescent lighting. In figure 15-20, you can see the rows of lights in the ceiling. The good thing about photographing theses spaces is that the lighting is usually designed by an architect and engineered to provide fairly uniform light at a level that is adequate (though certainly not optimum) for photography. If your goal is to photograph the room as a whole, you can probably do it by available light. You may need to add supplemental lighting if you want to show people in the scene, or you have a foreground object that exhibits excessive shadows from the overhead lights.

Offices and commercial spaces often have large windows. The windows can help light the scene, but they can also be a problem if a bright window creates a backlight situation. Sometimes, the only effective solution to the backlight issue is to wait for darkness, or at least wait for the sun to move to the other side of the building. To control the brightness of the windows in figure 15-21, the photographer resorted to manipulating the image in Photoshop, matting windows from a darker exposure into the base image of the overall room.

15-20
Photo by Randy J. McCaffery

PRO TIP

Windows in commercial buildings are often tinted to control light intensities and heat gain through the windows. Some tints are a reflective silver or neutral gray that don't cause any color problems in a photograph, but others have a pronounced color cast — usually purple or greenish yellow. If a window has an objectionable color cast, try not to include it in your photograph. If necessary, shoot after dark when the window will not be a light source in the photograph.

15-21
Photo by Dean Lavenson

Shooting Residential Interiors

Residential interiors are usually characterized by lower ambient light levels and smaller spaces than commercial interiors. Some grand homes, such as the one shown in figure 15-22, feature high ceilings and open spaces, but low ceilings and small rooms are typical of the average home.

15-22
Photo by Randy J. McCaffery

Tungsten lighting is the norm. Unlike the engineered lighting scheme of a commercial building, a residential interior is usually lit by an assortment of floor lamps, table lamps, and perhaps a chandelier or some wall sconces. The overall light level is generally low, but with hot spots around each lamp. During the day, windows may admit enough daylight to create a good ambient light level as shown in figure 15-23, but the available artificial lights are rarely adequate for photography. Plan on providing at least some supplemental lighting.

15-23
Photo by Randy J. McCaffery

Small room sizes can be both a problem and an advantage when it comes to lighting the scene. The cramped space gives you very little room to work with to position your lights. However, the small space doesn't need as much light as a larger commercial interior. One light bounced off the ceiling above the camera may be enough.

SHOOTING INDUSTRIAL LOCATIONS

Industrial locations, such as factories and ware-houses, are the biggest indoor spaces you're likely to need to photograph. Scenes such as figure 15-24 are much too big to light effectively, so you must use ambient lighting for the overall exposure. Like commercial spaces, the lighting scheme was probably engineered to provide a certain light level throughout the space, although the light may not be as bright or as even as the normal office. If the light level is indeed lower, you may need to boost your ISO setting to get a decent exposure.

15-24
Photo by Randy J. McCaffery

Industrial locations frequently use high-efficiency, low-maintenance lights such as sodium vapor and mercury vapor. These lights give scenes such as figure 15-25 a distinct color cast that is markedly different from the tungsten, fluorescent, and daylight standards. These lights don't match any of the standard white balance presets, which makes setting the correct color balance difficult. The best way to deal with the color is to shoot Camera Raw and adjust the color when you process the Raw file. If that's not possible, try white balance bracketing to help find an acceptable setting.

15-25
Photo by Randy J. McCaffery

■ **Why do the colors look a little off in some industrial interiors, even after doing a custom white balance for the lights at the location?**

Some light sources, such as the mercury vapor lights used in many industrial locations, don't emit light in a smooth, continuous spectrum like daylight and tungsten lights. Mercury vapor lights emit disproportionately more light in some parts of the spectrum compared to others.

When you adjust the white balance, you are telling the camera what the average color of the light source is. That adjusts the overall color of the image, but doesn't fully correct for the inconsistencies in the color spectrum emitted by the mercury vapor light.

How can I use tungsten lights as supplemental lighting in a daylight scene, or use flash to supplement a scene where tungsten lights are dominant?

Try to avoid mixing light sources in this way, but it is possible to do. In fact, film and television lighting crews do it all the time. You can get special blue color filter gels to put on your tungsten lights that change then to daylight color balance. Similarly, you can use an orange filter gel to change a daylight-balance flash to match the color of tungsten lights. The filters drastically reduce light output, but they can effectively match the color of disparate light sources.

Note that not just any blue or orange filter will do. To get good results, you need to use filter gels that are calibrated to just the right colors for the daylight-to-tungsten or tungsten-to-daylight color shift. You can order them from a theatrical supply house or other outlet that supports the film and television production industry.

Recently a new product has come onto the market to make it easier to mix the output of an external flash unit with ambient tungsten or fluorescent lighting. It's a colored diffuser from Sto-Fen Products (www.stofen.com) that fits onto the flash head of most brands of external shoe-mount and handle-style flash units. There's a green diffuser that approximates the color of fluorescent lights, and a gold diffuser that approximates the color of tungsten lighting. To use this accessory, you set your camera's white balance for the ambient light color (tungsten or fluorescent) and then use the corresponding colored diffuser on the flash to make the flash output conform to that color. The result isn't always a perfectly color balanced image, but there isn't a stark difference between the ambient light and the flash, and the overall color is probably close enough that you can make it look good with just some minor adjustments in an image editor.

CONTRIBUTING PHOTOGRAPHERS

The wonderful images that grace the pages of this book are the work of a group of talented photographers. The images themselves are the best testament to the photographic skills of the contributors. I've included these profiles of the contributing photographers in order to provide some background information and insights about the people behind the photographs.

DAN DRY

Dan Dry (figure A-1) is one of America's most widely recognized photographers. He has won over 400 national and international photography, advertising, and design awards during his career. Dry received his profession's highest honor, being named the National Press Photographer of the Year by the National Press Photographers Association.

Dry was a member of The Courier-Journal's Pulitzer Prize winning photography staff from 1976 until 1982. While still in high school, Dry made history at age 16, when he was part of a team that finished as runner-up to The New York Times for The Pulitzer Prize for Public Service. The work was done for The Athens Messenger, a rural Ohio newspaper with a total circulation of only 12,000 readers.

Dry served two internships at National Geographic; he first began at age 19. Dry went on to work professionally for the publication for an additional eight years, traveling the world extensively and shooting a variety of assignments as a contract photographer.

Dry is the author of 14 coffee table books on colleges and universities, and has contributed numerous photographs to over 100 additional books, including *America 24/7* and *A Day in the Life of America,* the only book of photography to ever top The New York Times bestseller list.

For the past 18 years, Dry has turned talents to corporate and advertising photography for Fortune 500 companies and advertising agencies, producing work for advertisements, annual reports, Web sites and brochures. In addition, Dry is under contract as a staff photographer for the University of Chicago, Department of Development and Alumni Relations.

Web site: www.dandry.com
E-mail: dan@dandry.com

TONY GUFFY

Tony Guffy has been a professional photographer and photo educator for over twenty-five years. He teaches Commercial Photography at Jefferson Community College, in Louisville, KY, and he is a member of the National Association of Photoshop Professionals. Tony also is a member of the Kentucky High School Athletic Association Hall of Fame. He coached five state championship soccer teams and coached championship teams at three different schools; Westport, Male, and Ballard High Schools.

Web site: www.tonyguffy.com
E-mail: photos@tonyguffy.com

A-1

A-2
Photo by Tony Guffy

DEAN LAVENSON

Dean Lavenson is a commercial photographer serving local, regional, and national clients from his studio in Louisville, KY. He is a graduate of Brooks Institute of Photography and served as a staff photographer for one of the region's largest studios before opening his own studio.

Lavenson specializes in advertising illustration, including food, people, and products both large and small — shot on location or in his large, fully-equipped studio. He can shoot film or digital images in small, medium, and large format, with latest innovations in digital workflow.

Lavenson's clients include a long list of prominent advertising agencies and corporate names, such as Valvoline, Humana, Papa John's, Chevron, Jewish Hospital, Norton Healthcare, Fifth Third Bank, National City Bank, and the YMCA, to name a few.

Web site: www.deanlavenson.com
E-mail: dean@deanlavenson.com

A-3

CHARLOTTE K. LOWRIE

Charlotte Lowrie is a freelance editorial and stock photographer and an award-winning writer based in the Seattle, WA, area. Her writing and photography have appeared in newsstand magazines including *Popular Photography & Imaging,* and *PHOTOgraphic* magazines. She is the author of three books, the best-seller, the *Canon Digital Rebel Field Guide,* and *Teach Yourself Visually Digital Photography, 2nd Edition,* and she is the lead author for *Adobe Camera Raw Studio Skills* book, all published by John Wiley & Sons. Charlotte also teaches photography classes on BetterPhoto.com.

A-4
Photo by Charlotte Lowrie

RANDY J. MCCAFFERY

Artistic and technical expertise are skillfully displayed in the industrial and commercial photography of Randy McCaffery. A 20-year veteran photographer, his creative images have appeared in annual reports, brochures, and posters for local, regional, and national clients.

A-5

She was the managing editor of the discontinued MSN Photos Web site for more than four years, and she served as the managing editor of *Double Exposure* magazine for a year. She is also a featured photographer on www.takegreatpictures.com.

In stock and editorial assignment photography, Charlotte enjoys nature and portrait photography. Her images have been published in books, magazine articles, and advertisements. A selection of her photojournalism images were exhibited at a Midwest gallery.

Web site: www.wordsandphotos.org
E-mail: charlotte@wordsandphotos.org

McCaffery works in various film and digital formats photographing industrial subjects, architectural interiors, lifestyle, events, trade shows, and annual report publications. He has been a member of the American Society of Media Photographers since 1989. His studio, McCaffery Photography, is located in Louisville, KY.

Web site: www.mccafferystudio.com
E-mail: randy@mccafferystudio.com

ALICIA MCGINNIS

Alicia McGinnis is a freelance commercial and fashion photographer based in Louisville, KY. She has a diverse photographic background shooting all sorts of subjects from products to people.

A-6

She developed her skills as a staff photographer for one of the region's largest commercial studios, and then served as the house photographer for a major department store chain before striking out on her own as an independent freelance photographer.

McGinnis shoots fashion, model portfolios, and general commercial assignments using both film and digital media.

Phone: (502) 724-1308
E-mail: brmcginn9@aol.com

BRYAN MOBERLY

Serving clients around the globe from his 2,500-square-foot studio for nearly two decades, Bryan's work has appeared in major publications, on billboards, and in advertising. Moberly Photography's images have garnered awards for architectural firms, advertising agencies, and marketing companies. The Louisville Advertising Federation and Louisville Graphic Design Association have recognized Bryan's photography with Gold and Silver awards for excellence and impact.

A-7

Bryan's mastery of digital photography and software enhancements enable him to capture images that create the looks his clients seek to portray. He is versatile in the latest digital technologies and all film formats.

Web site: www.moberlyphotography.com
E-mail: bryan@moberlyphotography.com

FRED D. REAVES

Fred Reaves owns and operates Image One Photography Inc. and Image One Gallery in Henderson, KY. An award winning photographer and graphic designer, he has been working professionally for 35 years with his main emphasis on architectural and industrial photography and publication design. His client base includes such internationally based clients as Eli Lilly, Bristol-Myers Squibb, Mc Donald's Corporation, Whirlpool Corporation, Toyota Motor Manufacturing, Kimball International, Atlas Van Lines, and General Electric Plastics.

A-8

Reaves, a graduate of Murray State University with a degree in art is also an accomplished fine arts photographer whose work can be found in galleries and museum shops as well as in private and corporate collections both nationally and internationally.

He has taught in numerous photographic workshops for high school aged photographers and currently teaches Advanced Studio Lighting Techniques and Intermediate Photography classes in the Visual Communications Dept. at Ivy Tech State College in Indiana.

Web site: www.imageonegallery.com
E-mail: imageonefineart @yahoo.com

RAMON RODRIGUEZ

Ramon Rodriguez is a portrait and wedding photographer based in Louisville, KY. A recent graduate of the commercial photography program at Jefferson Community and Technical College, he brings a fresh style to his portraits of seniors, couples, families, and babies.

A-9

Web site: www.ramonsphotography.com
E-mail: rodriguez67@mac.com

ROB SHEPPARD

Rob Sheppard has had a long and nationally recognized commitment to helping photographers connect with digital imaging technology. He was one of the small group of people who started *PCPhoto* magazine nearly eight years ago to bring the digital world to photographers on their terms. He is the editor of *PCPhoto* as well as *Outdoor Photographer* magazines (second only to *Popular Photography* in circulation), group editorial director of all Werner Publication photo magazines (*PCPhoto, Outdoor Photographer,* and *Digital Photo Pro*) and is the author/photographer of over a dozen photo books, including *Adobe® Camera Raw for Digital Photographers Only,* published by Wiley Publishing.

A-10
Photo by Rob Sheppard

He also writes a column in *Outdoor Photographer* called Digital Horizons and teaches around the country, including workshops for the Palm Beach Photographic Centre, Santa Fe Photography and Digital Workshops, Digital Landscape Workshop Series, and the Great American Photography Workshop group. His Web site for workshops, books and photo tips is at www.robsheppardphoto.com.

As a photographer, Rob worked for many years in Minnesota (before moving to Los Angeles), including doing work for the Minnesota Department of Transportation, Norwest Banks (now Wells Fargo), Pillsbury, 3M, General Mills, Lutheran Brotherhood, Ciba-Geigy, Anderson Windows, and others. His photography has been published in many magazines, ranging from *National Geographic* to *The Farmer* to, of course, *Outdoor Photographer* and *PCPhoto*.

Web site: www.robsheppardphoto.com

ALSO

In addition to the contributors profiled above, the following photographers graciously allowed their images to be used in this book:

> Erin O'Mara

> Michael O'Mara

> Lance Sparkman

> Jon Sullivan of PDPhoto.org. (Ironically, Sullivan doesn't claim to be a photographer, but his images make a persuasive argument to the contrary.)

> Various photographers who contributed images to Wikipedia and WikiCommons, and placed those images into the Public Domain or licensed them for use under GNU Free Documentation License or Creative Commons.

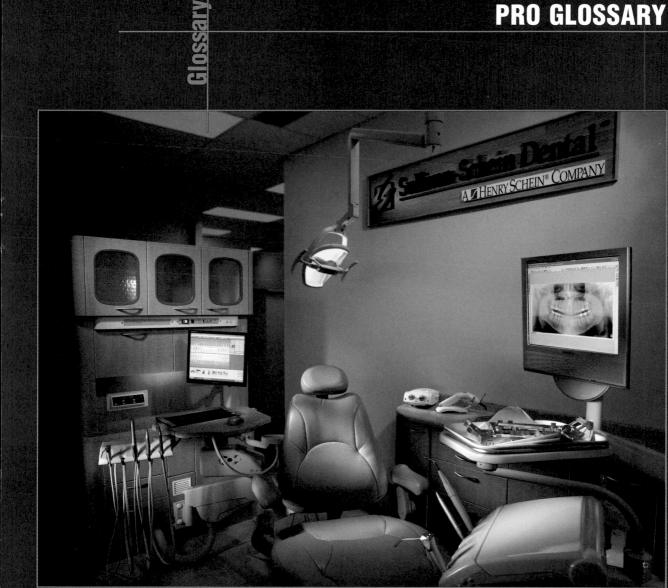

8-bit (24-bit) image: an image file format that allocates 8 data bits to record light intensity for each color channel of each pixel. An 8-bit image can record 256 levels of brightness. Most JPEG, TIFF, PNG, and other common image file formats are 8-bit images. Sometimes called a 24-bit image. The number 24 comes from counting 8-bits in each of the three color channels.

12-bit image: an image file format that allocates 12 data bits to record light intensity for each color channel of each pixel. A 12-bit image can record 4096 levels of brightness. The native Raw file formats of many digital cameras record 12-bit images. These images usually must be converted to 8-bit images for printing and other uses.

16-bit (48-bit) image: an image file format that allocates 16 data bits to record light intensity for each color channel of each pixel. A 16-bit image can record 64K (65,536) levels of brightness. The native Raw file formats of some digital cameras record 16-bit images. These images usually must be converted to 8-bit images for printing and other uses. Also called a 48-bit image. The number 48 comes from counting 16-bits in each of the three color channels.

32-bit image: an image file format that allocates 32 data bits to record light intensity for each color channel of each pixel. A 32-bit image can record a huge brightness range. None of the current digital cameras are capable of recording 32-bit images. Instead, they are created by merging multiple 8-bit images into a single image with an extended dynamic range.

Additive lighting: a lighting scheme in which the photographer adds light sources to illuminate the subject. The opposite of subtractive lighting.

Aperture: the exposure setting that controls how much light can pass through the lens at any given instant. The aperture is adjustable by means of a diaphragm that you can partially close restrict the amount of light that can pass through. Apertures are expressed as *f*-numbers, with the smaller numbers (*f*-4) designating a wider aperture opening and larger numbers (*f*-22) designating narrower aperture openings.

Aperture-priority: the automatic exposure mode that allows the photographer to select the aperture while the camera adjusts the shutter speed depending on the light level. Compare to shutter-priority exposure.

Average metering: a light metering mode that averages the light intensity across the field of view of the lens.

Back light: when the background is brighter than the subject itself, usually because the primary light source is behind the subject.

Background light: a light used to illuminate the background in a studio photograph. The background light is usually positioned so that it does *not* illuminate the primary subject.

Bounce lighting: directing a flash or other light toward a ceiling or other surface instead of directly at the subject.

Bracket: take multiple pictures of the same scene at slightly different exposures and choose the best one later.

Brightness range: the difference in the brightness of the darkest shadows and brightest highlights. Also called dynamic range.

Camera Raw: an image file containing minimally processed image data from the camera's digital image sensor, recorded in the camera manufacturer's proprietary file format. Raw files are usually 12-, 14-, or 16-bit images that must be processed and converted to another format for use.

Camera shake: motion of the camera during the exposure causing a blurred image.

Catch light: the highlight in the eye of a portrait subject, usually caused by the eye catching a reflection of one of the studio lights.

Chromatic adaptation: the tendency for the human eye and brain to automatically adapt to changing lighting conditions, adjusting color perception so that most changes in light source color go unnoticed.

Circle of confusion: a term used to define depth of field. Points of light that are closer or farther away than the focus point of a lens are blurred into disc shapes instead of single points. The edge of such a disk is known as the *circle of confusion*. Depth of field is the zone in which the circle of confusion is small enough that the average human eye can't perceive the difference between the disk and a single point.

Color temperature: a measure describing the color makeup of a light source. Color temperature is defined as the light that would be radiated by a *theoretical black body* heated to a given surface temperature. Color temperature is measured on the Kelvin temperature scale. For example, the warm light of an incandescent lamp has a color temperature of 3400 kelvin and the cool light of a north sky is approximately 7500 kelvin.

Cool lights: photographic lights that give off less heat than incandescent lights. Cool lights usually use specially color corrected fluorescent lamps.

Depth of field: the area in a lens' field of view where objects appear acceptably sharp. Objects within the depth of field zone appear sharp while objects outside the depth of field appear visibly blurred. Also see circle of confusion.

Diffuser: a lighting accessory, composed of translucent material, that is used to diffuse and scatter the light to achieve a softer effect. The diffuser may be attached to the lighting instrument or placed between the light source and subject.

Digital image sensor: the light sensing component of a digital camera.

Digital noise: an artifact of the digital image sensor and its processing software that shows up as grain-like speckles scattered throughout the image. Higher ISO settings exaggerate noise.

Discontinuous spectrum: the light emitting characteristic of certain lights, such as mercury vapor and sodium vapor, that produce large quantities of light within one or more narrow wavelength bands and very little light throughout the rest of the visible spectrum. This contrasts with the more uniform light distribution of sunlight and incandescent lights.

Dynamic range: the difference in the brightness of the darkest shadows and brightest highlights. Also called brightness range.

Effect light: any light that adds an effect (such as the highlight on the hair in a portrait) instead of being part of the primary lighting for the scene.

Equivalent exposure: any of the multiple combinations of aperture, shutter speed, and ISO that all produce the same exposure. A larger aperture paired with a faster shutter speed can deliver the same total amount of light to the image sensor as a smaller aperture paired with a slower shutter speed.

EV (Exposure Value): a numeric scale for measuring exposure in which each EV unit increases or decreases the exposure by a factor of 2 (doubling or halving the light). Equivalent exposures (combinations of aperture and shutter speed that result in equal exposure) all have the same EV number. EV was developed for use in exposure tables to calculate exposure, but now it's used primarily as a unit of measurement for exposure compensation.

Exposure compensation: a camera setting that allows you to increase or decrease the exposure calculated by the camera's automatic exposure system.

Exposure: the combination of aperture, shutter speed, and ISO that controls the amount of light reaching the digital image sensor.

Fill light: a secondary light used to fill in the shadows cast by the main light and increase overall illumination.

Flash fill: using a photographic flash as a fill light to open up the harsh shadows cast by direct sunlight.

Flash meter: a light meter designed to read the light from a photographic flash and calculate the correct exposure.

Flash sync: synchronizing the triggering of the flash with the opening and closing of the shutter.

Flash: a photographic light source of extremely high intensity and short duration. Examples of flash lighting range from the small built-in flash units incorporated into most cameras to large studio lights. Because of the short duration of the light, flash is unsuitable for video and motion picture lighting, but it works great for most film and digital still photography.

Gel: a transparent colored material used to filter the color of a light. The term is short for gelatin, the material originally used to make the filters, but most gels are made of acetate and other plastics today.

Gray card: a standardized reference target for light meter readings and white balance. The standard gray card is a neutral gray that reflects 18 percent of the light falling on it — the same reflectance as the theoretical "average" scene for which all light meters are calibrated. Since it's neutral gray, it can also be used for custom white balance.

Grid: 1) a structure suspended from the ceiling of a studio to provide attachment points for suspending overhead lights. 2) a lighting accessory that is attached to a light to restrict its spread. Also called a honeycomb.

Hair light: a light placed above and slightly behind a portrait subject to create a highlight across the head and shoulders.

Hard light: any point source light that creates sharp highlights and hard-edged shadows.

High Dynamic Range: an image with an extreme brightness range, recorded as a 32-bit image.

High key: a photograph composed mostly of very light tones. Compare to low key.

Histogram: an important and useful tool for evaluating exposure. It plots the distribution of tones in an image as an area chart, with the range of values from dark to light going from left to right along the base of the chart and the prevalence of a given value represented as height.

HMI (Hydrargyrum Medium arc Iodide) lights: a type high-performance, continuous output lighting with daylight color balance. HMI lights have twice the light output of comparable quartz or tungsten lights, and generate less heat, but they're very expensive and require bulky ballast/transformers and

long warm-up times. They're used primarily by big-budget film and video productions.

Hot lights: photographic slang for incandescent lights, so named because they generate a lot of heat, especially the high-output lights found in photography studios.

Hot shoe: the mounting point on a camera for an accessory flash unit. It includes electrical contacts that trigger the flash to fire in synchronization with the shutter when you take a picture.

Hyperfocal distance: the focus point at which the farthest reaches of depth of field extends to infinity.

Image stabilization: a technology built into some lenses (and cameras) that counteracts camera shake to produce sharp images at slower shutter speeds than would otherwise be possible.

Incandescent light: any light in which the light is produced by passing electrical current through a filament. Contrast to fluorescent lights, which produce light by exciting a gas.

Incident light meter: a meter that measures the brightness of the light falling on the subject instead of reflected from it.

Inverse square law: a law of physics that states that the intensity of light is inversely proportional to the square of the distance from the source. So, doubling the distance between a light source and the subject reduces the light intensity to one fourth.

ISO (International Standards Organization): a number indicating the relative sensitivity of the image sensor (or film) to light. A higher ISO indicates greater sensitivity (and increased digital noise).

Kelvin: the temperature scale used for color temperature readings.

Key light: the primary, dominant light that defines the shape and shading on the subject. Also called the main light.

Kicker light: an accent light used to create highlights to complement those from the main light.

Light meter: an instrument for measuring light levels and calculating exposure. May be a separate hand-held tool or built into a camera.

Light ratio: the ratio between the brightness of the highlights and shadows in a given scene, usually a portrait.

Low key: a photograph composed mostly of very dark tones. Opposite of high key.

LV (Light Value): a numeric scale representing the brightness of the light reflected from the subject. It's the same kind of scale as EV, but measures subject luminance rather than exposure. The LV for a gray card in mid-day sun is LV15.

Main light: the primary, dominant light that defines the shape and shading on the subject. Outdoors, the main light is usually the sun. Indoors, it's usually the brightest light — the one that provides the principal illumination for the scene. People with a background in film and video lighting usually call this a key light, but I prefer the term main light.

Matrix metering mode: another name for multi-segment metering mode.

Mixed light: a scene illuminated by a mixture of lights. The mixture might include ambient light and light supplied by the photographer and/or a mixture of different kinds of lights, such as daylight, fluorescents, incandescents, flash, and others.

Modeling light: a low-power incandescent light added to a photographic flash to aid in positioning the lights. You use the modeling light as a preview and the flash for the actual exposure.

Multi-segment metering mode: a light metering mode that samples light intensity at numerous locations across the image and calculates the best exposure for the brightness range it finds. This feature goes by several names, such as matrix metering. Also called Matrix metering mode, ESP metering, and other brand names.

Open shade: a scene that is shaded from the direct light of the sun but lit by a large expanse of open sky.

Over exposure: too much light reaching the sensor, resulting in an image that is too light overall.

Photoflood: a high-output tungsten light bulb made for photographic lighting. It looks like an oversized household light bulb.

Programmed exposure modes: preprogrammed camera settings for various common photographic situations, such as scenery, portraits, or sports action. The program presets the camera's automatic exposure mode, ISO setting, and white balance to what the camera manufacturer deems appropriate for the subject. Also called scenes by some camera makers.

Quartz halogen light: a high-output, tungsten-filament, incandescent light. These lights are better suited to photographic use than standard household lamps because they have higher light output and more consistent color temperature.

Reciprocity: the principle that states that there are multiple combinations of aperture, shutter speed, and ISO that all produce the same exposure. See equivalent exposure.

Reflective light meter: a light meter that reads light levels of the light reflected from the subject.

Reflector: a light reflecting surface. 1) the bowl-shaped surface surrounding the lamp of a photographic light that helps direct the light toward the subject. 2) a white or silver board or other portable reflective surface used to reflect light from a source onto the subject. Note that the color of the reflector affects the color of the light it reflects. A white or silver reflector reflects white light. A gold reflector, on the other hand, gives the reflected light a warm golden glow, and a blue wall gives the reflected light a cool blue cast.

Scenes (exposure settings): see programmed exposure modes.

Shutter speed: controls how long the image sensor is exposed to the light coming through the lens. Exposures are normally measured in fractions of a second and controlled by an electronically controlled shutter in the camera. For convenience, camera controls normally list only the denominator of the fraction, so a shutter speed of 500 is really 1/500 of a second.

Shutter-priority: the automatic exposure mode that allows the photographer to select the shutter speed while the camera adjusts the aperture depending on the light level. Compare to aperture-priority automatic exposure.

Slave flash: a flash unit that is triggered by a light sensor detecting light from another flash unit. There is no need for a sync cord connecting the slave flash to the camera.

Soft light: any light that creates diffuse highlights and soft-edged shadows. The effect is usually the result of a large natural light source, such as a large north-facing window, or a hard light that has been softened by bouncing and/or diffusing the light.

Spill: light that spreads or bounces beyond the subject at which the lighting instrument is pointed.

Spotlight: a lighting instrument that uses a shaped reflector and/or a lens system to achieve a focused beam of light. Spots produce a hard light and may be used with cookies and gobos to create shadow pattern effects.

Spot meter: a reflective light meter with a very narrow angle of view (usually about two degrees).

Stop: photographic slang for one EV unit. The term originated from the detents, or click stops, on the shutter speed dials and aperture rings of manual cameras and lenses. The detents were spaced in one EV increment.

Strobe: another name for a photographic flash lighting instrument. Normally used to refer to large studio lighting equipment as opposed to a small battery-powered accessory flash unit attached to a camera.

Subtractive lighting: a lighting scheme in which the photographer uses shades and diffusers to block or reduce the light falling on the subject. The opposite of additive lighting.

Sunny-16 rule: the exposure guideline which states that the correct exposure for an average subject in direct mid-day sun is equal to f-16 at a shutter speed equal to the reciprocal of the ISO rating. For example, at ISO 100, the exposure is 1/100 at f-16.

Sync cord: a small cable that connects a camera to an external flash unit and triggers the flash to fire in synchronization with the shutter when you take a picture. Not needed with on-camera flash units attached to the camera's hot shoe.

Tent lighting: a lighting technique used to photograph highly reflective subjects such as silverware. The subject is completely surrounded by a "tent" of translucent white diffusion material. The lights are placed outside the tent and the camera lens is inserted through a small slit.

Theoretical black body: a hypothetical construct used in calculating color temperature. It closely approximates the light emitting characteristics of both the sun and the filament in an incandescent light bulb.

Tungsten light: an incandescent light that uses a tungsten filament. Most standard household lights, photofloods, and quartz lights use tungsten filaments.

Under exposure: too little light reaching the sensor, resulting in an image that is too dark overall.

White balance: setting the camera to match the color temperature of the light source so the finished images will have the correct color.

Wireless remote triggering: a device for triggering a flash unit or camera remotely without wires or mechanical connections. Most devices employ radio-frequency (like garage door openers) or infra-red (like TV remotes) signals. Compare to slave flash.

Zone System: a system for visualizing and controlling how the brightness range of a scene will render as a range of values in a photographic print. The Zone System was developed in 1940 and popularized by Ansel Adams. It's built around a gray scale in which the steps, called zones, are each twice as reflective as the next darker step.

Zone V: the Zone System step that corresponds to middle gray — the same 18 percent reflectance as a gray card.

index

continued